Franco Ferrero

WHITEWATER **SAFETY AND RESCUE**

ESSENTIAL KNOWLEDGE FOR **CANOEISTS, KAYAKERS, AND RAFT GUIDES**

FALCONGUIDES ®

GUILFORD, CONNECTICUT
HELENA, MONTANA
AN IMPRINT OF THE GLOBE PEQUOT PRESS

To buy books in quantity for corporate use
or incentives, call **(800) 962–0973**
or e-mail **premiums@GlobePequot.com**.

FALCONGUIDES®

Text contributions from Loel Collins, Ray Goodwin, Dave Luke, and Geraint Rowlands
Interior photos by Franco Ferrero and Peter Wood unless otherwise credited

Library of Congress Cataloging-in-Publication Data
Ferrero, Franco.
 Whitewater safety & rescue : essential knowledge for canoeists, kayakers, and raft guides / Franco
Ferrero.
    p. cm.
 Includes index.
 ISBN 978-0-7627-5087-0
 1. White-water canoeing--Safety measures. 2. Rafting (Sports)--Safety measures. 3. Rescue work. I. Title.
 GV788.F47 2009
 797.122028'9--dc22

                                                                                                    2008046129

Printed in China
10 9 8 7 6 5 4 3 2 1

CONTENTS

Acknowledgments

Once again I'd like to thank all the people I acknowledged in the 1998 edition. In this edition, in addition to the other contributors Loel Collins, Ray Goodwin, Dave Luke and Geraint Rowlands, a special thanks is due to Bob Timms who organized our alpine photo-shoot with consummate professionalism. A special thanks is also due to my wife, Joan, for being a great proofreader and a supportive friend.

A big thank you to all of the people who acted as our "models": Bob Timms, Dino Heald, Torry Jones, Dave Luke, Loel Collins, Pete Catterall, Polly Salter, Richard Manchett, Mark Chadwick, Chris Murmin, Steve Macdonald and Dave Brown.

Thank you to all the people who sent us so many of the photos that have made this edition so different. They are all credited in the captions. Any photos not credited were taken by Franco Ferrero or Peter Wood.

▶ **DEDICATION**—To the memory of "Ack" Hairon. Without his encouragement and practical support, neither I, nor his son Derek, would have been able to take up kayaking and get into so many scrapes at such a young age.

RESOURCES The photos and diagrams used in this book are available free to use in presentations on whitewater safety. They are available on this Web site.

www.pesdapress.com

Introduction

This book started when I tried to put some notes together as course notes for the safety and rescue courses I was running at Plas y Brenin. It soon became clear what a huge topic it is, and in sheer frustration I explained to a friend that I would have to write a book to cover it properly. His answer was, "Why don't you?"

This is the result. I hope you find it enjoyable and informative.

▶ **WHAT'S NEW IN THIS VERSION?** — Apart from the obvious improvement of full color and new photos throughout, the following changes have been made:

1 The text has been completely revised and numerous small but significant improvements in the explanations in the text have been made.

2 The principles of safety and rescue have been unified and the mnemonic CLAP adopted. This is to make it easier to remember them and fall in line with current practice in the teaching of whitewater safety.

3 The rescue section has been reorganized to fit in more closely with the TRTTG. "low to high risk" model.

4 The rafting sections have been completely rewritten by Geraint Rowlands.

5 Chapter 3 on Planning a Descent has been extended to cover factors to be considered when traveling abroad.

6 One-handed signals as used by Paul O'Sullivan in his chapter in the *BCU Canoe and Kayak Handbook* have been adopted.

7 Conforms with new resuscitation guidelines.

▶ **LEARNING ABOUT SAFETY & RESCUE** — The point of safety and rescue training is that there is rarely the time to develop a technique during a life-threatening emergency. Paddlers must already be in possession of a range of techniques that will allow them to solve the problem quickly. There isn't the time to reinvent the wheel. New techniques are often developed in training and practice situations.

There are three parts to becoming a safe and effective paddler and rescuer: knowledge, training and experience.

KNOWLEDGE, TRAINING & EXPERIENCE

This book can only provide the knowledge. It is important that the reader should consider attending practical safety and rescue courses in order to evaluate a range of techniques under controlled conditions. This will also ensure that the techniques are fully and correctly understood.

For those who already have a good deal of training and experience the book will be useful as an aide-mémoire, and probably cover some areas that are new to the reader.

▶ **PRACTICE**—Like all skills, safety and rescue skills need to be practiced, initially to become competent and thereafter to maintain competence. Great care should be taken in selecting suitable sites, where the skills can be practiced in controlled conditions. Nothing could be worse than to be, or see a friend, injured while practicing how to stay safe! It is also important to try and practice as a team with the people you normally paddle with.

▶ **STRUCTURE**—This book is in four sections. The order they are in reflects the importance that I attach to them.

Whitewater SAFETY
    Section One deals with safety, which is about staying out of trouble in the first place.

Whitewater RESCUE
    Section Two is about rescuing people. This is what we do when our safety has failed.

CARE OF VICTIMS
    Section Three is about caring for and evacuating people who are physically or emotionally injured.

ACCESS & RECOVERY
    Section Four is primarily about recovering equipment.

▶ **TERMINOLOGY**—The following words are given specific meanings for the purposes of this book:

Paddler means anyone who paddles on whitewater.

Boater means kayakers and canoeists.

▶ **GENDER**—Despite being rich in words, English has a simple grammar that can't cope with the equal opportunities world we live in. Unless the context implies otherwise, "he," "him," and "his" are used as neuter words and could refer to a male or female person.

DISCLAIMER: MANY OF THE SAFETY AND RESCUE TECHNIQUES DESCRIBED IN THIS BOOK ARE INTENDED FOR USE IN SPECIFIC CIRCUMSTANCES, AND MAY BE HAZARDOUS IF APPLIED INAPPROPRIATELY BY UNSKILLED OR INSUFFICIENTLY TRAINED PADDLERS. THE ONUS IS ON THE READER TO APPLY THE TECHNIQUES DESCRIBED APPROPRIATELY AND CORRECTLY. **THESE TECHNIQUES ARE BEST LEARNED AND PRACTICED UNDER THE GUIDANCE OF A QUALIFIED INSTRUCTOR.**

About the Author

Franco Ferrero divides his work time between managing Pesda Press and freelance coaching. He is qualified as a BCU Level 5 Coach (Sea and Inland), is a REC first aid provider, a Rescue 3 Instructor and holds the Mountaineering Instructor Certificate. His passions are whitewater and sea kayaking, rock and ice climbing, and ski-mountaineering. He has paddled throughout the UK and in many parts of the world including Nepal, Scandinavia, the European Alps, Peru and Western Canada.

Franco Ferrero

Contributors

Loel Collins   *Ray Goodwin*   *Dave Luke*   *Geraint Rowlands*

Loel Collins has been paddling whitewater around the world. "In thirty years you get to paddle lots, swim a bit and throw loads of lines at your mates, colleagues and clients." He works as a senior instructor at Plas y Brenin, the National Mountain Centre, where he runs the canoeing and kayaking departments. Loel has worked with the BCU designing the safety training programs for the Coach Education Scheme and worked closely with the emergency services designing bespoke water safety training for rescue teams. Most of all he loves boating. Loel acted as technical proofreader and contributed many ideas to the development of the book,

Ray Goodwin has paddled throughout Britain and in North America and Nepal. He has a considerable reputation as a coach running his own business RayGoodwin.com. In 2005 he was featured on Ray Mears' BBC2 *Bushcraft* series. Ray is a BCU Level 5 Coach. Ray wrote two canoe chapters for the *BCU Canoe and Kayak Handbook* and wrote the canoe specific sections for this book.

Dave Luke has paddled throughout Britain, in the Alps, Corsica and in the United States. He represented Britain in the OC1 at the rodeo (freestyle) championships in Germany. Dave wrote and advised on specialist whitewater open boat matters.

Geraint Rowlands has worked as a commercial river guide on every continent apart from Antarctica. He is an instructor for Rescue 3 UK and a Level 5 Coach who works as Head of Rafting at Canolfan Tryweryn, the National Whitewater Centre. Geraint wrote the raft specific sections of the book.

CHAPTER 1
Principles of Safety

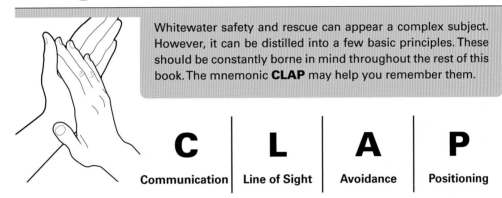

Whitewater safety and rescue can appear a complex subject. However, it can be distilled into a few basic principles. These should be constantly borne in mind throughout the rest of this book. The mnemonic **CLAP** may help you remember them.

C	**L**	**A**	**P**
Communication	Line of Sight	Avoidance	Positioning

COMMUNICATION

Misunderstandings must be avoided at all costs.

Signals, instructions and briefings must be simple, clear and concise. Do not make assumptions. If necessary, question to check understanding.

When using signals:

- **Point at where to go, rather than at the hazard.**
- **Confirm understanding by repeating the same signal.**

LINE OF SIGHT

Never run anything blind.

There are two facets to this:

▶ Paddlers can only choose a line and assess the level of risk if they are in a position to see what is coming.

▶ All members of the group should remain in the line of sight of at least one other member of the group.

AVOIDANCE IS BETTER THAN CURE

This covers a number of important guidelines:

- **Mutual Support—Paddlers should paddle as a mutually supportive team.**
- **Preparation and planning prevent poor performance.**
- **Clean Profile – No knots or handles on your throw line, no loose or unnecessary straps on your Personal Flotation Device (PFD), nothing that will increase the risk of snagging/entrapment.**
- **Assess the Risks – and make your own decisions accordingly.**
- **Talk, Reach, Throw, Tow, Go (TRTTG) – Go for the low risk options first.**
- **Plan B – Ask yourself "What if?" and work out a back-up plan.**
- **KISS – Keep it short and simple.**
- **Nothing a rescuer does should make the victim worse off.**

POSITION OF MAXIMUM USEFULNESS

Being in the right place at the right time is the key.

- **When protecting a rapid, paddlers should position themselves so as to cover the highest risk. This usually means covering the problems that are most likely to occur, rather than the most dangerous hazard.**
- **Look to your own safety – If you get into trouble you can't help anyone else.**

Big Sandy River, USA. Photo: Mark Rainsley

CHAPTER 2
Reading Whitewater

*Figure 2-1
Directions and flow
on straight section
of river.*

Knowledge is power. Only by understanding how moving water behaves can we use it, and by so doing avoid unnecessary or unacceptable levels of danger.

Directions

When giving directions or describing a feature on a river, it is important to use the same language so as to avoid misunderstandings.

*The terms we use for
giving directions on
the river.*

| river left | downstream | upstream | river right |

Upstream is where the water is flowing from and downstream is where it is flowing to. River right and left are simply right and left when facing downstream.

Straight Section of River

As a general rule, when a river is running in a straight line the current is strongest in the middle and weakest near the banks.

▶ **MAIN FLOW**—Away from the friction caused by contact with the banks, the current flows at its fastest. The layer nearest the river bed is the slowest and the layer just beneath the surface is the fastest. This is because the surface layer is slowed down a little by the friction caused by contact with the air.

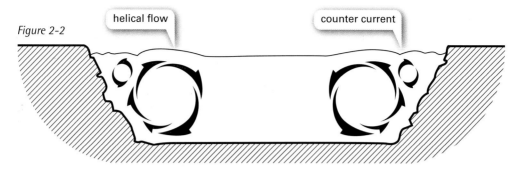

Figure 2-2

helical flow

counter current

Helical Flow

Figure 2-2 shows a cross-section of helical flow at river banks. There may be a shallow counter current very close in to the bank. These create minute eddies that can be exploited by the boater. However, because they are relatively shallow, they are of little help to a swimmer.

The friction provided by the banks slows the current down and causes it to spiral in such a way that the surface water near the edges of a fast flowing, straight sided river can push a swimmer away from the bank. Therefore one should never assume that swimmers are safe, even if they are swimming strongly, until they are actually out of the water and on the bank. Despite this, it is far easier to get ashore against the relatively slow helical flow than where the powerful main flow sets into the bank.

Flood Channels

Where the banks of a watercourse are smooth sided there may be no helical flow and the main flow runs right up to the bank. This usually happens in man-made structures such as flood relief channels and canalized rivers.

Bends in the River

Figure 2-3

The main current will always go towards the outside of a bend. On the outside of a bend the water is deep and fast where the main flow sets right into the bank. On the inside it is slow and shallow. Because of the erosion thus caused, undercut banks and overhanging trees are often a hazard. Undercut banks can be doubly dangerous as there may be tree roots or debris which can act as a "strainer" and trap a swimmer.

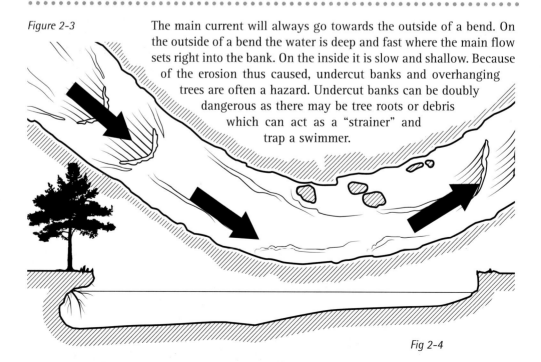

Fig 2-4

Upstream & Downstream *Vs*

Rocks that are just above or just below the surface are usually indicated by a *V* shape on the surface of the water. The point of the letter *V* is pointing upstream. Conversely, the route taken by the main flow of water is indicated by a letter *V* shape whose point is pointing downstream. This "tongue" of clear water usually indicates the best route.

Figure 2-5 right, V tongue of water pointing the way. Rio Chotohuasi, Peru.

Figure 2-6 below, upstream and downstream Vs, viewed from above.

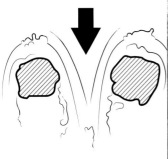

Rooster Tails

Figure 2-7 small rooster tail over a barely covered rock.

In a fast flowing river which has a steep gradient, a rock that is only just covered may be indicated by a "rooster tail," a plume of white frothy water.

Figure 2-8 going left to avoid the obvious rooster tail, Rio Susisa, Bolivia. Photo: Mark Rainsley

Eddies

Wherever flowing water is forced around an obstruction, an "eddy" is formed. This is caused by a counter current flowing in the opposite direction to the main flow, to fill what would otherwise be a hole!

eddy line

Figure 2-9 (left) an eddy formed behind a midstream boulder.

Figure 2-10 (right) an eddy formed by an obstruction on bank.

Eddies are usually places of relative calm in which we can rest, or pause to read the next section of rapid, before we commit ourselves to paddling it. We often paddle a river by hopping from one safe eddy to another. This can be visualized by imagining the main flow of the river as a fast moving conveyor belt and the eddies as a series of stable platforms which we can hop on to, in order to rest and get our bearings.

In slow flowing or low volume technical rivers, eddies are usually calm places. In fast flowing, high volume rivers, the counter current can be fast flowing and the water in the eddy fairly turbulent.

In the worst case scenario the recirculating current in an eddy can feed you straight back into the main current, or into a hazard you were trying to avoid.

▶ **EDDY LINES**—The eddy line or "eddy fence" is a visible line on the surface of the water that marks the border between the main flow and the counter current. Think of it as the point where the edge of the conveyor belt meets the platform. When one aims to eddy-out or eddy-in, at an angle of, say 45°, the angle is between the direction of travel and the main flow, which is not necessarily the same as the general direction that the river is heading in.

▶ **EDDY ZONES**—On less powerful rivers the line between the eddy and the main current will be quite distinct at the top of the eddy. However, the line will gradually become less distinct and broaden so that it becomes a zone rather than a line.

In very high volume rivers flows, the whole eddy may be huge and full of swirls and boils. On this type of river it may be better to stay out in the main flow until the rapid loses power and the eddies become calmer. When you go for an eddy, choose where to cross the eddy zone so that you end up in a quieter part of the eddy.

Figure 2-11 Sabretooth Rapid (Grade IV) Clearwater, BC. Note the huge boils in the eddy on river left (top right of photo).

Standing Waves

Standing waves are formed when fast flowing water hits a layer of relatively still water. The waves that are formed are of "green" water, i.e. water that isn't full of air bubbles, although the very top of the wave may curl over and therefore be frothy.

Figure 2-12 a huge train of standing waves, they appear to be jogging on the spot. Paddling downstream straight over them is like riding a roller coaster. Silverback, White Nile, Uganda. Photo: Mark Rainsley

On most rivers they make great play-spots, where boaters can practice their surfing skills. We can use them to surf from one side of the river to the other, thereby saving energy.

Last but not least, the top of a standing wave can be a great place from which to get a view of the river to come.

Stopper

Stoppers are formed when water that has speeded up as a result of flowing over a drop needs to get rid of the extra energy that has thus been created. It does this by sending the water that can't flow away normally rushing to the surface. Some of this water is then forced to recirculate back into the stopper. The technical term for a stopper is a "hydraulic jump."

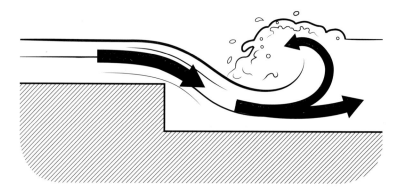

Figure 2-13 a hole.

▶ **HOLE** (Noisy)—There are different types of stopper and at one end of the scale is the hole. In this kind of stopper all the action takes place on the surface. Therefore, although it will hold a buoyant object such as a kayak or in the case of large ones, a raft, a swimmer would normally be flushed through the stopper in the green slab of water that is below the surface. The fact that the action is on the surface also means that they are visually very obvious and tend to be quite noisy.

Friendly holes make great play-holes, in which to learn the skills needed to get out of the not so friendly ones. Small holes can be deliberately "side-surfed" and used to stop and get a good look at the way ahead.

Figure 2-14 raft flip in huge hole. The good news is that the swimmers will be flushed through, although it will feel like a long time down in "the green room." The Bad Place, White Nile. Photo: www. swiftwater rescue.at

Figure 2-15 a more manageably sized hole or play-hole.

Figure 2-16 a deep recirculating stopper.

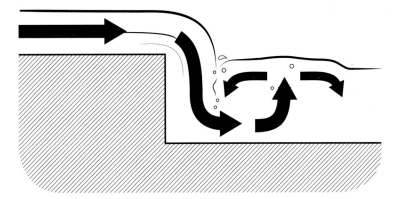

The angle of the face of a hole is usually relatively shallow. Steeper faces make side surfing difficult, if not impossible, and are often referred to as *pour-overs*.

▶ **HYDRAULIC** (Quiet)—At the other end of the scale is the hydraulic deep recirculating stopper. As the name implies, most of the action is happening below the surface. When the volume of water involved is taken into consideration, these stoppers are relatively quiet.

This is a dangerous type of stopper because the backwash will often hold a swimmer. They are also dangerously deceptive because the water isn't very aerated. This means that to the untutored eye it may appear as if the water is fairly calm.

The critical factor is the distance between the slot and the boil line, in other words, the length of the backwash. As a rough guideline, anything over half a boat length is probably worth walking around.

Natural stoppers are rarely 100 percent surface or 100 percent deep recirculating. Due to the uneven nature of the river bed they are normally a blend, and often exhibit different characteristics throughout their length. So you may find that one end of a stopper is very "grabby," while the other end is very forgiving.

Figure 2-17 jumping over a stopper that has no obvious outflow. The cameraman is also standing by with a throw line in case the paddler blows it. Sermenzina, Italy.

▶ **OPEN VERSUS CLOSED**—More importantly, most, though by no means all, natural stoppers will have one or more weaknesses where the recirculation is broken and the water flows through. These may be caused by a break in the underwater feature that is causing the stopper or by the fact that the stopper is not at 90° to the main flow. In the case of the latter, some of the recirculating water flows towards the downstream end of the stopper.

Unless you are 100 percent certain that you can power through, or in certain cases jump over a stopper, you should keep well clear of any stopper that does not have a weakness that will allow you to escape its clutches. These are called "keepers."

Figure 2-18 (left) smiling stopper viewed from side (Note how muddy water makes it harder to read the water).

Figure 2-19 (right) frowning pour-over stopper seen from upstream. Skeena River, BC.

▶ **SMILING OR FROWNING**—Many "surface" and "pour-over" stoppers occur when water flows over an isolated boulder in midstream. If, when facing downstream, the resulting stopper makes the same shape as a child's drawing of a smile, the backwash will be recirculating in such a way as to feed boats or people into the outflow and out of the stopper. If the stopper appears to be frowning, the backwash is recirculating back into the stopper, and is best avoided.

The Nature of the River

There are a number of ways to describe rivers that give us more idea what we are letting ourselves in for. High volume usually means that the water features are the hazards, large stoppers and standing waves, and boily eddies. Low volume means that rocks and the water features that form around them are problems.

The geology of the area that the river flows through will have an effect on the nature of the river. Rivers are often described as boulder gardens, pool drop or rock-slides. The following photos will help illustrate better than words.

| rock-slide | boulder garden | pool drop | high volume |

Figure 2-20 (top left) rock-slide (these usually form over hard rock such as granite, Grass River, New York State.

Figure 2-21 (lower left) boulder garden, Bugaboo Creek, BC.

Figure 2-22 (top right) pool drop (these usually form where the river cuts through a relatively soft bedrock), Rio Unduavi, Bolivia.

Figure 2-23 (lower right) a high volume river, a Grade 3 rapid on the Skeena, BC.

Photos 2-20 to 2-22: Mark Rainsley

Water Levels

Be aware that rivers and their hazards change dramatically as their water levels change. Most guide books describe rivers as they will be found in medium levels.

▶ **LOW WATER**—As water levels drop, rivers usually become more technical but more forgiving. This means that it is harder to make the line because there are more obstacles but due to the fact that the current is less powerful, mistakes are less costly.

Photos: Karl Midlane

Figure 2-24 (left) Cobdens Falls just too low to be worth paddling, Afon Llygwy, North Wales. (middle) Cobdens at a good paddleable flow, Grade IV. (right) Cobdens in high water, Grade IV+ (in floodstage this rapid is Grade V).

There are some notable exceptions, where even in low levels the current is powerful enough to make entrapment lethal. Due to the fact that entrapments are more likely in lower water levels, these rivers are more dangerous in low water.

▶ **HIGH WATER**—As water levels rise, some rapids will become simpler or even wash out altogether. Others will become much harder and low head dams, or weirs, that don't wash out will probably become killers. The current will become much faster, giving you little time to react, and more powerful, leaving little scope for errors. Trees that were just a nuisance become massive strainers.

River Ogwen, North Wales

"Five of us stood on the bridge above the village of Bethesda, looking at the distinctive boulder that served the locals as a water gauge. We all agreed that it was going to be high/exciting rather than high/terrifying, more an easy grade V than its normal grade IV.

"We set off and enjoyed the exhilarating ride, until we arrived at the confluence of the Caseg. This tributary drains off the Carneddau mountains. Normally it carries far less water than the Ogwen itself, but today was different. A huge mass of grey snowmelt water thundered in, swelling the already high Ogwen. It was like being hit by an express train.

"It didn't take long to work out that our estimates of water level and difficulty were going to have to be altered radically. By the time we got to the hard bit all bar two of us decided to walk. I got such a spanking that when I finally managed to break out (eddy in), I decided to walk the last hard rapid, even though I only had 100m [328 feet] to go. After all, how much adrenaline do you need?"

Flood

A river is said to be in flood when it has either burst its banks or it has exceeded the normal maximum flow.

You should only run flood-stage rivers when you are very competent and know the river well. Everything now happens so fast that if you go for a swim you are on your own. On all but the easiest rivers any other boaters will probably be too busy surviving to come to your rescue. You will be moving so fast that any bank-based rescuers will be unable to keep up on foot. Should they manage to get a line to you, the current will be so powerful that you may well be unable to hold on.

William Neally, in his book *Kayak*, stated that there are three reasons for running a river in flood: Accident (flash flood), misadventure (ignorance of river level), or choice (defective genetic programming). He went on to say that lots of paddlers do run flood-stage rivers, because it's exciting. You must, however, have first-class river reading skills, a bombproof roll, a cool head and a cavalier attitude.

Flood-stage rivers are extremely high risk. If you need to ask another paddler if they think you are ready for it, you aren't! If you think you are, you had better be right!

*Figure 2-25
left, after flash flood
and right, before.
Photo: Mark Rainsley*

FLOOD STAGE RIVERS ARE EXTREMELY HIGH RISK

Big Drops & Waterfalls

From a safety point of view, any drop over 9 feet (3m) is the same as a waterfall, so from now on I will use the term "drop" for anything over 9 feet and "small drop" for anything smaller. The good news is that remarkably few people have been killed paddling drops. The bad news is that quite a number of people have been badly injured. The reason I use 9 feet as my definition of a big drop is that it has

Figure 2-26 high volume drop, easy approach but you'd better have a bombproof roll. Kalagala Falls, White Nile, Uganda. Photo: www.swiftwater rescue.at

been proven in research with crash test dummies that, if you land bow first onto a hard surface from that height, you will fracture your lower legs. A flat landing onto non-aerated water from that height could result in spinal damage. Having said that, drops of 131 feet (40m) have been paddled; so what's the difference between a good drop and a bad drop?

In my way of thinking there are three types of drops: Easy drops, hard drops, and drops that will probably hurt you.

Figure 2-27 waterfall on the River Rivanese, Corisca. Although the take-off and landing of this fall are uncomplicated, its sheer height makes the angle of entry critical. Freefall can be avoided by scraping down the rock on the extreme (river) right of the fall. Photo: Dan Yates

▶ **EASY DROPS**—Easy drops demand only raw courage or a lack of imagination; skill doesn't really come into it. They have deep plunge pools full of aerated water to provide you with a soft landing. They also have an easy approach that requires little or no technical skill to set yourself up so that you go over the lip pointing in the right direction. Runnable drops of over 23–26 feet (7–8m) usually consist of very steep slabs rather than vertical drops. This is because if you free-fall for a considerable distance it becomes difficult to ensure that your boat hits the water at a safe angle. If the boat lands too flat there is the risk of spinal compression. Another requirement is that, if there is a stopper at the base of the drop, it isn't a hazard in itself.

▶ **HARD DROPS**—Hard drops require technical skill and a cool head. These are essentially the same as easy drops in terms of the landing. The difference is that the approach to the lip of the drop is technically difficult and may be close to the limit of your paddling skill. Failure to get the entry right may result in landing at a bad angle or missing the plunge pool altogether. The most technically difficult drops of all are complex falls that require the paddler to maneuver during the descent. To a degree, the difference between a hard drop and an easy drop is subjective, as it depends on each individual's skill level.

▶ **DROPS THAT WILL HURT YOU**—I don't run these! Into this category go any drop where the landing is so poor that, no matter how perfectly you run the drop, there is a reasonable chance of ending up in the hospital. Landings that come into this category include: bare rock, barely covered rock, shallow or obstructed plunge pools, non-aerated water and killer stoppers. Hitting water that has not had its surface tension disturbed can be like landing on concrete!

HEALTH WARNING

REMEMBER THAT UNLIKE WEIRS **THERE MAY BE NO WARNING CHANGE IN THE NATURE OF THE FLOW** OF THE RIVER UPSTREAM OF THE DROP. YOU WILL HAVE TO RELY ON GOOD SCOUTING TECHNIQUE AND SIGNS SUCH AS NOISE TO FOREWARN YOU.

CHAPTER 3

Hazards

Figure 3-1 new hazards can be created after heavy rain. Don't assume the river hasn't changed. Photo: Bob Timms Boating & Trekking

This chapter looks at hazards that, as paddlers, we need to identify and in most cases avoid. The mere presence of these hazards on a section of river does not automatically mean a portage. Providing we identify the hazard in good time, it is usually easy to choose a line down the river that keeps well clear of them. However, if the degree of technical difficulty involved in avoiding one of these features exceeds, or even comes close to, the limits of our paddling ability, it's time to get out and walk!

Overhanging Branches

These are usually found on the outside of bends where the current tries to set you into the bank. They are usually easily avoided, although novices seem to have a morbid fascination for them.

EMERGENCY ACTION—If unable to avoid overhanging branches, and they are *only thin ones*, you should not hold on to them as this will capsize boaters and pull rafters into the water. Paddlers in this situation should lean forward, make themselves as small as possible and allow the current to push them through. For thick branches see *strainers*.

Strainers

A strainer is any obstruction that leaves gaps that are large enough for the current to flow but not big enough for a boat or swimmer to pass through. Examples are tree branches or roots, fences, eroded and exposed steel reinforcing rods and virtually any junk you can think of that has been thrown into the river. Avoidance really is the name of the game here.

PADDLING AWAY FROM THE STRAINER AND AVOIDING IT IS THE BEST BET

Figure 3-2 a naturally formed strainer. Photo: www.canoecontrol.com

EMERGENCY ACTION—If swept into a strainer, the only hope is to jump or climb over the obstacle rather than be swept under it. Open boaters have a definite advantage here, as it is much easier to "Get out of the kitchen if you don't like what's cooking!" That said, the chances of success are slim and paddling away from the strainer and avoiding it is the best bet. What to do as a swimmer is covered in Chapter 14.

Boulder Sieve

This is essentially the "mother of all strainers," where the whole or a large portion of the river is strained through the gaps in a mass of boulders. Avoidance is the only answer.

Figure 3-3 portaging a boulder choke, Manns Creek, West Virginia. Photo: Mark Rainlsey

Broaches

Broaches usually happen on boulders but can involve other obstacles. It involves being swept sideways onto and being held against one or more obstacles. On easier rivers this is a common occurrence with novices who lack the skill to take evasive action. In gentler waters it is not usually too much of a problem, but if the current involved is very powerful, it may cause serious damage to the boat or raft, or even trap the boater.

▶ **EMERGENCY ACTION: KAYAKS**—If avoiding action has been unsuccessful and being pushed sideways onto a rock is inevitable, immediately lift the upstream edge of your boat by snapping up the appropriate knee and lean onto the offending obstacle. This will allow the water to pass under the boat and leave you in a stable, if unenviable, position. Unless getting off the rock will put you in a worse position than you are already in, work your way off the rock by pushing or pulling your way along the obstacle, while at the same time keeping your edge up.

Figure 3-4 emergency action. for a broached kayaker.

If you don't react quickly enough and the current catches your upstream edge, the boat will rotate towards the current and the pressure rapidly builds up on the spray deck and deck as the pressure wave transfers from the rock to the deck of your boat. Your best bet is to get out of the boat as quickly as possible, before the deck collapses. This is one of the situations where a keyhole cockpit is a very desirable design feature, as it will make it much easier to get out quickly and reduce the likelihood of your legs being trapped. (See Chapter 12.)

EMERGENCY ACTION: OPEN BOAT—In an open boat you will have to throw your weight hard towards the offending object and onto the downstream side of the boat. If you don't manage this maneuver it is easier to bale out of a canoe. Make sure that you get your legs clear of kneeling thwarts before the boat wraps.

However, because of the extra surface area involved, a wrap, even in a relatively slow current, can result in a complete write-off. Even worse, it is possible for the ends of the boat to fold right around the rock and trap the paddler. This is known as being "bear trapped."

Figure 3-5 if you don't manage to lean onto the rock in time, get your legs clear of kneeling thwarts quickly! Photo: Whitewater Consultancy

▶ **EMERGENCY ACTION: RAFTS**—As with all dangers, avoidance is certainly your main priority. The seconds before impact are crucial, and fast decision making is required. If contact with a boulder or other object in the flow is imminent, you should make all efforts to turn your raft so that you make contact with either the bow or the stern as this will decrease the potential of a broach. Before impact it is essential that you call a "hold on/hold on, get down" bracing command to avoid the rafting crew being catapulted towards the direction of the rock.

If a raft impacts with an object sideways, the downstream tube will rise up against the face of the object exposing the internal compartments to the full force of the water, wrapping the raft around the object. The upstream tube meanwhile is being pushed under the surface by the force of the water. This rising and sinking action can sometimes be avoided by moving the rafting crew to the downstream tube thus effecting a weight shift similar to that of a kayaker leaning onto a rock in a broach situation. The command for this weight shift is a "high side left/right" depending on your orientation. Guide anticipation of the situation, linked with an early high side command, is vital if a high side is to be successful! Raft crews will need to practice this procedure as the response needs to be immediate.

As the pin occurs your objective is to try and stabilize the situation as soon and as much as is possible. Your first action is always to "count heads" and ensure you have a grasp of where all your crew members are. Following this your actions may involve ensuring that all crew members are located on the downstream tube and are holding on tightly to the perimeter line, signaling to another member of your flotilla or safety kayaker to rescue a swimmer from your raft who may have fallen in during impact, or in a worst case scenario rescue a crew member who may have become lodged between the boulder and the raft. Raft guides have been known to rescue victims caught between a boulder and a raft by making an incision into the raft's fabric!

Low to high risk, simple to more complex, methods are now employed to free the raft. Moving crew members either to the bow or stern of the raft can be enough to dislodge you and this is your first course of action. Be warned that rafts have been known to flip over as they come off. Keep the downstream tube weighted! If weight shifting hasn't worked, it is time to evacuate the raft and transport the raft crew to a safe location before more complex raft extrication methods are employed. Remember your priority is always the safety of your crew before considering any raft extrication methods.

Should the raft go on to wrap, the crew should climb up over the high side of the raft and onto the obstacle or into the eddy that will have formed behind it.

Figure 3-6 raft pin on the Marsiangdi, Nepal. Having stabilized the raft and made safe the crew, bank support arrives swiftly from the safety boaters.

Figure 3-7 as an added hazard this abandoned boat has become vertically pinned among boulders. River Dart. Photo: Mark Rainsley

Vertical Pins

This is where water flows over a vertical drop that has obstacles and shallow water at its base rather than a deep plunge pool. If the bow of a boat gets lodged, the boater ends up pinned vertically, rather than broached horizontally. If a vertical pin looks like a possibility, you should not run the drop unless you are sure that you have the technique required to boof the drop, keeping the bow up. Even then, as a precaution you should ensure that other members of the team can get in position to help should there be a case of pilot error. What to do in this situation is covered in Chapter 16.

Undercuts

An undercut is wherever a current flows under some form of over-hanging obstacle, such as an eroded bank, undercut bedrock or overhanging boulder. If a boater is swept under an undercut, he will almost certainly be capsized. In some cases it may be possible to hold on to the rock above the undercut and work your way along the obstacle without being fed under it. The real danger is that there is some form of strainer hidden under the undercut, or that the undercut narrows and that the paddler is thus trapped underwater. Once again avoidance is the only real answer.

▶ **SPOTTING THE UNDERCUT**—Undercuts are usually formed where the current sets onto a rock and erodes it. When the current sets onto a rock that isn't undercut, it forms a cushion wave. If there is no cushion wave, or it is smaller than the power of the water would lead you to expect, suspect the presence of an undercut.

Figure 3-8 the cushion wave indicates that the boulder is probably not undercut.

Sometimes undercuts are obvious because the rock has been eroded at high water and the river is being run in low or medium water. In this case, if the current sets under an overhanging section of rock, you should assume that the rock is further undercut beneath the water.

WHITEWATER SAFETY AND RESCUE

Figure 3-9 undercuts will often make it impossible to reach a swimmer, and even so they make extraction difficult. Photo: www.swiftwaterrescue.at

Siphons

Figure 3-10 (below)

① + ② pinned in a siphon, Rio Santa Clara, Mexico. It was impossible to arrange anchors so that the boat could be pulled back at the correct angle.

③ success came five and a half hours later when a line was attached to the bow and the kayak was pulled down through the siphon.

④ Simon Drinkwater somewhat the worse for wear but happy to be out of the boat.

A siphon is where water flows through a tunnel formed by a pothole in the bedrock or a gap between boulders. They can be a lot harder to spot than undercuts. In all other respects the dangers posed are of the same nature.

▶ **SPOTTING THE SIPHON**—The only sure way to spot siphons is to inspect the river bed in drought conditions! In normal river flows, if there seems to be less water coming out of a pool than is flowing into it, suspect the presence of a siphon. If the mouth of the siphon is near the surface it may cause the same sort of vortex effect on the water as you see when water goes down a plughole.

Sometimes the mouth may be inconspicuous but the exit point obvious, in which case you can make an educated guess as to where the water is coming from. Inspecting by working your way upstream is a good way to spot siphons.

Photos: Lara Tipper

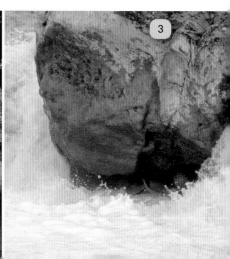

Dangerous Stoppers

As discussed in the previous chapter, hydraulics will hold a swimmer whereas surface stoppers usually don't. Nonetheless, a hydraulic may not be a killer. It may have a weakness, indicated by a tongue of water flowing through in the opposite direction to the backwash on either side. Through this weakness a bold and sufficiently skilled paddler could break through, or a swimmer could make his escape. Most, but by no means all, natural stoppers have one or more weak spots. Whether an individual paddler has the skill or is cool-headed enough to be able to use them is another matter.

▶ **ASSESSING RISK**—By looking at whether a stopper is even or uneven, deep or surface, we can assess just how dangerous it is. There are other factors to take into account such as the size of the stopper, depth of the water and the power of the current, underwater and downstream hazards and the technical skill of the paddlers involved. If in any doubt, get out and walk!

Figure 3-11 assessing a stopper:
a) a fairly deep hydraulic that is open will be an awkward hazard.
b) a hydraulic that is closed will be a deadly hazard.

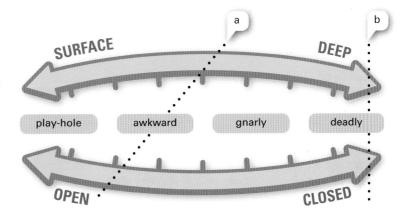

Double Recirculation

A particularly lethal kind of stopper is formed where water has undercut the base of a drop. This can cause a double recirculation. Should a person end up recirculating in the undercut his chances of survival are slim.

▶ **SPOTTING A DOUBLE RECIRCULATION** - Any vertical or near-vertical drop with a decent flow of water running over it should be considered suspect. Look for signs of erosion at the base of the rock face, behind or to the sides of the flow of water. Look for signs of water recirculating behind the waterfall.

Figure 3-12

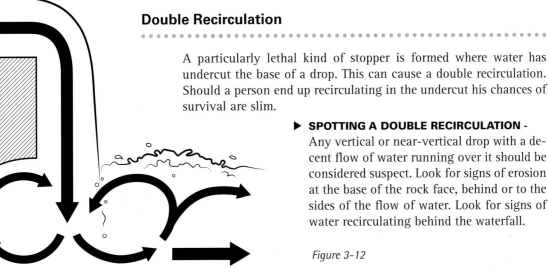

River Goeddol, North Wales

"Kevin and I finished inspecting the two drops. On the first, the water divided and fell as a near vertical fall on "river right" and a shallower angled but more turbulent looking fall on river left. Both options looked straightforward, so we decided that whoever was not running it would stand by with a throw line by the second fall.

"I had gone first on the last big drop so it was Kevin's turn. I signalled to confirm that I was ready and he paddled over the right-hand fall of the first drop, vanishing from sight into the plunge pool.

"When after a few seconds neither he nor his boat had reappeared, I ran back up to the plunge pool and, my heart pounding, scanned the foaming water. After what seemed an eternity his boat reappeared but there was still no sign of Kevin. Time passed, and I began to wonder how I was going to break the news to his pregnant wife.

"Suddenly he burst to the surface. He had kept his cool and, on feeling his foot touch bedrock, had kicked off it for all he was worth. Milliseconds later my throw line landed in his hands and I pulled him to safety.

"We reinspected the fall, and ruefully I realised that we had missed the signs. They weren't obvious but they were there. The back of the fall was undercut, producing a double recirculating stopper. I felt physically sick at the thought that because we had missed the vital clues my friend had come close to losing his life.

"I'm not sure who was more shaken, but the decision to get off the river and retreat to Pete's Eats for a monster pig out was unanimous."

Low Head Dams

Figure 3-13 (left) dangerous low head dam, R. Oetz, Austria. Note the long backwash, and relative lack of aerated water. Photo: Paul O'Sullivan

Figure 3-14 (right) Salmon Steps low head dam on the Exe, with safe passage down the fish ladder. Photo: Mark Rainsley

Low head dams, or weirs, often produce dangerous stoppers. This is because (being man-made) they are symmetrical. Therefore they produce stoppers that are regular and have no weaknesses through which a jet of water can flow. To make matters worse the ends of the stoppers are often blocked off with high walls that offer no holds for a swimmer to grab hold of. Horseshoe low head dams are particularly bad as they recirculate their victims to the middle of the river where it is hard to get to them. Anti-scour low head dams have a "lip" which is designed to prevent erosion, dissipating energy by creating a particularly powerful deep recirculating flow of water which will hold a swimmer. In Britain the governing bodies of this sport are campaigning to stop any more of these lethal low head dams being built.

Other ways that have been used to reduce the flow of the water include placing steel stakes, concrete "dragon's teeth" and "gabions," (wire-mesh baskets filled with rocks), on the bed of the river. As "gabions" erode, the damaged wire mesh is particularly hazardous.

Some low head dams are built with weaknesses designed into them, and broken ones sometimes provide good play spots because, through damage or neglect they have become uneven. Beware, nonetheless, because broken low head dams may have dangerous spikes in the form of exposed reinforcing steel rods.

Fish passes are best avoided. It is sometimes illegal to even paddle near them and they are often made in such a way that it is possible to become entrapped.

HEALTH WARNING

LOW HEAD DAMS ARE EITHER STRAIGHT-FORWARD, OR THEY KILL YOU. THEREFORE, IF IN ANY DOUBT, PORTAGE. THE ONLY WAY TO BE SURE IS TO ASK THE LOCALS. ALWAYS INSPECT LOW HEAD DAMS AND THE STOPPERS THEY CREATE.

POSSIBLE SIGNS THAT YOU ARE APPROACHING A LOW HEAD DAM ARE:

Calm Deep Water—Low head dams are designed to hold water back, so upstream of the obstruction there is a "low head dam pool."

Noise—Created by the overflow of the low head dam. Be wary; some dangerous recirculating stoppers are very quiet.

An Event Horizon—Due to the sudden drop created by the low head dam, you will see a foreground, a false horizon, and a background. The middle ground is missing, giving you an unusual perspective and a valuable early warning sign.

A Change in Height—A change in the height of the river banks.

Concrete Constructions—Concrete walls or small buildings.

Mill Buildings—Older low head dams built during the Industrial Revolution in Britain were often built to power cotton mills. Old multi-story buildings are a useful warning sign.

A Warning Notice—These are common in parts of continental Europe where canoeists are seen as a valuable tourist resource. Even if you can't read French, Italian, or German the skull and crossbones is pretty clear in its meaning!

Don't get complacent! The absence of a warning sign doesn't necessarily mean that the low head dam is safe.

Figure 3-15
an event horizon. Photo: "Spike" Green

Other Paddlers

Other paddlers are potentially a very real hazard particularly at popular and crowded playholes or playwaves. There is a form of etiquette that is best to follow:

Playboating Etiquette

1 On slalom sites it is usual to keep out of the gate-line and get out of the way of anyone who is doing a timed run or obviously training seriously.

2 If the normal line of descent of a rapid goes through a playwave or hole, boaters descending the river have right of way. Having said that, someone who is struggling at their limit to master a play-hole may not be looking upstream. It is therefore a good idea to stop where they can see you and wait for them to clear the hole. If you are playing the hole, be courteous and make a point of signaling them to come on down.

3 Don't drop in uninvited, even if the person concerned has been hogging the hole. The unwritten rule is that if there are other people waiting, you only stay on the wave or in the hole for two minutes. If somebody is hogging the hole, have strong words with them when they are in the eddy rather than risking physical injury by trying to barge them out of the hole.

Environmental Hazards

I have included a number of items in the final part of this chapter that the reader may have expected to find in the chapter on first aid. There are two reasons for this:

1 They are conditions brought about by environmental hazards.

2 They are all conditions that are easily preventable.

Sudden Immersion

In very cold water this can stop a paddler from thinking clearly and reacting. Prevention is simply a case of wearing a foam-lined helmet or a neoprene skullcap under your helmet and suitable protective clothing. (See Chapter 12.)

Another effect is a form of hyperventilation. The cold causes people to keep trying to breathe in and feeling unable to breathe out. With habituation, cold water immersion is less likely to have this effect. Some raft guides brief their clients to counter this by shouting as loud as they can when they surface. This has the effect of expelling air from their lungs as well as attracting the raft guide's attention.

Hypothermia

Hypothermia is a condition brought about by a lowering of the body's core temperature, which can ultimately result in death. It is caused by a person being unable to generate enough heat to counteract the effects of cold due to exhaustion, or, more commonly with boaters, through the rapid lowering of the core temperature caused by immersion in cold water.

EVEN IN ITS MILDEST FORM, HYPOTHERMIA CAN DRASTICALLY AFFECT A PERSON'S JUDGMENT

Figure 3-16 doubt creeping in on the Grass River, New York State. Photo: Mark Rainsley

Being mammals, humans need to maintain the vital organs of the body at a constant 98.6°F (37°C). The critical thing about hypothermia is that even in the early stages, in its mildest form, it can drastically affect a person's judgment. Therefore if you are feeling very cold, you should take remedial action or get off the river before you start making dangerous mistakes.

▶ **PREVENTION**—The emphasis should be very much on avoidance.

1 Avoid taking long swims by careful scouting, thorough assessment of the risks involved and skillful paddling.

2 Maintain a suitable level of personal fitness.

3 Eat well before and during a river trip. Complex carbohydrates such as rice, pasta, bread, and cereals provide energy in a form that is made available to your body at a steady rate and over several hours.

4 Wear suitable clothing for the conditions and type of paddling.

5 Buddy up and keep an eye on each other for the early signs of hypothermia.

6 Be prepared to shorten or abort a trip if members of the party show signs of getting too cold.

7 If one member of the party is suffering from hypothermia, there is a good chance that the conditions that affected them are affecting everyone else. Therefore action should be taken to protect the team as well as treat the victim.

▶ **SIGNS AND SYMPTOMS**—The good news about immersion hypothermia is that if someone takes a long swim in glacial melt water it is obvious that we should suspect its onset. Unfortunately exhaustion hypothermia can easily go unnoticed in its early stages. Paddlers can fall prey to either form or a mixture of both. Therefore whenever we paddle in cold conditions or someone goes for a swim in cold water it is important to look out for the signs and symptoms.

In a hospital, doctors would take a core temperature. This involves the use of a rectal thermometer which is not very practical on the river bank and would probably result in the first aider being assaulted by the victim! The signs and symptoms are what matter. The figures below indicate the core temperature at which they normally occur. Note that a victim may not exhibit all of the signs and the order they appear in may vary slightly.

Figure 3-17 in an alert group of boaters who work as an effective team, hypothermia would rarely be able to progress beyond the early warning stage unnoticed or untreated.

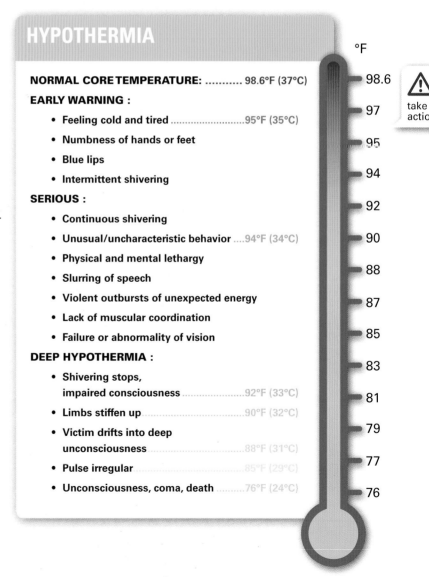

HYPOTHERMIA

°F

NORMAL CORE TEMPERATURE: .... 98.6°F (37°C)

EARLY WARNING :

- **Feeling cold and tired** ....95°F (35°C)
- **Numbness of hands or feet**
- **Blue lips**
- **Intermittent shivering**

SERIOUS :

- **Continuous shivering**
- **Unusual/uncharacteristic behavior** ....94°F (34°C)
- **Physical and mental lethargy**
- **Slurring of speech**
- **Violent outbursts of unexpected energy**
- **Lack of muscular coordination**
- **Failure or abnormality of vision**

DEEP HYPOTHERMIA :

- **Shivering stops, impaired consciousness** ....92°F (33°C)
- **Limbs stiffen up** ....90°F (32°C)
- **Victim drifts into deep unconsciousness** ....88°F (31°C)
- **Pulse irregular** ....85°F (29°C)
- **Unconsciousness, coma, death** ....76°F (24°C)

take action

98.6
97
95
94
92
90
88
87
85
83
81
79
77
76

▶ **TREATMENT**—In the case of immersion hypothermia, the body hasn't depleted its energy reserves. This means that victims will respond more quickly to treatment and are more likely to make a complete recovery. The field treatment for both types of hypothermia is essentially the same, except that if exhaustion hypothermia is suspected, one should assume that victims are unfit to continue, even if they appear to have made a full recovery. If remoteness means that the easiest way to evacuate them is to continue paddling, they should be made to rest and eat for as long as is practicable before setting off.

▶ **EARLY STAGES**—treat the early signs of hypothermia as follows:

1 **Prevent Further Use of Energy**—Exercise will draw warm blood away from the core where it is needed and use up energy reserves which the body needs to generate heat for the core.

2 **Prevent Further Heat Loss**—Provide shelter from wind and rain. Put extra clothing on victims. Put them in a bivouac bag (a 7 by 3 foot [2 by 1 m] plastic bag). If available put them in a sleeping bag. Be aware that the insulation in a sleeping bag keeps heat out as effectively as it keeps heat in. Therefore it is best to put a warm-bodied person in with the victim.

3 **Slowly Reheat Victims**—This is best achieved by providing an environment in which they are breathing warm moist air. In this way they are rewarmed from the inside. In a house this can be achieved by sitting them down in a steam-filled bathroom heated to 104°F (40°C). In a hut or tent heat and humidity can be provided by boiling a pot of water on a stove, being careful not to knock it over and burn the victims. On the river bank the most effective way is to get all the members of the party in a "group shelter." Once inside, everybody's body heat and breath soon provides a warm moist environment. This has the added bonus of ensuring nobody else develops hypothermia as well as rewarming the victims.

4 **Encourage the Victims to Eat**—Give them food that will rapidly provide energy with which the body can quickly digest and generate heat; glucose and sugars (simple carbohydrates). Follow this up with food such as pancakes, cereal bars, biscuits and sandwiches (complex carbohydrates) in order to stabilize their blood sugar levels and provide a longer term energy source.

Figure 3-18 group shelter.

▶ **SERIOUS HYPOTHERMIA**—As for early stages plus:

- **Seek Hospital Treatment—Even if the victim appears to make a full recovery.**

- **Stretcher Evacuation—Unless the victim appears to make a full recovery he should be evacuated on a stretcher and not permitted to use energy by walking or paddling.**

SOME THINGS TO AVOID:

- ## DO NOT RUB VICTIMS
- ## DO NOT PLACE WARM OBJECTS ON THE VICTIMS' BODIES
- ## DO NOT GIVE THE VICTIMS ALCOHOL

The body's natural defense involves shutting off circulation to the limbs and surface blood vessels. This ensures that warm blood is retained in the core where it is needed and cold surface blood isn't allowed to cool the core further. All of the above "treatments" have the opposite detrimental effect.

Sunshine

Paddlers in summer climates are well aware of the potential damage from the sun.

Hyperthermia

Hyperthermia is caused by the body overheating and can be divided into two distinct stages: *Heat exhaustion* is caused when the body overheats, and having lost too much water and salt through sweating, is struggling to maintain a normal body temperature.

Untreated it can lead to *heat stroke*. This occurs when the body is no longer able to sweat and the body's temperature rises unchecked. This condition can become life threatening.

Figure 3-19 dehydrating on the trek into the Bio Susisa. Photo: Mark Rainsley

▶ **PREVENTION**—Prevention is simple, In warm climates *drink plenty of water*; don't put your wet suit on until just before getting on the water and have rest/lunch breaks in the shade. On whitewater stretches the constant splashing with cold water keeps paddlers cool. On long flat stretches it may be necessary to splash yourself or roll from time to time.

▶ **HEAT   EXHAUSTION**—Beware! Although not in itself a serious condition it will progress to heat stroke if the casualty is not re-moved from the source of heat.

▶ **SIGNS AND SYMPTOMS**

- Feeling unwell; headache, dizziness, nausea, cramps

- Weakness

- Moist skin

▶ **TREATMENT**

- Remove to cool area

- Give fluids

HEAT STROKE

▶ **SIGNS AND SYMPTOMS**

- Confusion/loss of consciousness

- Skin hot and dry

- High temperature

▶**TREATMENT**

- Reduce temperature by removing to cool area

- Bathe with tepid water. (Drenching them with very cold water could cause heart failure)

- Fan the casualty

- Seek urgent medical attention

- If the casualty is unconscious, place in the recovery position

Dehydration

Peeling off layers of paddling clothing is very inconvenient. It is therefore tempting to drink as little as possible to avoid having to go to the toilet. This is a great mistake both in terms of the risk of hyper- and hypothermia and in terms of reduced performance. Paddlers should drink frequently in hot and cold climates.

Sunburn

Paddlers abroad are particularly prone. If they are used to paddling in the rain at home, they don't realize how quickly and badly they can burn.

▶ **PREVENTION**

- Avoid the noon day sun and rest in the shade whenever possible.

- Wear long sleeved garments and sun hats to protect the ears and neck.

- Use waterproof sun block on all exposed skin and apply frequently.

▶ **TREATMENT**

- Cool affected area by bathing in cool water for 10 minutes.

- Prevent infection by not bursting any blisters and covering any that have burst with a sterile dressing.

- Prevent any further exposure to direct sunlight.

- Ensure that the victim drinks plenty of fluids.

- If the sunburn is severe and covers an extensive surface area, medical attention should be sought.

Eye Damage

Sun reflected off water can cause eye damage in the same way as sunlight reflected off snow. In the short term this can cause extreme discomfort and in extreme cases temporary blindness. In the long term the accumulated permanent damage can lead to cataracts and other forms of eye damage.

Figure 3-20 sunglasses and a peaked hat for eye protection.

▶ **PREVENTION**

- Wear sunglasses and peaked hats

▶ **SIGNS & SYMPTOMS**

- Headaches
- Tears
- Gritty painful eyes

▶ **TREATMENT**

- Rest in a dark room and seek medical treatment

Ear Damage

Aural osteomata is a condition also known as "swimmer's ear" or "surfer's ear." Subjecting your ears to frequent incursions of cold water causes bony growths to develop, which narrow the ear passage. Eventually this causes frequent ear infections and even deafness.

One method of prevention is to wear earplugs. Even with the earplugs in place, you can still hear well enough for normal river communication. It is also a good idea to tape up the earholes on your helmet during the colder months.

Some manufacturers now make very thin neoprene or Lycra skull caps. These fit easily under a helmet to cover the ears and are designed to prevent surfer's ear.

*Figure 3-21
a thin neoprene
skull-cap is unobtrusive
underneath your helmet
and affords additional
ear protection as well
as warmth.*

The wearing of earplugs or skull-caps can also help in the prevention of pierced eardrums which can occur when the ear is subjected to violent water pressure at the foot of larger waterfalls or on big volume rapids.

Polluted Water

*Figure 3-22
noseplug.*

On our crowded planet it is a fact of life that many whitewater rivers or sites are polluted to some degree. Rivers that are heavily polluted with industrial effluent are out of the question, but many less polluted rivers are paddled regularly. In "developed" countries where sewage is treated, the risk of getting a viral infection is least in the warm summer months when water levels are low. This is because the "bugs" used in the treatment plants to break down the sewage are at their most efficient in the warm months.

Periods of higher flows are higher risk, summer or winter, because accumulated rubbish is washed out of storm drains and the treatment tanks of sewage plants may overflow. This means that untreated or partially treated sewage gets into the river.

PERIODS OF HIGHER FLOWS ARE HIGHER RISK

In poorer countries, the disposal of rubbish and feces and, in some places, the bodies of those too poor to afford a funeral pyre, take place on the river bank. This is deliberately done above the normal high water mark. This means that the water is as clean as it can be for most of the year. In the monsoon all this detritus is swept downstream to fertilize the plains. During the early part of the monsoon almost everyone, canoeists and locals, are ill with some form of stomach bug.

▶ **PREVENTION**

- Avoid paddling polluted rivers in periods of high flow.
- Remove wet clothing and wash hands and face in clean water, or better still, take a shower before eating or drinking.
- If you have to paddle on polluted water consider using a nose plug.

▶ **IN COUNTRIES WHERE TAP WATER IS UNTREATED**

- Treat your drinking water. Either use one of the commercial systems where you pump through a filter that also adds iodine at the required dose, or add two drops (more if the water is heavily polluted) of tincture of iodine (available from any drugstore) and allow to stand for an hour before drinking. (Note that chlorine based water purifying tablets will not kill the cysts that transmit amoebic dysentery.)
- Only eat food that has been thoroughly cooked and is still hot.
- Don't take milk in tea or coffee unless it has been boiled.
- Don't eat locally made ice cream or items such as salads which have probably been washed in polluted water.

 **HEALTH WARNING**

ALTHOUGH SAFE IN SMALL QUANTITIES, IODINE IS A POISON THAT BUILDS UP IN THE THYROID GLAND. THEREFORE IF YOU ARE GOING ABROAD FOR AN EXTENDED PERIOD IT MAY NOT BE A SUITABLE SOLUTION.

Leptospirosis or Weil's Disease

This is a potentially serious disease that is transmitted when rats' urine is washed into water courses. The main symptoms are very much like those of flu. Weil's Disease is not very common and is usually associated with sewage workers. This means that many doctors in general practice are unlikely to suspect it.

It is just as prevalent among paddlers as sewage workers. Therefore if you suspect you may have it, you may have to insist that they send off a sample of blood for testing urgently. If undiagnosed and untreated, Weil's disease can be fatal.

CHAPTER 4
Planning a Descent

Whether it be an eight-day unsupported trip in Nepal or a day's paddling on one of the local rivers, the factors that affect our planning from a safety viewpoint are the same (there may be additional concerns when paddling abroad):

- **Your team's skill level and experience**
- **The difficulty of the rivers you would like to paddle**
- **Water levels**
- **How committing or remote the river is**
- **Transport to and from the river**
- **How you feel on the day**

The Team

It is important to create a team environment. On wild rivers you should paddle with people who will support each other. Competition is a luxury we can only afford on safe sites and playwaves!

A sizeable portion of the time I have spent teaching on whitewater has involved rebuilding individual paddlers' shattered confidence. The story is nearly always the same. Their "friends" tell them not to worry that it's a grade harder than they've ever paddled. "It's easy for the grade. You'll be fine." What the so-called friends really mean is that they are determined to paddle a given river for their own selfish reasons, and if our paddler isn't up to it, tough! Inevitably our paddler gets trashed and his self confidence plummets.

PADDLE WITH PEOPLE WHO WILL SUPPORT EACH OTHER

Figure 4-1 the team mellowing out, Rio Chotohuasi, Peru.

Rivers should be chosen on the basis of what the least able paddler can manage. Many rivers have sections of differing levels of difficulty. This allows the extreme whitewater paddlers, or "hair boaters," to warm up on the easier section while the less able paddlers have a stretching but enjoyable time. The more able paddlers then go on to test themselves on the harder section and everyone goes home happy.

If you are choosing a trip for a team that includes people you haven't paddled with before, be careful. When some people say they paddle grade 5, they mean that they have paddled the odd 5 where a positive mental attitude and good reactions will get you down in one piece. Their boating skills and ability to work the water may not be up to more technically demanding grade 5s.

Difficulty

When taking on a river that has rarely or never been run before, paddlers have to make some guestimates about the difficulty of the river based on its volume and its gradient. The steeper a river is, the less volume of water it needs to be a difficult paddle. Equally, the more volume it has, the less gradient it needs to reach the same level of difficulty, albeit in a very different way. Most of us are quite happy to gather information on a river from a guidebook or paddlers who have first-hand knowledge of it.

Figure 4-2 planning a day's boating.

Guidebooks

IT IS YOUR PROBLEM, NOT THE GUIDEBOOK WRITER'S

It is important to remember that a guidebook's function is to give a rough idea of what we are in for. It is not supposed to be a substitute for our eyes, ears, brain and river sense. In my view a guidebook should provide the following information:

- The general layout and character of the river system

- The volume and gradient

- The overall difficulty of the river

- The difficulty of any rapids or drops that are markedly harder than the rest of the river

- The position of any mandatory or advisable portages

- Information on any hidden or easily overlooked hazards

- Where to start and finish

- Other points at which it is possible to take out (escape routes)

- Local customs and attitudes (This can be a very important safety factor)

Everything else should be down to personal observation and judgment. Trees fall across rivers, boulders move, eroded bedrock collapses, water levels change. If you get into difficulties, it is your problem, not the guidebook writer's.

▶ **ONLINE GUIDES**—The Internet is an increasingly useful resource. In seldom paddled areas guidebooks are not commercially viable. However online guides do not require huge print costs so individuals often share their knowledge of an area via Web sites. A few key words in a search engine and away you go. However, be aware that the accuracy of the information offered will vary enormously.

▶ **RIVER GRADES OR CLASS**—The way we try and define difficulty is by use of a grading system. Although adequate, this system has lots of flaws. How can a 177 cubic feet per second (5 cubic meters per second) creek, so steep you get vertigo, be given the same grade as a river like the Sun Khosi in Nepal, which has a very low gradient but can run at 14,126 cubic feet per second (400 cubic meters per second? As outlined in Chapter 3, I feel that the system breaks down completely when it comes to big drops.

The truth is that the system does work quite well, providing the guidebook also tells you if the river is low, high or medium volume and continuous or pool/drop.

Only with experience will we get to know what a high volume grade 3 or grade 5 is like, and what makes a low volume, steep creek just as difficult, although in a completely different way.

Figure 4-3 (below) the international river grading system. Note: "Pressure areas" refer to boils and cushion waves. Low head dams are not classified here as they are either easily navigable or very dangerous.

▶ **THE INTERNATIONAL RIVER GRADING SYSTEM**

GRADE 1	GRADE 2	GRADE 3	GRADE 4	GRADE 5	GRADE 6
Free Passage	Free Passage	Recognizable route	Route not always recognizable	Route difficult to recognize	Generally speaking impossible
Regular stream	Irregular stream	High irregular waves	Inspection mostly necessary	Inpection essential	Possibly navigable at particular water levels
Regular waves	Irregular waves	Larger rapids, stoppers, eddies, whirlpools & pressure areas	Heavy continuous rapids, stoppers, whirlpools & pressure areas	Extreme rapids, stoppers, whirlpools & pressure areas	High risk
Small rapids	Medium rapids, small stoppers, eddies, whirlpools & pressure areas	Isolated boulders, small drops & multiple obstructions	Boulders obstructing stream, big with undertow	Narrow passages, steep gradients and drops with difficult access and landing	
Simple obstructions	Simple obstructions & small drops				

At normal water levels you might translate the table as follows:

▶ **GRADE 1**—Even complete novices could paddle on this provided they can be kept away from overhanging trees.

▶ **GRADE 2**—The ideal grade on which to learn and hone basic white-water boating skills. There are some dangers but they can be easily maneuvered around, provided you recognize them.

▶ **GRADE 3**—At this grade you can come across nearly all the water features and hazards there are. However, a "line" down the rapid is clear enough that a competent paddler could tackle it without the need for a bank inspection. Dangerous hazards are few and easily avoided by those with the skill to maneuver. Bank-based protection may, in places, be a good idea with relative novices.

▶ **GRADE 4**—The line can be scouted from your boat but it is advisable to bank inspect. The line is difficult to manoeuvre down, even for skillful paddlers. Mistakes can be costly. Bank-based rescuers, positioned in advance may be helpful, especially with less experienced paddlers.

▶ **GRADE 5**—The line is complex due to the increased number of dangerous hazards that have to be avoided. Bank inspection is essential. Staying on your chosen line will require a high skill level and a cool head. Mistakes will involve risk to life and limb. Where feasible, bank-based rescuers, positioned in advance, are the norm.

▶ **GRADE 6**—Only runnable at specific water levels. The slightest mistake will involve risk to life. Even the most skillful and cool-headed paddlers will need to feel at peak form to take one of these on.

Figure 4-4 running deep in a sheer sided gorge, the rapids on this section give a heightened sense of severity. River Cuileig, Torridon.

HEALTH WARNING

DON'T PUSH YOUR LUCK ON UNFAMILIAR WATER. ARE STEEP RIVERS OR BIG VOLUME NEW TO YOU? DROP A GRADE WHILE YOU LEARN THE NEW STYLE, SKILLS AND APPROACH NEEDED FOR A BIG WATER OR STEEP CREEK ENVIRONMENT. THEY ARE VERY DIFFERENT.

▶ **OTHER SYSTEMS**—In many guidebooks there are variations on the 1-6 system. Many guidebook writers use the symbols + or - to let you know whether a rapid is at the harder or easier end of the grade. It is also common practice to use brackets to indicate isolated rapids that are harder than the rest of the river and easily portaged. If a river was mostly grade 3 but had a couple of short sections of 5, it would appear as 3(5).

Many guidebooks use symbols or letters to give additional information. For example the Scottish and English Whitewater guides use these symbols:

 Full-Face Helmet—"a short boat run of a rocky or precarious nature, come equipped with full-on gear."

 Footprint—"the approach to this run requires a significant walk in."

 Dagger—"this section is not a tried and tested descent, the authors may have run it once or twice, or the rapids may be subject to periodic change, proceed with due caution."

Maps

On remote rivers it is essential to carry maps in case you are forced to walk out, through boat loss or injury.

I find that conventional maps are of little, if any, use once you are afloat. They are however very useful in the planning stages for identifying access and egress points and finding landmarks to warn you of the approach of major rapids or portages. In Switzerland and other parts of Europe there are maps made specifically for boaters that contain the above information. They also use a color code to let you know at a glance what grade any given section of river is. These maps *must* be used in conjunction with the guidebook as they give no indication of what "normal" water levels are.

Water Levels

As discussed in Chapter 2, changes in water levels can make your intended paddle considerably harder or easier. Most guidebooks will tell you how to work out what the average or guidebook level is. This will usually involve water gauges, which are often positioned near bridges, or failing that, local landmarks such as prominent boulders. Study them carefully and try and find out how much these changes affect the river you have in mind. If no information is available, assume that the higher the water level, the more serious/dangerous the river becomes.

▶ **SEASONAL CHANGES**—All the river systems of the world are either fed by melting snow/glaciers or rain. Snow and ice act as a reservoir, making the release of water predictable on a seasonal basis. So, if for example you are planning a trip with the Wild Bunch, you would go to the French Alps in May and the rivers would almost certainly be huge. On the other hand, if you wanted to paddle some of the more technical gorges, you might choose to go in early August when the rivers are low but still runnable.

*Figure 4-5
water flow on
fast-flowing
rivers.*

▶ **DAILY VARIATIONS**—In snow-melt rivers the water is usually lower in the morning and at its highest in the late afternoon, due to the influence of the midday sun.

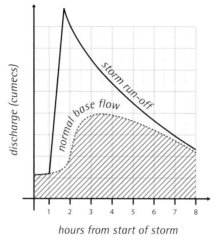

discharge (cumecs)

storm run-off

normal base flow

hours from start of storm

In rain-fed systems water levels go up and down like yo-yos. Keep an eye on the weather charts for some days before your planned trip. Contact local paddlers who won't mind you phoning them for a rain check. Fast-flowing rivers come up far faster than they go down. Therefore it is safer to get on them when they have reached the optimum level and are on the way back down. Mature rivers, fed by heads of water such as large lakes, come up more slowly and hold their water for longer.

Commitment

*Figure 4-6 (below)
a committing paddle,
the canyon walls rise
nearly 10,000 feet
(over 3,000m). Canon
del Chocolat, Rio
Colca, Peru.*

If a river trip involves being several hours from help should someone get injured, it raises the seriousness stakes considerably. A multi-day trip will involve you paddling a boat that is much heavier and therefore less responsive. I believe that such considerations take a good half or even a whole grade off what I am prepared to paddle. A laden boat increases the probability of error and remoteness increases the consequences.

Trips Abroad

Factors to consider when planning a trip abroad:

▶ **INSURANCE**—Make sure your medical/travel insurance covers whitewater boating and the costs of rescue/evacuation.

▶ **MEDICAL**—Have a check-up before you go and ensure, well before the event, that you have had any necessary inoculations. Find out whether you will need to take anti-malarial precautions in that part of the world and consult your doctor for up-to-date advice.

▶ **TRANSPORT**—Getting to and from your chosen rivers can be a logistical nightmare. If you have plenty of time but a very limited budget, kayakers can get around on local transport, though in some countries this will probably be the most interesting and most dangerous part of the trip.

If you are tight on time, anything that can be done to minimize logistical problems is a good idea. For some trips you can use a local outfitter; this costs but saves all the hassle of getting boats and equipment out there and covers local transport arrangements. Another alternative is to use a local travel company to arrange for a vehicle and driver, hire of boats, accommodation and in some countries, permits. Wherever possible, try and use people who come recommended by other boaters.

The sheer volume of equipment involved in rafting means that, where possible, it is usually cheaper and more practical to hire from a local company/guide than freight equipment out.

Figure 4-7 (below left) raft accompanied trip. River Skeena, BC. Photo: Dave Walker

Figure 4-8 (below right) in countries like Canada where distances are vast, flying in may be the only practical method.

Figure 4-9 whatever your method of transport, don't get separated from your boats. Rio Chotohuasi, Peru

Kayakers can team up with raft trips so that they don't have to carry any food or camping equipment. Personally, I prefer lightweight unaccompanied trips. Rafters carry so much luxury equipment that the hardest work of the day is helping load and unload the rafts!

Whatever you do, don't get separated from the vehicle, donkeys, elephants or whatever is carrying your boats and equipment. Travel at their pace. It can be tempting to arrange to meet them and travel at your pace but a simple misunderstanding can mean hours or even days of frustration while you try to find them again.

How You Feel on the Day

This factor really can't be emphasized enough. When planning a day's river running, paddlers should always have a number of rivers on their list. This allows considerable flexibility to take into account unseasonable water levels or members of the party feeling off peak form. On multi-day wilderness trips consider the option of a rest day.

Tamba Khosi, Nepal

"After a twelve hour bus journey on the most frightening roads imaginable, a meal of Dhal Bhat at a local tea house, and a bivvi at the water's edge, I was raring to go. I had already packed and was watching Ray check, for the third time, that he had packed everything.

"I couldn't help chuckling. Untypically, he had been very disorganized at the start of the trip. We had even had to take a detour into Central London on the way to the airport to pick up his visa. I had given him no end of stick about this, as you do.

"At long last he looked up, a satisfied grin on his face. 'No, I haven't forgotten anything,' he announced. I looked down at my boat and suddenly felt as sick as a chocolate parrot, 'Ah,' I groaned, 'I have. I've left my helmet at the hotel!'"

TACTICS
Reading Whitewater
Choosing a Line
Spatial Awareness

TECHNIQUE
Paddle Strokes
Edge Control
Body Movement
Timing

BOAT POSITIONING

MENTAL PREPARATION
Control of Anxiety
Psyching Up

FITNESS
Stamina
Strength
Flexibility

Figure 5-1 skillful paddling.
Photo: Dino Heald

CHAPTER 5

Skillful Paddling

The best way to become a safer paddler is to be a better paddler! Combined with the ability to read water, skill is a far better guarantee of safety than a full-face helmet and body armor.

Skill

Skill in paddling whitewater is the ability to choose a line and paddle down it smoothly and efficiently. A truly skillful paddler makes it look effortless.

The diagram above shows a profile of all the parts that have to come together for a paddler to perform skillfully. When all these factors combine, what we see is in essence good boat positioning. It doesn't matter in what proportion the parts are mixed, as long as the end result is that the paddler is in the right place at the right time. They also need to be pointing in the right direction, moving at the right speed and the right way up!

Mental Preparation

This subject is covered in Chapter 6.

Tactics

Reading whitewater is covered in Chapter 2.

Choosing a line is the ability to "see" a way down a rapid that avoids all the hazards and uses rather than fights the water wherever possible. It is your brain's contribution to good boat positioning.

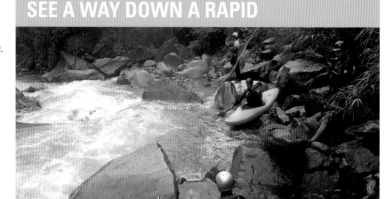

CHOOSING A LINE IS THE ABILITY TO SEE A WAY DOWN A RAPID

Figure 5-2 choosing a line, Rio Calaya, Bolivia. Photo Mark Rainsley

When choosing their line paddlers need to ask themselves the following questions:

1 Which way is the water flowing?

2 What hazards need to be avoided?

3 Will the water take the paddlers where they want to go?

4 Where it won't, what do they need to do to stay on a line that avoids any hazards?

5 Are they capable of making the moves necessary?

Technique

Good technique will serve a paddler far better than brute strength.

It would take another book to cover technique, so for now I will refer the reader to other books. However, as it has a direct bearing on safety, we will look at some techniques that, when performed poorly, can lead to injuries.

In both the following cases poor technique can and frequently does lead to shoulder dislocations. If this injury ever occurs, help should be sought from a specialist sports physiotherapist. It is vital to build up the various groups of muscles that prevent instability of the shoulder joint. Repeated dislocations could lead to irreparable damage and the end of that person's paddling days. Prevention is better than cure. Nonetheless, treatment is dealt with in the chapter on first aid.

*Figure 5-3 (left)
a poor high brace.*

*Figure 5-4 (right)
a good high brace
support stroke.*

▶ **HIGH BRACE—**A kayak technique, the high brace is used to prevent a capsize. The kayaker reaches out at 90° and gains support by laying the drive face of the blade on the water and pulling down, with his wrists underneath the paddle shaft. The stroke can be used statically, as a brace, where a water feature provides so much uplift that it feels like one is resting the paddle on a firm cushion. Alternately, it can be used dynamically, as a support stroke. In this case the paddler gains enough support to bring the boat back upright by pulling down powerfully on the paddle.

Good technique consists of keeping the mid-point of the shaft no more than forehead high and keeping both elbows bent . Bent elbows act as shock absorbers relieving the pressure on the shoulder joint.

Bad technique is illustrated in Figure 5-3. The shoulder joint is already at the extreme end of its range and the elbow is already fully extended. Should there be a sudden increase on the force applied to the paddle there is no way to safely absorb the energy. The only way of relieving the pressure is for the shoulder to dislocate, or for the paddler to let go of the paddle. Unfortunately it often happens too quickly for the latter to be an option.

▶ **BOW RUDDER—**The bow rudder, or "Dufek stroke," is a very variable stroke. It has been suggested that a better name for it would be the Vertical Paddle Turn. The blade that is in the water may, depending on the situation, be held in a position that can range from almost touching the hull of your boat forward of your knee, to reaching out to the side level with your hip. In the latter case the placement should be achieved by rotating the trunk, rather than by just using your arms.

*Figure 5-5 (left)
unsafe example of
a bow rudder.*

*Figure 5-6 (right)
a good example of
a bow rudder.*

Try the following exercise

Sit upright on a bench or hard backed chair. Now hold one arm so that your elbow is touching your side and your forearm sticks horizontally out in front of you at 90° to your upper arm. Keeping your upper body still and your elbow at your side, rotate your forearm out to the side and see how far it will go. The position your arm is now in is the extreme range of movement permitted by your "outer rotator cuff muscles." In most male paddlers the range of movement will be about 80°. In female paddlers it may be over 100°. Memorize this position and then go back to the original position.

This time, by rotating your trunk, turn your shoulders through 90° and place your forearm in the same place it reached in the first movement. Now try to rotate your forearm even further. You should find that because you have rotated your trunk you can now rotate your forearm through another 20°+. This represents the safety margin that is introduced through good technique.

Fitness

A paddler inactive for months and then jumping straight onto a demanding whitewater run, may find their body unable to deliver the fitness component of the skill required.

The best way to get fit for paddling is to paddle regularly. Even if paddlers live a long way from whitewater they can still paddle on flat water to build up stamina and strength, and maintain flexibility. If you have had a long break from paddling, build up slowly.

Geographical location and work patterns may make it impossible to paddle as regularly as is necessary to maintain the required standard of fitness. A carefully thought out fitness training regime, designed to build up strength and stamina in the right proportions, and at the same time maintain flexibility, can pay dividends.

Seek expert advice. Poorly thought out training can do more harm than good. If the right muscle groups are not built up in a balanced way it can set up an instability in the muscles that affect the shoulder joint. This can make paddlers more prone to dislocations. Strength training must be complemented by stretching in order to maintain flexibility. Research shows that over-flexibility in the shoulder joint can make paddlers more prone to dislocations. The shoulder is a very poorly designed joint and it is only the tension of the various muscle groups that hold it in place.

Stretching should be used to promote the normal range of movement required for paddling.

Figure 5-7 playboating—improving skills and fitness by having fun.

Boat Positioning

There are four ways paddlers can go about hitting their chosen line:

- **By moving faster than the current**
- **By choosing to drift at the same speed as the current**
- **By moving slower than the current**
- **By using water features**

Figure 5-8

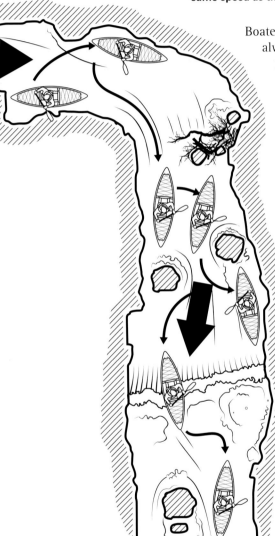

Boaters involved in competition such as slalom try to always move faster than the current. They need to be fast and accurate.

Traditional open boaters and rafters generally try to go slower than, or at the same speed as, the current. They need to use their buoyancy to ride over the waves, because if they go fast and plough through them, they will get swamped.

Kayakers, closed deck C1 paddlers and specialist whitewater open boats (with asymmetrical hulls, saddles and buoyancy bags) will benefit from using a mixture of all three approaches.

▶ **FASTER**—The times you need to be moving forward are to accelerate into or out of an eddy, to "punch through" a stopper, or when paddling across a fast-flowing current to avoid an obstacle or hazard. In each of these cases there needs to be a distinct change of pace. If you are only paddling forward because you have chosen to in preference to other methods, then you can afford a more leisurely pace. In both cases good forward paddling technique will pay dividends, either gaining more speed or saving energy.

▶ **SAME SPEED**—If the flow of water is taking you where you want to go, then you can afford to drift. Your paddles should still be in the water, either moving the boat sideways using draw strokes to make small corrections to keep you on line, or in the low brace position to keep you stable.

WHEN DELIBERATELY ALLOWING YOURSELF TO DRIFT, YOU SHOULD BE VERY AWARE OF WHERE THE WATER IS TAKING YOU

When deliberately allowing yourself to drift you should be very aware of where the water is taking you and ready to change mode when the flow is no longer going your way.

▶ **SLOWER**—By reverse paddling with your stern pointing directly upstream, you slow your boat down, or even hold your position in relation to the bank. By reverse paddling and angling your boat to the current (reverse ferry glide) you slow down and move across the current. This allows you to adjust your position and stay on line while moving slower than the current.

Apart from not swamping open boats, the main advantage of slowing your boat down is that you get more time to see what is coming and plan your moves.

In modern whitewater playboats that have very low and flat back decks, it is necessary to lean right forward when reverse ferry gliding. Failure to do this may result in an involuntary tail stand.

Changing Gear

When paddling on whitewater you need to be either idling, paddling at a steady rate or, if only briefly, going flat out. It is important to:

1 Know when to paddle in which mode.

2 Be able to change gear instantly.

A good exercise is to set up a circuit on a section of easy rapid. Plan your line, decide how you are going to stay on your line, where you can afford to idle, where to paddle at a steady rate and where you need to accelerate. Then paddle the circuit, consciously and deliberately changing speed at the points you identified earlier. At the points where acceleration is called for, shout "NOW," and paddle flat out. The shout will let your companions know at which point you intended to speed up, allowing them to feed back to you how effective your acceleration was.

Figure 5-9 surfing a wave to cross the river. Photo: Dino Heald

Using Water Features

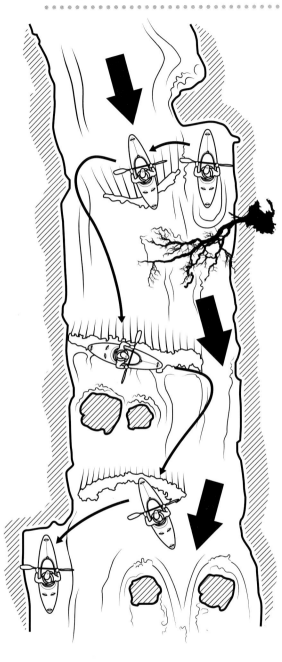

Figure 5-10

Every paddler must be able to read white-water well enough to choose a line down a rapid. The sign of an advanced paddler is the ability to read the water well enough to make use of water features, large and small, to accurately work his way down a rapid with the least effort. A tired paddler makes mistakes, so whenever possible use the water rather than fight it. With modern short length/flat hulled boats that lack forward speed but can surf the merest hint of a wave, this is more important than ever. The most commonly used ways of doing this are:

- **Surfing standing waves**
- **Side-surfing stoppers**
- **Using the edge of a stopper to turn**

These skills are best practiced by getting involved in playboating, or freestyle as the competitive version is known. All that is needed is a standing wave, a "friendly" stopper and a group of friends.

TRAIN HARD, PADDLE EASY

It is quite possible to have a grade 3 and a grade 5 rapid that require the same level of technical skill to follow the chosen line. If the paddlers end up off line on the grade 3, they will probably be able to fight their way down anyway. If they lose the line on the grade 5 they are in serious, possibly life threatening, danger.

I believe that grade 2 is where we should learn our basic whitewater skills. Beginners shouldn't move on to harder rivers until they are in control at this level. That is to say that they can follow a predetermined line down a rapid and make a number of predetermined eddies on the way, rather than simply getting to the bottom of the rapid still upright.

Grade 3 is where we hone our skills and ensure that we are sufficiently skilled to cope with the demands of hard whitewater paddling before we move up the grades. Before considering themselves ready to move on to harder things, paddlers should practice until they are competent, confident and fluent on grade 3. They should also make the relatively safe grade 3 that they are paddling as technically difficult as grade 4 and 5, by deliberately choosing the most difficult line down the rapid, and making as many eddies as they can. In this way it is possible to simulate the difficulty of grade 4 and 5 paddling without paying such a high price if mistakes are made.

Coaching

GOOD COACHING IS A VALUABLE INVESTMENT

Good coaching is a valuable investment. It can lay firm foundations for future skill by ensuring that the basics are learned well and that bad habits are not embedded. Experienced paddlers can benefit from it to help them get over a learning plateau or iron out bad habits.

Practice

Practice, and lots of it, is what is needed but beware, practice doesn't make perfect. Practice makes permanent. So, when training, someone else needs to observe the paddler, and give constructive feedback that will help him improve.

The other important thing about practice is that it should be as varied as possible. Use different locations, practice on the left and right, vary the angles, speeds, stroke work and approach.

Figure 5-11 Stu Morris at the UK Freestyle Championships, Holme Pierrepont, Nottingham.

CHAPTER 6
Mental Preparation and Warm Up

As mentioned in the previous chapter, mental preparation is a crucial aspect of skillful boating. A skillful paddler, who stays in control, is safe.

Stress

It is important to create a team environment. On wild rivers you should paddle with people who will support each other. Competition is a luxury we can only afford on safe sites and playwaves!

Figure 6-1 mental rehearsal helps turn "seeing the line" into "making the line." Verzasca River, Italy. Photo: Sarah Nash

To paddle well, you have to be sufficiently stimulated or "aroused." The right amount of stress heightens awareness, speeds up reactions and ensures that brain and body are on full alert (excitement or healthy fear).

Too little stress and we "wind down." This leads to a lack of concentration and a tendency to make stupid mistakes. Most boaters can think of times when they have run a difficult rapid perfectly, only to foul up on the easy section.

Too much stress and we become over-anxious. Our performance decreases dramatically to the point where a paddler may even "freeze" (unhealthy fear or terror).

Catastrophe Curve

Figure 6-2
the catastrophe
curve. Curve
A represents a
stress resilient
person and Curve B
represents a stress
prone person.

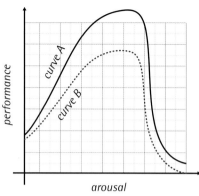

performance

curve A

curve B

arousal

As we become more stimulated, the standard of our performance steadily increases. Eventually we reach the point where the stress becomes harmful and our performance starts to suffer. The bad news is that after a brief initial gentle decline, performance doesn't decline steadily . . . it plummets!

▶ **RECOVERING**—Recovering from such a plummet requires a slow and methodical build-up of confidence. If people "crash" on a grade 5, paddling grade 4 won't allow them to recover. They will have to go right back to something they can cope with without any stress at all, probably grade 2/3 and only build up once they have relaxed and started to really enjoy their paddling again.

▶ **INDIVIDUAL DIFFERENCES**—Some individuals can cope with much higher levels of stress than others (curve A). Other people's performance curves peak at a much lower level (curve B).

Some people perform well at high levels of stress but are easily stimulated and have to be careful not to become overstressed. Others only perform well when highly stressed and find it difficult, on all but the most dangerous rapids, to be sufficiently stimulated to perform at their best.

Figure 6-3
comfort zones.

▶ **COMFORT ZONES**—If we look at Figure 6-3 we can think of how an individual reacts to different levels of stress in terms of three zones:

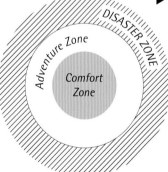

DISASTER ZONE

Adventure Zone

Comfort
Zone

▶ **THE COMFORT ZONE**—If we never allow ourselves the stimulus created by straying into the adventure zone, our comfort zone (i.e. the amount of stress we can deal with without becoming at all anxious) will shrink.

▶ **THE ADVENTURE ZONE**—If we constantly jump in and out of the adventure zone, our comfort and adventure zones expand. The closer we go to the outer edge of the adventure zone, the quicker we expand and the better we become at controlling anxiety.

▶ **THE DISASTER ZONE**—This is where anxiety changes to uncontrolled terror. If we misjudge our abilities or allow others to pressure us into a situation where we step over this line, our self-confidence takes a massive blow and our comfort and adventure zones shrink dramatically.

Coping with Stress

It is important that we recognize that we are all different, and develop mental preparation strategies to suit our individual requirements.

The presence of physical danger obviously induces stress and anxiety. As paddlers become more technically proficient, if they wish to paddle on harder, more dangerous rapids, they will have to learn to control their anxiety levels.

Figure 6-4 when getting on the river at a place like this it is important to warm up mentally and physically before getting on the water. Rio Camata, Bolivia. Photo: Mark Rainsley

Habituation

By gradually exposing themselves to more challenging situations, people find that they get used to the feelings produced by these situations. This has two effects on the persons concerned:

1 **They are able to cope with higher levels of stress**.

2 **The situation becomes less stressful**.

IT IS VITAL THAT WE MANAGE THIS PROCESS OF HABITUATION CAREFULLY

▶ **RITUAL**—Before getting on the water, there are a number of things everyone must do, such as getting changed and checking their equipment. There are also a number of things that perhaps we ought to do, such as a physical warm-up and mental preparation exercises. If we learn a routine and do these things in the same order and the same way, they become a kind of ritual. Their familiarity is in itself reassuring, and has a calming effect.

People who need to increase their stress levels may benefit from deliberately varying the way they prepare and the order in which they do things.

▶ **MUSIC**—People who need to lower their stress levels should listen to peaceful, soothing music on the way to the river. People who need to "psych-up" should travel in another car and wind themselves up with some "heavy metal" music.

▶ **WARM UP**—If you need to "psych-down" you should plan your physical warm-up sessions so that they are slow and gentle. That way they will have a calming, rather than stimulating, effect.

If you need to psych-up you should start your warm-ups gently so as not to cause any injuries. As the warm-up progresses the pace should become fast and frenetic.

▶ **BREATH CONTROL**—This is an exercise, borrowed from yoga that can be performed just prior to running a difficult rapid or drop. It is a technique that I have taught a number of paddlers I have coached, most of whom found it beneficial.

Figure 6-5 breath control. This exercise helps you relax and reduces physical and mental tension. People who need to "psych-up" can perform the breathing exercises described later in this chapter. These can be performed in a much more energetic manner so that you get the physical benefits without the calming effects.

1 Sit in an upright but relaxed posture.

2 Think only of the act of breathing.

3. Take a long, slow, deep breath. Visualize the air flowing into every corner of your lungs.

4 When your lungs are full, hold your breath for three seconds.

5 Breathe out, visualizing the air flowing out of your lungs.

6 When your lungs are completely empty, pause and repeat the exercise three or four more times.

▶ **VISUALIZATION**—Perform this exercise immediately after the breath control exercise and immediately before running the rapid or drop.

NEVER PUT YOUR BODY WHERE YOUR MIND HASN'T BEEN FIRST

1 In your "mind's eye," picture the rapid, complete with the flowing water, obstacles and hazards.

2 See yourself paddling in complete control down the line that you have chosen.

3 Picture yourself arriving in the safe eddy at the bottom of the rapid, smiling with pleasure at the successful outcome.

This act of visualization has a number of positive effects:

1 It habituates you to that particular rapid, even though you haven't physically been there yet.

2 It prepares you mentally and physically for the demands that are about to be made of you.

3 It instils a positive view of the outcome which reduces anxiety.

IF YOU CANNOT VISUALIZE A SUCCESSFUL OUTCOME, DON'T RUN THE RAPID!

▶ **MENTAL REHEARSAL**—Experienced paddlers, who have had considerable practice of visualization, will be able to take this a stage further, visualizing the sequence of maneuvers, even the stroke sequence that will be needed to stay on a complex and technical line.

It has been shown that athletes who are practiced in these techniques actually send the same signals through their nervous system that they will use when they perform the actual task they are visualizing. The difference is that the brain sends much weaker versions of the signals so that they don't actually result in physical movement.

Figure 6-6 mental rehearsal.

▶ **POSITIVE FOCUS**—When deciding whether or not to run a rapid, the risks posed by the level of difficulty and the seriousness of the hazards are assessed. Once the decision to run the rapid is made we must focus our minds on where we want to be, not where we don't want to be. If you are thinking of the stopper that you wish to avoid, that is precisely where you will end up! Focus your attention on the route that you have chosen, on the path that you wish the boat to follow.

Psyching Up

There are a few things that people who feel the need to psych up ought to consider seriously:

1 Although it works for them it may be the last thing that other members need.

2 Is it really for them, or do they do it because their teammates have always done it?

3 At what point should they stop? No matter how high their optimum arousal level, once they go beyond that point their performance will crash as quickly as anyone else's.

Warming Up

If there is a long easy section at the start of your river run, then the very act of paddling gently is sufficient to warm you up before the more difficult sections make sudden and strenuous demands on your body. However, if you are going to be committed to difficult and demanding paddling within minutes, or even seconds, then a more formal warm-up session is essential. These can be done on the river bank or on the water, providing there is at least a short easy section above the first rapid or drop.

Physically warming up before taking on a demanding section of whitewater has a number of benefits:

▶ **INJURY PREVENTION**—If the body isn't properly warmed up before strenuous exercise we run the risk of torn muscles and ligaments. Having warmed up, we are able to use the whole of our normal range of movement without risking injury and have therefore, in effect, increased our range of available movement.

▶ **REACTIONS & COORDINATION**—If the body is thoroughly warmed up, the efficiency of the transfer of messages from the nerve ends to the muscles is increased. This results in improved coordination and faster reactions.

▶ **MENTAL PREPARATION**—It is worthwhile going through a formal, bank-based, warm-up even on easy rivers. This is because it enables paddlers to develop a routine, so that when they warm up before a difficult run it becomes part of a calming, reassuring ritual.

Techniques

A good start to the process, when paddling in cold climates, is to change in a warm place and travel to the river in a warm car.

gentle exercise

↓

moderate exercise

↓

mobility exercise

↓

breathing exercise

Those with a background in physical training will probably already have a warm-up routine that they can easily adapt to the needs of whitewater paddling. The following approach to warming up is one that most people can use, even if they aren't into fitness training.

In my view, a warm-up session should contain all four elements in the order shown.

▶ **GENTLE EXERCISE**—This should last for a minimum of five minutes, preferably nearer ten. On dry land a gentle jog along the river bank is fine. On the water a leisurely paddle, against the current if necessary, is all that is required. The pace of this session should be such that the paddler is breathing deeply but never out of breath, and should carry on until he develops a light sweat.

▶ **MODERATE EXERCISE**—This should only last for one or two minutes, as we don't want to build up lactic acid. On the bank, this could consist of a short run at a pace which would no longer allow you to talk, followed by standing still and going through the movements involved in normal forward paddling. The arms, shoulders and trunk should start at a gentle pace and then move on to a brisk pace, (not flat out). On the water, a short brisk paddle will suffice.

▶ **MOBILITY EXERCISES**—These are intended to warn your body of what is to come and ensure that your body will not be caught by surprise if it is asked to suddenly operate at the ends of its range of normal movement. The joints and groups of muscles that paddlers need to prepare are in the following areas:

- **Neck**
- **Shoulders**
- **Trunk (especially rotation)**

- **Wrists**
- **Hamstrings (in kayak)**
- **Ankles (in canoe)**

▶ **NECK**—Stand in a relaxed but upright posture, feet slightly apart, looking straight ahead. Keeping your eyes at the same level, gently turn your head so that you are looking over your shoulder. Stop when you feel your muscles beginning to resist, hold the position for a couple of seconds, then face forward again. This initial movement is to warn your muscles of the movement to come. Repeat the movement and this time hold the position for a minimum of a slow count to ten. As you feel your muscles relaxing turn your head a bit further till you feel resistance again. (At no time should you feel any pain or even discomfort.) Repeat the whole of the procedure, this time looking over the other shoulder.

This exercise can be done sitting in your boat.

▶ **SHOULDERS**—*Exercise One:* Standing in the same position as for the neck exercise, starting with your hands by your sides, gently swing your arms forward till they are above your head and then behind you in a circular motion. Repeat the action without stopping so that it is a continuous action. Keep the action going for a slow count to ten.

In your boat, start by sitting upright and relaxed, holding your paddle so that it is resting on the front deck of your boat or on your knees. Hold your paddle with your hands wider apart than usual. Keep your arms fully extended and slowly lift the paddle with the shaft vertical and raise it above and then behind your head, stopping before you experience discomfort. Hold this position only for a couple of seconds and return to the start position. Repeat the procedure, this time holding the position for a slow count to ten.

Exercise Two: Stand in an upright position again and, keeping your hands by your sides, shrug your shoulders and then keep the movement going so that they move in a circular fashion. Keep it up for a slow count to ten and then repeat the action with your shoulders rotating in the other direction.

This exercise can be performed sitting in your boat.

▶ **TRUNK ROTATION**—Stand with your feet shoulder-width apart and your hands on your hips. Keeping your feet still, slowly rotate your upper body, once again stopping before you experience discomfort. Hold the position for a couple of seconds and then return to the start position. Repeat the movement, this time holding the position for a slow count of ten. Repeat the whole sequence, this time rotating in the other direction.

Figure 6-7 trunk rotation. In the boat you can use the same sequence except that you are sitting down. Instead of putting your hands on your hips, reach around with your paddle blade and place it across the back deck.

▶ **HAMSTRINGS**—Stand with your feet together, bend at the waist and reach down to touch your toes. Once again only bend as far as it takes to feel some resistance. Stop before you feel any real discomfort. Hold the position for a couple of seconds and stand up. Repeat the exercise, this time holding for a slow count to twenty.

In your boat, reach forward to touch your toes and try and kiss the deck of your boat at the same time. In order to fully relax the hamstrings after this exercise try laying back on your deck for a slow count of ten. This will also gently stretch your lower back.

Figure 6-8 (left) gently stretching the hamstrings. (right) Relaxing the hamstrings.

These actions can be performed equally well on the bank or in the boat.

▶ **WRISTS**—*Exercise One:* Stand with your elbows at your side and your hands held out in front of you. Extend your fingers so that they are fully spread out and then curl them up to make a fist. Repeat this action twenty times.

Exercise Two: With your hands forming the same shape they would make if they were holding a paddle shaft, gently roll your hands around in a circular motion. Ten rotations in one direction, and then ten in the other.

This exercise can be performed on the bank or in an open boat.

▶ **ANKLES**—Sit down, keep one leg extended and cross the other so that your ankle is resting on your thigh. Hold the crossed leg in position with one hand and using the other hand to guide it, gently rotate your foot in a circular motion, ten times in one direction, and then ten in the other. Repeat with the other ankle.

▶ **BREATHING EXERCISES**—These can be done purely for the physical benefits of increased oxygenation of the blood and the flushing out of fatigue by-products, and also as a mental relaxation technique.

On the bank immediately after your mobility exercises, start by standing upright with your hands held above your head. Crouch down so that your knees are touching your chest and your hands are on the ground. At the same time breathe out so that your lungs are empty. Hold this position for a second or two and then stand up and reach for the sky. Take a deep breath as you do so and hold your breath and the outstretched position for a couple of seconds. Repeat the cycle several times.

▶ **WARM DOWNS**—After strenuous exercise it is a good idea to warm down with five to ten minutes of gentle exercise. This ensures that well oxygenated blood flows throughout your body, flushing out harmful fatigue poisons, ensuring a more rapid recovery and preventing sore muscles. The pace should be even gentler than the warm-up. Whereas on the warm-up exercise you should be able to talk in short sentences interspersed with a breath or two, on the warm down you should be able to hold a continuous conversation.

▶ **POSTURE CORRECTION**—Sitting in a kayak forces paddlers to adopt a very poor posture. The spinal column is designed to remain curved. By sitting in a kayak we straighten out this natural curve in such a way that the discs that separate our vertebrae are squeezed outwards. This results in stiffness and even considerable discomfort if the disc bulges sufficiently to put pressure on nearby nerve bundles. Picking up a heavy plastic boat with your discs already weakened could easily result in a slipped disc.

The following exercise is a good way to help your spine recover.

Figure 6-9 posture correction exercise

Lie face down on the ground and leaving your hips where they are, raise your shoulders off the ground in a press-up-like motion. Hold this position for about a minute. Repeat if necessary.

Upper Conwy, North Wales

"Ian sat in the eddy staring at the entry to Bryn Bras Falls. We had inspected from the bank, chosen our line of descent and positioned other members of the group with throw lines. He didn't look too confident, so I decided to give him a final pep talk.

"'Forget the obstacles and focus on being on the line.' He didn't look convinced, so stupidly I went on to leave him with a negative mental image, 'Come on, you've decided to do it because the worst that can happen is a cold swim. You'll do fine, but if you do go for a swim, remember: positive mental attitude. You're not a victim, you're a canoeist in temporary difficulties.'

"Ian nodded, so I paddled to an eddy halfway down the rapid, got out of my boat and positioned myself where I could help anyone who didn't manage to avoid a rock that the main flow of the current ran straight into.

"I gave the signal and after a brief hesitation Ian set off. I couldn't help but notice that the other paddlers waiting at the top of the rapid were rolling about, shaking with laughter. Needless to say, Ian blew the line and was swept up against the 'magnetic rock.' When later I asked the others what had struck them as so funny, they told me that as Ian set off they heard him muttering: 'Positive mental attitude, you're not a victim, you're a temporary canoeist in difficulties.'"

CHAPTER 7

Scouting Techniques

Figure 7-1 a massive landslide changed the river overnight; the newly created rapid now runs through the trees. Never run anything blind . . . even if it was okay the day before. River Guil, French Alps.

Throughout this chapter, when reference is made to a group, it can mean a group of boaters or a number of rafts traveling in convoy. The lead paddler or raft guide has to:

1 Spot potential hazards.
2 Work out which way the water is flowing.
3 Choose a line that all the members of the group will be able to paddle.
4 Decide at what point to get off the water and inspect from the safety of the bank.

Factors Affecting Choice of Technique

NEVER RUN ANYTHING BLIND

One of the basic principles of safe river-running is that you never run anything blind (the line of sight principle). If the river is straightforward and the lead paddler can see a reasonable distance ahead, decisions can be made without even needing to slow down. On a technically difficult stretch of river where visibility is limited by tight bends and drops, it may be necessary to inspect every rapid from the bank.

The above examples represent the two extremes of a continuum. In between there are a whole range of techniques we can employ. As the river becomes more difficult (in relation to the group's ability), and visibility deteriorates we have to "change down a gear" and adopt a slower but more appropriate approach. As the river gets easier and we can see farther, we can speed things up again.

Figure 7-2 continuum of scouting technique.

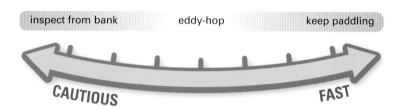

The above examples represent the two extremes of a continuum. In between there are a whole range of techniques we can employ. As the river becomes more difficult (in relation to the group's ability), and visibility deteriorates we have to change down a gear and adopt a slower but more appropriate approach. As the river gets easier and we can see farther, we can speed things up again.

▶ **TECHNICAL DIFFICULTY/LEVEL OF ABILITY—**The smaller and more skilled a group, the more difficult the stretch of river they can paddle without changing to a more cautious approach. Whereas one group may decide to bank inspect a grade 3 rapid, another may choose to leap-frog from eddy to eddy down a grade 4. If both parties have correctly assessed their ability, then both parties have made the correct decision and shown good judgment.

▶ **VISIBILITY—**This is an entirely different matter. If a flat but fast-moving stretch of water disappears around a blind bend and there is no other way of seeing what lies around the corner, someone has to get out and have a look. This is as true of the most technically competent extreme whitewater paddler as it is of the complete novice. If there is a river-wide strainer caused by a recently fallen tree and they decide not to inspect, the only difference is that there will be a few more famous paddlers at one of the funerals.

Technique

By constantly switching techniques as the nature of the river changes, we can descend a river quickly but safely. The following techniques are available to us:

- **Keep paddling**
- **Slow down and maneuver**
- **Move from eddy to eddy**
- **Scout, using micro-eddies**
- **Lead paddler inspects from the bank**
- **Whole group inspects from the bank**

▶ **KEEP PADDLING**—On straight sections of river where it is possible to see far enough ahead to assess the difficulties and choose a line, the whole group can move together, as fast or as slow as they wish.

▶ **SLOW DOWN & MANEUVER**—As the river gets more difficult or bends reduce visibility, it may be necessary to slow down, or even reverse paddle to give the lead paddler more time to assess the situation and make decisions. In order to get a better view of the way ahead, the lead paddler may decide to go around a bend as far on the outside as possible even though this may mean going close to overhanging trees and other obstructions. The lead paddler will probably therefore signal the rest of the team to take a safer route.

Open boaters in non-specialist boats can, in addition, stand up in the boat to get a better view.

▶ **MOVE FROM EDDY TO EDDY**—Where visibility is further reduced, it may only be possible to see the line as far as the next eddy or pool. If the line is straightforward and the eddies large, the group may move down to the next eddy one behind the other. If the lead paddler isn't sure if the whole group can fit in the next eddy, or exactly how difficult it is going to be to make the eddy, he may choose to run the rapid first, then signal the rest of the group to come down or not.

If the eddies are obvious but small, the group will have to leapfrog or eddy-hop (see Chapter 9).

▶ **SCOUT USING MICRO-EDDY**—Often it will be possible for the lead paddler to get to a position where it is possible to see round a bend by getting his boat into a micro-eddy. It doesn't matter if he is the only member of the group who has the skill to make the eddy. This is because, from his observation post, he is able to signal the rest of the group (see Chapter 10) to either follow on down, run it one at a time, or get out and inspect.

▶ **LEAD PADDLER INSPECTS FROM THE BANK**—If there is no way the lead paddler can inspect from the water, he will have to get out and inspect from the bank. If the way forward turns out to be straightforward, the lead paddler simply gets back on the water and leads the team down.

Especially useful in open canoes and rafts where it is much easier to hop in and out of the boat than in a kayak.

▶ **WHOLE GROUP INSPECTS FROM THE BANK**—This technique is the only option when the way forward involves a complex line that has to be memorized, or a risky line where each individual will need to decide whether to run it or not (see Chapter 8).

Figure 7-3 keep paddling.

Figure 7-4 ferry gliding to position the boat, slow down and have more time to choose the line.

Figure 7-5 lead paddler inspects from bank. Rio Chotohuasi, Peru.

Markers

When scouting a rapid and discussing or memorizing a line, paddlers will refer to markers. These will be used to indicate a change of direction or the position of a feature that can be used. These may be bank features or, particularly on big volume rivers, water features. There is plenty of room for misunderstandings here; to less experienced members of the party one standing wave may look much the same as another. One way around this is to throw a stone at the feature to ensure that everyone is talking about the same one.

Early Warning Signs

The two main reasons for a loss of visibility are a tight bend or a sudden drop. Other signs may tell us that there is a dangerous hazard immediately around the bend or that the drop is large enough to be considered a hazard in itself. If these signs are present, a prudent lead paddler will get off the water well ahead of the hazard and not risk trying to get as close as possible using micro-eddies.

▶ **NOISE**—When paddling on a river we soon get used to the general background noise of the rushing water. If the roaring of a particular rapid or fall can be heard above this background noise, it is probably worth getting out and inspecting from the bank.

▶ **SPRAY**—Big drops on volume rivers are often indicated by the spray created by the mass of falling water.

▶ **TREE LINE**—Sometimes it is possible to see across the land in a bend in the river, even when it isn't possible to see around it. If you are level with the tops of the trees that grow on the river bank on the far side of the bend, there must be a considerable increase in the gradient of the river ahead.

The tree line is often a useful indicator of gradient on straight sections of river, where it is possible to see some distance ahead.

▶ **EVENT HORIZON**—Upstream of a drop, a paddler will be able to see the foreground, the background, but not the middle ground. Trees and other tall objects in the middle ground will appear to have their lower parts missing. This odd perspective gives the impression of a false horizon, and is a warning sign that should not be ignored.

▶ **LANDMARKS**—There are some hazards where the river is fast-flowing and lacking in eddies for a considerable distance upstream. Wherever a guidebook, or information from other paddlers, indicates this to be the case, it is imperative that paddlers inspect the section on foot before running the river and choose landmarks that will warn them when to get off the river.

There is a serious rapid just below the bridge to Cwm Penmachno on the Afon Conwy in North Wales where this is the case. It is notorious, and it is clearly indicated in the guidebook that it should be pre-inspected and that it is normally portaged. Nonetheless, every year, groups of paddlers find themselves huddled on a large boulder in midstream, waiting to be rescued by local paddlers on their way home from work, or by the local Mountain Rescue Team. They are the lucky ones; others have been drowned there.

HEALTH WARNING

LEAD PADDLERS CAN MAKE MISTAKES OR OVERESTIMATE OTHER PADDLERS' ABILITY. IF YOU FEEL THE NEED TO BANK INSPECT A RAPID THAT THE LEAD PADDLER THINKS THE GROUP CAN RUN ON SIGHT, **HEAD FOR THE SIDE.** QUITE OFTEN LEAD PADDLERS MAY CHOOSE A MORE DIFFICULT LINE THAN NECESSARY BECAUSE IT WILL ENABLE THEM TO SEE FARTHER; THEREFORE **BE PREPARED TO MAKE YOUR OWN DECISIONS** AND CHOOSE A DIFFERENT LINE.

Figure 7-6 whole group inspects from the bank. Rio Colca, Peru.

CHAPTER 8

Assessing Risk

Figure 8-1 looking ahead and making quick decisions on the move. River Guil, French Alps. Photo: Dino Heald

All adventure sports involve taking risks. Whether making lightening fast decisions as they descend a river, or calmly weighing up the various factors from the safety of the bank, paddlers should always assess the level of risk involved. They also need to decide what level of risk they are prepared to take on. Although a leader can advise, and where they have a legal or moral responsibility, reserve the right to veto a rash decision, all paddlers should make their own individual risk assessment.

When deciding whether or not to run a rapid, it is best to break the rapid down into sections, i.e. from one place of safety to the next. When trying to work out the level of risk you have to ask the following questions:

1 What hazards are there?

2 What are the consequences should you fail to avoid any of the hazards on a given section?

3 Does the flow of the water avoid or feed into the hazards?

4 What line will you need to stay on to paddle the rapid safely?

5 What maneuvers will you have to effect to stay on your chosen line?

6 What is the probability of you being unable to stay on your chosen line and avoid the above hazards?

Consequences

When working out the consequences of failing to avoid a particular hazard we are looking at the objective dangers. That is to say that if a river-wide strainer is terminal, it will just as surely kill an expert as a novice should they get swept into it.

Figure 8-2 inspecting a rapid, checking out the line and assessing the risk. Euthanasia Falls, River Dart, SW England. Photo: Mark Rainsley

▶ **RATING THE CONSEQUENCES**—One way of trying to quantify the consequences of falling foul of a hazard or series of hazards (which can have a cumulative effect in terms of exhaustion and hypothermia) is to rate them on a scale of 1-5, 1 being the least serious and 5 the most. On this scale the consequences of failing to stay on your chosen line would be rated as follows:

1 An easy swim

2 Knocks and bruises and/or a long cold swim

3 The potential for serious injury and the certainty of a considerable fright

4 A risk of death and a high risk of serious injury

5 Almost certain death

It is important not to rely on a guidebook's assessment of the possible consequences. Each paddler should make his own observations and assessments. Besides, rapids change. Trees fall, boulders move, sections of bedrock collapse and water levels fluctuate wildly.

Probability

When working out the probability of avoiding hazards we are trying to quantify something that is very subjective. That is to say that it will be different for each individual. It is quite possible to have a hazard that is positioned in such a way that an expert will almost certainly be able to avoid it and a novice will almost certainly be swept into it. The key safety factor here is the ability to make an honest self-assessment of your own capabilities.

Variables affecting the probability:

- **The technical difficulty of staying on line**
- **The skill of the individual paddler**
- **How the individual feels on the day**

The importance of the last of these variables cannot be emphasized enough. It doesn't matter if you've run the rapid a hundred times before. If it doesn't feel right, don't do it! If we look at the scale below, a skilled paddler, looking at a relatively straightforward section of grade 3, could rate his chances of a successful outcome at anything between 1 and 3, depending on how well he was paddling on the day.

▶ **RATING THE PROBABILITY** — On this scale, the probability of blowing the line and failing to avoid the hazards would be rated as follows:

1 Almost certain success.

2 It would require a major "pilot error" to end up sufficiently off-line and it may be possible to avoid the hazards by paddling a different line than the one you had in mind.

3 A simple mistake could result in failing to avoid the hazards, but prompt remedial action would probably retrieve the situation.

4 It would only require a small error to end up off-line and in trouble.

5 Almost certain failure.

Risk Factor — Combining Probability & Consequence

In order to decide how high the risk factor is, we need to combine the probability of failure with the consequences. In practice, it will be a case of: "I don't like the look of that. There is quite a difficult approach. I'm not paddling particularly well and if I do end up under that undercut it could get very serious. I'll portage." However, purely to illustrate various combinations of factors and the risk they pose, we can give a number to the risk factor by multiplying the probability rating by the consequence rating. This gives us a scale of risk that runs from 1 (negligible) to 25 (almost certain death).

Figure 8-3 a hydraulic that is difficult to run and almost impossible for a rescuer to access and safeguard. Rio Chotohuasi, Peru.

It is relatively low risk to run a rapid where failure to make the line would result in certain death (5), if the chances of blowing the line are virtually nil (1), 5x1=5. Equally, the risk factor is relatively low where the paddler is deemed to be almost certain to end up in the hazard (5), if the consequences of such an action are only an easy swim and a dented ego (1), 5x1=5.

On the other hand, if the consequence was almost certain death (5) and the probability almost certain failure (5) the risk factor would be unthinkable, 5x5=25.

IN PRACTICE IT'LL BE A CASE OF "I DON'T LIKE THE LOOK OF THAT"

Profiles

Consider the four people in Figure 8-4. Each of them will come up with a different risk rating for the rapid they are looking at, and each of them will have a different level of risk that they are willing to take.

The rapid is serious enough to rate a consequence rating of 3, this being an objective factor which is the same for all the paddlers. The rapid is also technically tricky which means that some skillful maneuvering will be required to ensure success.

Figure 8-4 decision time. Cartoon: Danny Jones

▶ **JANE** enjoys paddling whitewater and taking reasonable risks. She would rate her risk factor limit at 12.

She is a highly skilled paddler and feels at peak form. Therefore she rates her probability factor as a 3. When combined with the consequence rating of 3 this gives Jane a **risk factor of 9**. She therefore has no qualms about running the rapid.

▶ **ERIC** has a similar outlook to Jane and also rates his risk factor limit as a 12. However he is only an averagely skilled paddler and is feeling off peak, having missed a few simple breakouts higher upstream. He therefore rates his probability factor as a 5. When combined with the consequence factor of 3, this gives Eric a **risk factor of 15**. He has no qualms about portaging.

▶ **SUE** enjoys whitewater paddling and playboating. However, she doesn't particularly enjoy risk taking and is very aware of her responsibilities to her young family. She would rate her acceptable risk factor as 8.

Sue is also an averagely skillful paddler but unlike Eric is feeling at peak form. She therefore rates her probability factor as a 4. Combined with the consequence factor of 3, this gives Sue a **risk factor of 12**. Sue will also hit the portage trail.

▶ **PAUL** enjoys risk taking and regards the prospect of "a good trashing" as part of the learning process. His awareness of his lack of experience and skill means that he will "only" accept a **risk factor of 16!** As he improves he will probably go on to accept a risk factor as high as 20.

Despite the fact that he is feeling at peak form, he is almost certain to blow the difficult line. He therefore has a probability factor of 5. Combined with the consequence factor of 3 this gives Paul a risk factor of 15. Despite being the least able paddler in the group Paul will run the rapid. He does so knowing that his actions pose no threat to the other members of the group and in full knowledge of the risks involved.

Remember that the numbers are only there for us to make a comparison. In reality each individual has assessed the risk and decided that it is either acceptable or too high. Most people don't think numbers in reality!

Assuming the above people to be a group of friends, every member of the group has made a careful risk assessment and behaved accordingly. However it is worth pointing out that in a situation where a leader has a legal or moral responsibility for the other members of the group, it would be foolish of the leader to allow Paul to run the rapid. No responsible leader could allow a person in his charge to tackle something he was almost certain to fail on where there was a potential for serious injury.

CHAPTER 9

Organization

Figure 9-1 a small group of experienced boaters who have paddled together before need very little organization. River Guil, French Alps. Photo: Dino Heald

Once afloat, small groups of experienced paddlers often find that they have no need for a leader as such. Each paddler assumes a position or role they are happy with and, should a decision be necessary or a rescue need dealing with, whoever is in the best position to do so temporarily assumes the role of leader/coordinator.

Unfortunately this state of perfect cooperation is rare. Teams are seldom so well matched. The greater the disparity in experience and the larger the group, the greater the need for more formal organization and leadership.

No matter how little need there is for a formal leader, any group that wishes to paddle in safety will need to be organized to a degree. Each member of the group needs to know:

- **The role of each team member**
- **The way in which the group is going to tackle the river**
- **The order of descent**

Roles

In order to make a safe descent of a river each member of the group will have to accept responsibility and take on one or more roles.

▶ **TEAM MEMBER**—All members of a team must have the safety and well-being of the whole group as their top priority. We all paddle for our own selfish reasons; however, if these come before our concern for the safety of the other members of the team we are a liability.

All team members need to be honest about what they have to offer, and their own limitations. It is better to say that you are not prepared to take on a certain role than to accept it and foul up through lack of skill or confidence.

▶ **THE "BUDDY" SYSTEM**—This system involves every member of the party pairing up with another. From that point on, as well as their normal responsibility for the other members of the team, each person is particularly responsible for the welfare of their buddy. This is particularly useful in large groups where it might otherwise be possible for someone to go missing without anyone realizing.

▶ **LEAD PADDLER/RAFT GUIDE**—This person is not necessarily the leader. This role is often taken on by the more experienced and skilled paddlers or by the person in the group who has paddled the river before. Because of the linear nature of rivers, whoever is out in front has the following responsibilities:

- **Choosing a line**
- **Spotting and avoiding hazards**
- **Deciding when to bank inspect**
- **Getting the group off the water well above any portages**

Figure 9-2 lead raft with the guide looking well ahead. Scheif'seck Rapid, River Sanna, Austria. Photo: www .swiftwaterrescue.at

Being lead paddler is an exciting, challenging and satisfying role, (see Chapter 7). Taking a turn at being lead paddler on a suitable stretch of river is an important part of a paddler's personal development. If you don't normally take the lead, insist on having a turn out in front on the easier sections. Don't let anyone hog the lead and have all the fun.

▶ **BACK MARKER**—Sometimes known as "Tail-End Charlie." This is another role that is usually taken by one of the more experienced paddlers. This is because they have to pick up the pieces and therefore must be able to take on the role of chase boater. They are also at extra risk because everybody else tends to look downriver. If they get into trouble there is the possibility that it won't be noticed for some time. When boating, I prefer to have two people take on this role, frequently changing places as back marker. That way they act as a team within a team and feel a special responsibility for each other (the buddy system).

▶ **CHASE BOATER**—Chase boating is the art of rescuing swimmers or their equipment from your boat rather than from the bank (see Chapter 14). It is a high-risk activity requiring a high level of skill and confidence, fast reflexes, even better judgment and the ability to think on the move. In some groups every paddler will be able to take on this role. In others there may be only one or two people willing and able to take it on.

Figure 9-3 chaseboating, the paddler has dislocated his shoulder. River Guil, French Alps. Photo: Peter Knowles

▶ **SPECIALIST RESCUE ROLES**—There are some situations that may require specialist knowledge, skills or aptitude. Examples are rescues that might involve ropework skills or where there is a risk of ending up in or a need to enter the water. In the case of the latter it is important that such roles be taken on by people who are strong swimmers and water confident. Should such a rescue situation arise, time will be precious, so it is better to identify who can take on these roles in advance.

HEALTH WARNING

IF YOU WOULD RATHER NOT TAKE ON A RESCUE ROLE, DON'T BUY A CHEST-HARNESS PERSONAL FLOTATION DEVICE.

WHITEWATER SAFETY AND RESCUE

▶ **MOTIVATOR**—Not all team roles involve paddling skills. Everybody needs a shoulder to lean on or a sympathetic ear at some stage.

▶ **TEAM LEADER**—The leader takes on a multitude of roles. At the very least he is an organizer, motivator, risk assessor and communicator. He may well find himself having to be counselor, psychologist, coach, pillar of strength and wisdom, to name but a few!

A team leader will also have a role as a safety advisor. Where there is a legal or moral obligation, or the consequences of someone else's poor judgment puts the welfare of the team at risk, he may have to veto an individual's decision.

Tackling the River

How a group is best organized will depend on:

• **The size of the group**

• **The nature of the river**

• **The nature of the group**

Figure 9-4 (below) two rafts traveling in convoy with a kayaker acting as scout and chase boater. River Sanna, Austria. Photo: www .swiftwaterrescue.at

▶ **SIZE OF GROUP**—It is seldom a good idea to solo paddle on whitewater. To paddle as a pair is acceptable, although if one paddler gets into trouble that only leaves one potential rescuer, which would limit the number of options available. With two rafts working in tandem this is less of a problem as there will be plenty of person power, even if only the two raft guides are experienced. If you decide to paddle as a pair, bear this in mind when assessing risks and err on the cautious side.

Three is a good number from a safety point of view. Four is probably the ideal. This is because it allows people to buddy up and operate as two pairs who, although still members of the team of four, are particularly responsible for the welfare of their buddy. It is also a small enough team to operate with a minimum of organization.

► **THE RIVER**—Different types of river require different approaches.

Figure 9-5 moving together. River Guisane, French Alps. Photo: Bob Timms Boating & Trekking

► **EASY LOW & MEDIUM VOLUME RIVERS**—On low and medium volume rivers that are fairly straightforward it is usually best to travel as one small group, one behind the other, keeping fairly close together. If the leader is not the lead paddler he may well position himself in the center of the group so that he can see both the lead paddler and the back marker.

► **HIGH VOLUME RIVERS**—On high volume rivers the distance between safe eddies, and the size of the water features mean that there has to be a reasonable gap between each paddler. It is probably best to travel as semi-independent buddy groups (pairs). One of the good things about the buddy system is that you can pair a young hot-shot paddler with an experienced paddler. The experienced paddler will have the eyes to choose a safe line and the hot-shot the skills to stay on it. With this arrangement, instead of being able to see the whole group, paddlers will only be able to see the pair immediately in front and behind them, and only then intermittently, from the top of waves. It is therefore vital that the lead pair stop whenever they find a large enough eddy to regroup and count heads.

► **TECHNICAL RIVERS**—On technically difficult low and medium rivers it may also be better to travel as semi-independent groups of two or three paddlers. The twists, turns and drops restrict visibility and the technical difficulty means that paddlers need more space.

A group of six would split into two semi-independent groups of three or three semi-independent pairs. Each group of three would act independently, obeying the line of sight principle within the sub-group. Whenever the back marker of the first group lost sight of the lead paddler of the second group, the first group would stop and wait until the second group came back into view.

Group Control

In the above section we looked at how different factors might make us choose different ways of moving together as one group. On some sections of river, it may be preferable that not all paddlers are on the move at once. With all the following techniques it is essential that every member of the group understands what is required and that a simple and efficient system of signals is agreed on (see Chapter 10).

▶ **ONE AT A TIME**—In its simplest form, the lead paddler runs the rapid first and then makes a signal. On seeing this, a second member of the group runs the rapid. Everyone else stays put until the lead paddler/raft guide signals again for the third person and so on.

Figure 9-6 running the rapid one at a time on the lead paddler's signal. Rio Chotohuasi, Peru

On harder rapids where a bank inspection has taken place, most or even all of the other members of the team may provide bank protection while one member of the team runs the rapid. In a large group it is essential that the group are well briefed and that the leader uses a clear set of signals to keep things moving.

As soon as the paddler reaches the bottom of the rapid he must get out and change places with one of the people on the bank who is then free to get ready to run the rapid. If possible it is best to keep two people free of bank protection jobs. That way, while one person is running the rapid, another is getting ready to run it. This speeds up the process considerably.

Figure 9-7 running the rapid one at a time with bank protection. River Guil, French Alps. Photo: Dino Heald

▶ **LEAPFROGGING**—This works particularly well with small groups of boaters on rivers where there are lots of small eddies that will only take one boat at a time. A large group of paddlers would have to break into two or more sub-groups to make this work. Often this technique and eddy hopping are only used for short technical sections, the group reverting to moving together, or one at a time, as the river becomes easier or harder.

With this method every paddler in the group takes it in turn to be lead paddler and back marker. The lead paddler signals the back marker, who leapfrogs the whole group, becoming the new lead paddler and so on.

*Figure 9-8
leapfrogging:*

1 *the lead paddler signals down tail end charlie to the next safe eddy below, becoming the lead paddler.*

2 *the new back marker makes the eddy in the bottom right, becoming the lead paddler.*

3 *+ repeat.*

Photo: Dino Heald

▶ **EDDY HOPPING**—This works in similar situations to leapfrogging. A possible advantage over leapfrogging is that the order of descent doesn't change. Strangely enough the disadvantage is that it is harder to keep control of the group. This is definitely easier if the group splits into semi-independent pairs.

The lead paddler moves down to the next eddy that he thinks all the other members of the group will have the ability to paddle into. On the lead paddler's signal, the rest of the team move down one eddy. It is vital that paddlers do not set off until the paddler downstream of them is well clear of the eddy they want to move down to.

Figure 9-9
eddy hopping:

1. *the lead paddler breaks out in the next safe eddy below.*

2. *the next paddler moves to occupy the eddy left by the lead paddler.*

2. *the back marker moves to occupy the eddy left by the paddler in front.*

3. *+ repeat.*

Photo: Dino Heald

Order of Descent

With a group of evenly matched paddlers it is only really necessary to decide on who is the lead paddler and who are the back markers. Everyone else can paddle in any order they like, as long as they keep an eye on the person in front and the person behind them. With a mixed ability group it is best to pair people up so that the more skilled/experienced paddlers are teamed up with the less able, the exception being the back markers who both need to be good paddlers.

CHAPTER 10

Communication

Good communication avoids misunderstandings, and their subsequent mistakes. Over the years, I have been asked to look into a number of kayaking accidents. In almost every case such misunderstandings were key contributory factors.

Briefings

In some ways, avoiding misunderstandings is much more difficult when paddling with a group of friends than as a group of people who have paid or formally asked someone to guide or instruct them. In the latter case, people will expect the leader to allocate roles and give a formal briefing so that everyone knows what's happening.

▶ **FORMAL BRIEFINGS**—At the beginning of a trip a number of things need to be made clear to all members of the team:

- **The nature of the river and likely hazards**
- **Who is taking on which role and the responsibilities it entails**
- **The order of descent**
- **Who is whose buddy, if you decide to use the buddy system**
- **Who is carrying what items of rescue equipment**
- **What signals the group is going to use**
- **Any pre-arranged actions in the event of someone getting into trouble**

Leaders should ensure that their briefings and any instructions given are clear and concise. They should know exactly what they are going to say before they say it, rather than thinking out loud.

USE QUESTIONS TO CONFIRM UNDERSTANDING

Members of the party may be apprehensive or distracted, so it may be a good idea to use questions to confirm that they have understood. The end of a briefing might go something like this:

"If anyone goes for a swim on this section, leave the chase boating to Angela and me. If you see someone swimming, shout SWIMMER to let everyone else know; make your way to the side and then run down the bank and offer what assistance you can.

"Eric, if you see a swimmer, who does the chase boating?"

▶ **INFORMAL SITUATIONS**—In a less formal situation, it may not be at all clear who is responsible for what. Even worse, different members of the group may have completely different views of what their roles are. Often people are loath to offer leadership which they believe may be unwelcome.

Here, a more subtle approach may be needed. If you feel that all is not as clear or as organized as it might be, it may be better to ask questions, rather than try to give orders. For example:

"Hey, just so there is no confusion, what signals do you use?"

Or: *"I've brought a first aid kit. Who's carrying the split paddles?"*
Or: *"I'm feeling a little off form today; I'd feel a whole lot better if we buddied up."*

If paddlers feel that they or other members of the group are not clear on what is going on, they owe it to themselves and the rest of the group to clear things up.

> ## IF YOU AREN'T SURE OF WHAT IS GOING ON, YOU CAN BE SURE THAT YOU'RE NOT THE ONLY ONE!

Signals

A clear set of hand and/or paddle signals can help avoid confusion, save time and increase flexibility. Often, when on or near whitewater it is difficult to hear, and visual signals are the only practicable option.

▶ **BASIC CRITERIA**—It really doesn't matter what signals are used, providing they meet the following criteria:

1 Each member of the party is using the same signals.

2 Each signal used has one specific meaning, i.e. is not a mime.

5 Signals can be given one-handed.

4 Signals are visually sufficiently different that they can't be confused with one another.

3 Signals are kept to a workable number (unless you paddle regularly with the group, I would suggest no more than four).

▶ **ACKNOWLEDGE SIGNALS**—When a signal has been given, the people to whom it is being sent should, if they are not too busy staying upright, repeat it. This achieves three things:

1 The signal is passed on to any member of the group who is out of sight of the original signaler.

2 It confirms that the correct signal has been received and understood.

3 It acts as an acknowledgment so that, if for some reason you can't act on the signal immediately, the person sending it knows that you have seen and understood.

Figure 10-1 (above) always point away from danger. River Guisane, French Alps. Photo Bob Timms Boating & Trekking

▶ **FAIL-SAFES**—The following two rules ensure that people don't get into trouble because of a simple misunderstanding:

1 **If someone is in a safe position waiting for a signal, the rule is: No signal, no move!**

2 **Always point away from the danger, and in the direction of safety.**

FAIL-SAFE NO. 1

NO SIGNAL, NO MOVE!

FAIL-SAFE NO. 2

ALWAYS POINT AWAY FROM THE DANGER

Four Basic Signals

These are some basic signals that are in fairly common use:

▶ **STOP**

Palm held upright, motionless

Meaning:
Depending on the situation, it can mean:

- Get to the nearest safe eddy
- Hold your position

▶ ONE PERSON TO COME DOWN

one finger held upright
followed by a beckoning action

Meaning: One person only to leave the eddy and paddle the rapid. The next person should not set off until he is signaled to do so.

▶ GO MORE LEFT OR MORE RIGHT

hand or paddle extended montionless
in intended direction

Meaning: Move in the direction the paddle or arm is extended. Used to help other paddlers to stay on line; if necessary a sense of urgency can be imparted by using a short jabbing motion.

▶ EVERYBODY COME ON DOWN

fist raised with elbow at right-angle
up and down motion

Meaning: Everybody follow the lead paddler, leaving a suitable distance between each paddler or, if the lead paddler has gone ahead to inspect the rapid, everyone paddle the rapid and join him, again leaving a suitable distance between each paddler.

Two Other Useful Signals

If people paddle regularly together it is worth learning a few more signals that will enable the team to communicate more effectively.

▶ PUT YOUR BOAT OVER THERE

finger raised to indicate one paddler then pointed at the intended location

Meaning: This is usually used when the signaler doesn't want the other boater to eddy into the same eddy that they are in. It can also be used to position the stronger paddlers in such a way that they are in the best place to effect a rescue prior to the less able boaters shooting the rapid.

▶ COME TO ME

hand placed on top of head as if patting oneself on head

Meaning: Send whoever has been designated down to join the lead paddler. (This is usually one of the better paddlers who is able to chase boat, often the paddler who brings up the rear.)

Alternatively, if no one has been designated, it just means the next paddler down should "come to me."

Often, when the lead paddler has gone ahead to inspect a rapid, he may decide that it can be adequately protected by having one good paddler stationed near a hazard that is halfway down the rapid and another stationed at the bottom of the rapid. By having the above signal, this can be arranged quickly, allowing us to have the best paddlers where they are going to be of use, rather than sitting in a safe eddy at the top of the rapid where people don't need any assistance.

Sound Signals

Other paddlers may use different signals so check it out before getting on the water.

In the noisy environment of a whitewater river it is best to keep these to an absolute minimum. I only use two:

1 A single whistle or shout means: "Look this way."

2 Continuous whistling or shouting means that someone is in serious trouble.

Mobile Phones & Radios

Mobile phones can be really helpful in an emergency. However, even where coverage is good, river gorges and deep wooded valleys are often masked from transmitters.

Radios can be useful to communicate with shuttle drivers or to another paddler scouting the far bank. However, they can be easily damaged and a signal is only line of sight. Therefore no plan should rely on the use of radios or mobile phones.

Figure 10-2 radios can be useful but should not be relied upon. Photo: Mark Rainsley

Briefing a Novice Raft Crew

As a raft guide the contact time you have with your rafting crew during initial raft briefing is very important. You must set the tone for the trip, gain your crew's confidence, and create a fully trained and highly responsive team all in a very short space of time. The response you get from your crew will depend on your professionalism, people skills, organization, and ability as a guide. A high degree of empathy for a person who might be experiencing the whitewater environment for the very first time is paramount. As a guide it is important to be honest about the inherent risks involved in whitewater rafting.

▶ **PRE-TRIP BRIEF**—Having introduced yourself, the next step is to gain more information about your raft crew and also deal with individual/group needs. The pre-trip briefing is generally carried out before the issuing of specialist rafting equipment.

Relevant issues include:

- **Have all crew members signed relevant participation agreement forms?**

- **Can all crew members swim or are they confident in and around water?**

- **Are any crew members under the influence of alcohol or drugs (banned/prescribed)?**

- **Anybody with an impaired state of consciousness must not go rafting.**

- **Less confident individuals can be placed towards the rear of the raft, closer to you, or even in the middle of the raft as a non-paddling participant.**

As a raft guide you will also need to be aware of any medical conditions or injuries that your raft crew may have. It is important that you carry essential medication on behalf of your crew members throughout the duration of the trip. Note that it is important that you are assessing your crew's coordination and mobility while you coach paddling and safety commands on dry land.

Rafting crew may not want to reveal medical conditions or injuries in public; therefore it is important that you provide them with an opportunity to inform you in private. All medical information gathered should then be communicated in private and in confidence to all other raft guides, bank support crew and rescue kayakers. Medical information may be essential should an incident occur on the river.

It is also important to brief the raft in detail as to what personal items they should bring, or should explicitly leave behind.

▶ **GLASSES/CONTACT LENSES**—There would be little consequence of wearing glasses on a flat water float trip. However as you are far more likely to be unseated while running rapids, wearing glasses increases the severity of a facial injury should there be an impact to the face. This should be balanced against the risk of injury through having limited eyesight by not wearing glasses, e.g. a decreased ability to receive a throw bag! Contact lenses are usually the best choice; raft crew wearing contact lenses can be positioned towards the back of the raft where there is a better chance of lenses staying in! If glasses are to be worn, ensure they have a retainer attached to them; this may be improvised using a shoelace.

▶ **ENVIRONMENTAL CONSIDERATIONS**—In colder climates you will need to brief your crew on appropriate thermal layers to wear in addition to any specialist rafting equipment such as a wetsuit. In warm conditions suntan lotion and carrying fluids may become a priority. Brief your crew not to apply suntan lotion on their foreheads as this will inevitably end up in their eyes; furthermore there is no danger of sunburn to this area as crew will generally be wearing helmets. Crew members should not apply suntan lotion to the backs of their legs either, as this results in people sliding about inside the raft.

WHITEWATER SAFETY AND RESCUE

▶ **PERSONAL EFFECTS**—Jewelery, or indeed anything valuable, should not be taken on the rafting trip and any clothing including shorts and footwear (warm weather) should be securely fastened as they can become forcefully removed in turbulent flows!

▶ **RAFTING SAFETY BRIEF**—If each raft guide briefs his crew individually, this always produces a more responsive, technically able crew than if a safety brief is conducted en masse. Briefs conducted en masse don't allow for variations that may exist between guides as regards paddling commands, and the ability to confirm understanding on an individual basis is severely impaired.

Key Points

1 Highlight the various areas you are going to talk about. Explain that this will take fifteen to twenty minutes and that it is very important that you have everyone's attention. The key areas are:
   • Introduction of equipment
   • Paddling commands
   • Safety procedures

2 Ensure that your brief follows a logical progression; this will help you remember everything you need to mention.

3 Give a good demonstration of all techniques involved.

4 Confirm raft crew understanding through questioning and asking them to physically demonstrate the skills they have been taught.

5 Give a brief summary, and then provide the rafting crew with an opportunity to ask any questions they may have.

▶ **INTRODUCTION TO THE RAFT**—Point out the relevant features of the raft you will be using; this will include the identification of the safety perimeter line, carrying handles, construction of the raft as regards its separate inflatable compartments, foot cups/straps if applicable, thwarts, and drainage system. Any potential risks of becoming entrapped in the perimeter line, under the thwarts, or in the guttering system will be highlighted at this point, as well as the danger of straining the limbs of the lower body if feet are pushed too far into foot straps.

▶ **POSITION IN RAFTS**—It is important to balance the left and right-hand side of the raft according to weight and power for optimum performance. This is largely guesswork at this stage; fine-tuning takes place once on the river, conditions allowing. It is important that you demonstrate a seating position where crew are sitting on the outside tube, not on the thwarts, and that feet and legs are positioned so that they act as a brace to decrease the chance of crew members falling out of the raft. A good exercise to perform on dry land is to ask crew to sit in the raft, brace, and then lean out; this enables you to gauge how securely they are positioned.

▶ **PADDLES**—The paddle consists of a T-grip, shaft, and a blade. Having handed out the paddles you should demonstrate how to hold them. It is important to stress that the T-grip should remain covered at all times when in the raft. A T-grip that isn't covered flails around and can cause serious facial injuries to rafters. The T-grip rule should be strictly enforced during a rafting journey especially when crew are required to move about the raft.

Paddling Commands

Be sure to practice all paddling commands extensively before you really need them!

▶ FORWARD / HARD FORWARD

Periods of maximum effort are required when rafting, for example, to punch through a stopper. However raft crews will become fatigued and ineffective if they paddle at maximum effort for any extended period of time. It is therefore important to be able to control the amount of effort a crew puts into their paddling, hence the use of the "Forward" and "Hard Forward" commands. Timing is achieved by asking the two crew members in the front compartment of the raft to keep time with each other; crew members sitting behind these two lead paddlers will then follow the pace of the person in front of them.

▶ BACKWARD

Backward motion can be achieved by asking crew members to use their lower hand (holding the shaft) as a fixed pivot point against the side tube while pulling back forcefully with a straight top arm (holding the T-grip), using the whole body motion.

▶ LEFT BACK/RIGHT FORWARD or vice versa

As the time period you have for training your crew is often short, this command for turning the raft is simply seen as a combination of the two strokes that you have already taught. Note that it is important to communicate the side of the raft you are talking to, e.g. "left," so that you have their attention, followed by the action required, e.g. "back." It is also preferable to standardize this command so that backward paddling is instigated first. By standardizing your commands you will find that fewer communication errors occur.

▶ STOP

The paddle is removed from the water immediately on hearing this command word, even if crew are halfway through a paddle stroke. With the ability of being able to generate half or even quarter paddle strokes comes the control required to finely maneuver a raft. When in the stop position, the paddle shaft should be rested on the knee and the body should lean slightly into the center of the raft.

Safety Commands

▶ HOLD ON

This command may be used when you foresee the raft experiencing a small amount of jolting or movement that may result in a crew member becoming unbalanced and slipping into the water. Instruct crew members to remove their bottom hand from the paddle shaft. The bottom hand then passes over the top of the paddle shaft and grips the perimeter line thus securing the crew member to the raft, as well as securing the paddle under the arm. At the same moment instruct the crew to tuck their chins to their chests and lean in towards the center line of the raft. The hand holding the T-grip should be in a low position away from the face, which reduces the likelihood of an injury and also lifts the paddle blade clear of the water.

▶ HOLD ON, GET DOWN

This command is used when you foresee large forces acting on the raft, e.g. impact with a large stopper or rock, both of which may stop the raft dead, resulting in crew members being flung forward unless they are braced correctly. Instruct your crew to adopt the same position as in the "hold on" position, and then sink to the floor of the raft; knees are brought to the chest and the back arches to form a compact shape with the chin tucked into the chest. Be aware that it does take some time for crew to move from this position to a position where they can perform a paddling stroke. If you allow for this delay when scouting this needn't be a big issue. Note that it is not uncommon to use your crew for generating a lot of forward momentum and to achieve the correct approach on the lead-in to a rapid and then negotiate large sections, or even the whole rapid with the crew in the "hold on, get down" position, while you control the raft from the stern!

▶ JUMP LEFT/JUMP RIGHT

Other utterances of this command include—"high-side left"/"high-side right" and "over left"/"over right." This command has many verbal mutations but the actions involved are identical. Situations that warrant a high-side include evasive action during a potential broach (Chapter 3). If "jump left" is called, all crew on the left hand tube adopt the "hold on" position as described earlier. Crew sitting on the right-hand tube release the paddle shaft with their bottom hand, locate a space between those sitting on the left tube (generally in front of their opposite partner) and lunge towards it, the bottom hand comes across the body and grabs the perimeter line on the left-hand side of the raft, the top hand covering the T-grip remains in position and crosses the body from left to right so that the top hand ends up next to the right hip thus keeping the paddle out of the way. To reiterate, it is very important that the T-grip remains covered at all times.

Situations Involving Swimmers (Crew overboard)

The rafting crew's three golden rules in a situation involving a swimmer are:

- **Try to stay calm.**
- **Never stand up in moving water.**
- **Always listen to your guide.**

The recovery procedures are taught as a series of situations that see a raft crew member fall in and progressively move farther and farther away from the raft.

If crew members have very fast reactions, it is possible to make a grab for the perimeter line as they fall out of the raft. Still being attached to the raft makes it easy for a rescue to be performed. It is useful to operate a buddy system whereby the person sitting opposite you is responsible for pulling you back into the raft; this ensures that there isn't complete chaos involving the whole raft crew moving to aid a swimmer. Demonstrate how to pull a swimmer back into the raft (Chapter 14).

A swimmer that has become removed from the raft is more difficult to rescue; again fast reactions are key to a successful recovery. If a swimmer is still close to the raft it is possible for any crew member to perform a simple reach rescue by extending their T-grip out towards the swimmer. This is the only time that crew members should let go of their T-grips while in the raft. A swimmer can also extend his/her T-grip out towards a member of the raft crew to perform a rescue in the same way.

If the reach rescue has not been successful immediately, it is time for the swimmer to adopt the defensive swimming position (Chapter 14). The paddle is hugged tightly to the chest with one arm, and the other is used to stabilize or alter course. All the while swimmers should listen for commands from raft guides or safety kayakers, such as swim left, swim right, or swim towards me.

Introduce the throw bag rescue from a raft as the next link in the continuum (Chapter 14); a demonstration is vital for this skill. Remember that you will only be able to effect an overarm throw from a raft as the outside tube will act as a barrier to throwing underarm. If you need to be in full control of your raft due to the presence of downstream river hazards, paddling after a swimmer who has come out of your raft and alerting other potential rescuers is your next course of action. Therefore it is essential that you inform your crew that they may need to get ready to paddle powerfully in the event of there being a swimmer.

The next in the continuum is a scenario that calls for self-rescue. If possible show crew members an example of an eddy from where you are briefing, or do this when you are on the water. If swimmers find themselves washed into an eddy they should swim in the defensive swimming position to the bank, pull themselves out of the water if possible, and then stay in position until reached by a raft guide or safety kayaker.

As a final word, there is always the potential for there being multiple swimmers. Therefore a combination of swimmer retrieval methods as previously described may need to be put into action simultaneously!

▶ **FALLING OUT AS A GUIDE**—In this situation inform the crew that they should listen for paddling commands, as you will be trying to bring the raft closer to you. Once you make contact with the raft, assistance from the closest crew member to help you back into the raft is gratefully received, although slightly embarrassing!

▶ **FLIPS**—For details of how to cover eventualities encountered during a flip situation, see Chapter 14.

▶ **DRY LAND GAMES**—While still on dry land, simulating conditions that could be encountered during rafting is a good way of warming up, practicing what has been learned, and improving mental alertness. Calling all paddling and safety commands in fast succession is a fantastic preparation game and involves crew members throwing themselves into a flurry of activity. Add to this game another key word such as "in the water" and you have an insight into how quickly crew members can get into the defensive swimming position.

Getting everyone on the left tube to simulate falling out of the raft and then being pulled in by their opposite partner on the right tube and vice versa improves group bonding. These activities can be interspersed during the brief to stimulate interest or can also be used on calm sections of water at the start of the trip if appropriate.

► **MANUAL HANDLING**—When maneuvering rafts with clients, all reasonable care must be taken to ensure good manual handling practice is adhered to. Teams should lift together and clients must be informed of correct lifting technique.

1 Assess the terrain that you will be traveling over. Warn clients if it may be slippery or uneven; avoidance of difficult terrain is preferable whenever possible.
2 Arrange raft crew so that they are opposite a person of similar height.
3 Position of feet: feet apart giving a stable base for lifting, leading leg as far forward as is comfortable, and if possible, pointing in the intended direction of travel.
4 Posture: bend the knees, keep the back straight, maintaining the natural curves of the spine (tucking in the chin and not looking straight ahead helps).
5 Grip: get a firm grip on the raft handle.
6 Commands: "Lift together when I say 'lift.' Hands on handles 1, 2, 3, and lift."
7 Placing the load down should follow the same procedure. "When I say 'down' slowly lower the raft to the ground as a team. 1,2,3, and down."

Please note that lifting rafts above shoulder height dramatically increases the load on the lifting crew and that rafts are generally carried in much the same way as you would carry a suitcase.

► **PERSONAL PROTECTIVE EQUIPMENT CHECK**—Whenever raft crew are close enough to the river to trip and fall in they need to be wearing a Personal Flotation Device and a helmet, and these need to be fitted correctly and checked. Ask crew not to adjust any of this equipment while on the water without consulting you, thus enabling you to reassess the fit.

► **COMMUNICATION WHILE ON THE WATER**—A great deal of background noise is generated in a rapid, which can make communication difficult. Crew can reach such a high state of excitement or fear that they suffer from a sensory overload and find it difficult to respond to any form of communication. The following are a few suggestions on how to tackle these problems. While negotiating a rapid it is important to keep any communication with the crew to a minimum, using only the pre-arranged command words. Interspacing all paddling commands with "stop" if your maneuvers allow, is also an effective way of minimizing confusion. Your head should be turned so that you are projecting your voice towards your crew. Ensure that your voice is reaching the front two crew members; this is particularly important as the people sitting behind them are likely to follow their lead! Stopping and briefing crew members about a rapid that is coming up next can be effective in improving their reaction time, simply because they are more prepared. A guide will generally give a brief outline of the rapid along with some generic reinforcement of what he/she expects from them, e.g. *"If you hear me say "hard forward," I really need you to put everything into it."*

CHAPTER 11

Leadership

Good leadership is an essential aspect of paddling a white-water river in safety. Whereas previous sections have dealt with many of the tasks that usually fall to a leader, such as planning and organizing, this section concentrates on how a leader behaves. A planner works with ideas; a leader is the person who can get a group of individual people to work as a team and make the plan work.

"Natural born leaders," if such a thing exists, may not need to think about what leadership entails, they just do it. The rest of us may well benefit from consciously trying to improve our performance, through a better understanding of the processes involved.

Once the planning and organizing are done and we actually get on the river, the leader's main concerns are the safety and well-being of the team members, morale, and making decisions. How they perform in the eyes of the other paddlers will depend on:

1 Their personal qualities
2 The way they go about leading, (their leadership style)
3 The way they go about making decisions
4 The effectiveness of their leadership

Leadership Qualities

If you asked a number of people to list the qualities they would expect to find in an effective leader they would come up with similar answers. What would differ is the amount of emphasis they would place on different qualities. One person would say that decisiveness was far more important than, say, honesty. Another would put the emphasis the other way around.

Every quality has a dark side. Decisiveness can become inflexibility. Honesty can become insensitivity. An effective leader will have these qualities in the right balance. Some qualities, such as decisiveness, determination and assertiveness are essential in terms of getting the job done. However, they need to be counterbalanced by other qualities such as honesty, empathy and openness, which help a leader to understand and manage people.

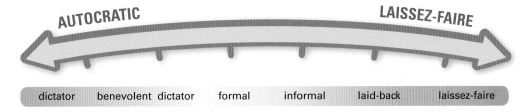

AUTOCRATIC   LAISSEZ-FAIRE

| dictator | benevolent dictator | formal | informal | laid-back | laissez-faire |

Leadership Styles

Figure 11-1 a spectrum of leadership styles.

Both Mahatma Gandhi and Attila the Hun were great leaders. Their approaches or styles of leadership couldn't be more different, but they were both effective!

A leadership style is not the same as a leader's personality, although a leader's personality will affect which styles he is happiest using. If we think of the range of leadership styles available to us, at one extreme we have authoritarian, a dictatorship, and at the other laissez-faire, in other words, let everyone get on with it. Between the two extremes there are a whole range of styles available. Most leaders will tend to operate left or right of center but nowhere near either of the extremes.

Factors affecting which style will be most effective or appropriate are:

- **The leader's own personality**
- **The expectations/personalities of the individuals he is leading**
- **Time or the lack of it**
- **Immediate danger**
- **The nature of the task being undertaken**

▶ **PERSONALITY**—Because of their own personalities, leaders will tend to have a preferred style of leadership that, all other factors being equal, they will work within. The most effective leaders will, subconsciously, use different styles in different situations. It is possible for leaders to increase their effectiveness by consciously trying to expand the range of styles they are comfortable using.

▶ **GROUP EXPECTATIONS**—People's background will affect their view of what effective leadership is. So if, for example, a person who is comfortable with a very laid back approach finds himself asked to lead a group from a military background, he may well find that the group's expectations force him to adopt a more authoritarian approach than usual. Otherwise the group may refuse to accept what they perceive to be weak leadership.

Equally, an authoritarian leader, faced with the average anarchic group of paddlers, will have to adopt a more relaxed style, or there will be a mutiny. Given enough time, a group will accept that a leader is effective and the leader may be able to revert to his preferred range of leadership styles.

WHITEWATER SAFETY AND RESCUE

▶ **INDIVIDUAL EXPECTATIONS** — Certain individuals within any group may, due to their own personality, feel that certain approaches give them more confidence than others. An effective leader will soon realize that John is happiest if he is told what to do, whereas Anna will be a more willing and effective team member if she is consulted; her views having been taken into account, she will probably offer to take on a particular task.

▶ **TIME** — If there is no need for an instant solution, it may be that a far more relaxed approach is advisable. A calm, unhurried approach will reduce tension. Consulting other members of the group may produce a less risky solution to the problem that the leader hadn't considered.

If time is precious, this will greatly restrict the choice of leadership styles available. If there are only minutes or even seconds in which to act, then I'm afraid that Attila the Hun is your man. There simply isn't the time to consult and cajole. This is particularly true when lack of time is combined with the element of danger. The good news is that in these emergency situations even the most anarchistic people will accept an authoritarian style because the need for it is obvious. All other needs are irrelevant compared to the need to get a friend out of a dangerous situation quickly.

▶ **THE TASK** — Sometimes the nature of the task being undertaken will virtually dictate what style the leader must adopt. Imagine a complex rescue where each member of the team has to do a different job at the same time and the noise of the rapids makes communication difficult. In addition, the leader has to do one of these jobs himself as the team is a small. The leader will have little choice but to delegate, and having done so, to let them get on with it.

Figure 11-2 not the time for laissez-faire. Overtime Rapid, White Nile. Photo: www .swiftwaterrescue.at

► **FLEXIBILITY**—The most effective whitewater leaders will probably have a preferred style but will switch styles as appropriate. It is quite possible to use the whole range of styles we have identified on a single trip.

Imagine the following:

Our leader, Lisa, has been asked by a group of club paddlers to lead them down a river they haven't paddled before. Lisa starts the day in a formal style. She hasn't paddled with them before and wants to ensure that everyone is clear about how they are going to run the river. The river is at the easy end of grade 3 at this point. She stays in this mode for a while, keeping tight control of the group and telling everyone exactly what she wants them to do. Eventually she realizes that everyone is working well together and that the group is more competent than she was led to believe. She therefore allows herself to change to a more "informal" style, allowing group members more freedom of action.

Eventually they get to a short but technically demanding grade 4 rapid which they inspect from the bank. Everyone decides to portage except Wayne, who is only 15 years old, and for whom our leader has therefore, a greater legal and moral responsibility. What's more, it is obvious to Lisa that Wayne's wish to run the rapid isn't matched by his ability as a paddler. Wayne seems determined to ignore good advice. Having sent the others off to start the portage, Lisa goes into benevolent dictator mode and lets Wayne know that he isn't going to run the rapid this trip and that's that.

Farther down, one of the group loses concentration and is pinned on a rock in a potentially life-threatening situation if not dealt with immediately. For the minute that it takes to solve the problem Lisa becomes a dictator, issuing orders, expecting and getting instant obedience.

The emergency dealt with, everyone feels euphoric with relief. Lisa reverts to a formal style until the group settles down.

The last couple of kilometers of river are of pleasant straight-forward grade 2. The group is quite capable of running this section without much guidance so she adopts a much more laid back style.

► **DECISION MAKING**—Most decisions have to do with picking one of a number of ways of solving a problem. Problems range from: *"Shall I wear my sports sandals or my wet suit booties today?"* to: *"How do we get Wally's boat out of that strainer without killing anyone in the process?"*

There are a number of ways in which we can come to a decision. Which way a leader decides to operate will be influenced by the same factors that affect his choice of leadership style. The nature of the decision being taken plays a very important part in this. There are some decisions that must have the backing of the whole group.

▶ **AUTHORITARIAN**—This is the method where the leader makes the decisions without any reference to the rest of the team. Even if the leader has involved the rest of the team in thinking up or brainstorming possible solutions, he doesn't take into account the team members' preferences when it comes to deciding which plan they are going to use.

PROS: Fast, appears very decisive, which can be good for morale.

CONS: The team may have little faith in the leader's plan causing morale to plummet.

▶ **DEMOCRATIC**—This is where the various options are compared and the group agrees to accept the plan that the majority approve of.

PROS: The group feel more involved in the decision-making process and may well try that bit harder to make the solution work. Reasonably quick.

CONS: Can result in a split in the group where a significant minority feel their views have been ignored. Doesn't necessarily come up with the best solution, only the most popular one.

▶ **CONSENSUS**—This is where the matter is discussed until every member of the group accepts that the plan decided on is the best one.

PROS: Every member of the group is committed to and feels a part of the solution.

CONS: Can be a very slow process. Usually only works with small groups.

▶ **FALSE CONSENSUS**—This is where one or more members of the team accept a decision even though they don't actually believe it to be the best solution. This is normally done to preserve unity or because they have had enough of discussions and would rather get on with it.

> THERE'S NO "RIGHT ANSWER," NO ONE WAY TO LEAD A GROUP. ALL LEADERS HAVE TO FIND A WAY THAT WORKS FOR THEM AND FOR THE PEOPLE THEY ARE LEADING.

Whichever system is used a decision must eventually be made. An effective leader will seek consensus if it is necessary and if he thinks it can be obtained. If a degree of acceptance is essential for the plan to work but it is obvious that one or more members of the group will never agree with the majority, then seeking consensus is a waste of time. The leader will go for majority rule. If time is of the essence or the group expects the leader to make all the decisions, then the leader will have to make the decision unaided.

There's no "right answer," no one way to lead a group. All leaders have to find a way that works for them and for the people they are leading.

CHAPTER 12

Safety in Equipment Design

In recent years there has been a great deal of effort on the part of innovative paddlers and equipment manufacturers to design and make equipment with safety as a major consideration. While this has made safe paddlers even safer, there has been a down side. This is that many paddlers seem to believe that if they have the right technology they are safe. This in turn led to equipment being designed with rescue in mind rather than paddling. Personal Flotation Devices (PFDs) were produced that were great for swimming in, but so restrictive that paddling skill suffered. In the very worst excesses, PFDs have been produced with so many unnecessary loops and attachment points for rescue equipment that they can easily be snagged.

NO MATTER HOW WELL EQUIPPED PADDLERS ARE, WITHOUT AWARENESS, JUDGMENT AND SKILL, THEY ARE STILL UNSAFE

Simple Design

Well designed and manufactured equipment is a wonderful bonus. However, no matter how well equipped paddlers are, without awareness, judgment and skill, they are still unsafe.

The more forward looking and responsible manufacturers have started to address these concerns by improving and simplifying their equipment, and providing more comprehensive written instructions.

Helmets

A good helmet should:

- Protect the wearer's head from direct contact with hard or sharp objects which would otherwise lead to cuts, lacerations and fractures of the skull.
- Absorb the energy of blows to the head that would otherwise cause concussion.
- Protect as much of the head as possible without impairing vision, hearing or balance.
- Stay firmly in position, even if the wearer is being thrown around in turbulent water.

Figure 12-1 a range of good helmets.

In order to check that a helmet will be able to achieve the above, paddlers should look for the following features:

▶ **OUTER SHELL**—The outer shell should be made of a tough but lightweight material, such as plastic, carbon/kevlar or other Glass Reinforced Plastics. Color is also important because, when you are a swimmer, your helmet may be the only part of you that is visible. There is some debate as to which colors show up best if someone is under the water. It would seem best to steer away from colors that are too light or too dark. White or pale yellow won't show up in aerated frothy water and black won't show up in peaty or muddy water.

▶ **SHOCK ABSORBING LAYER**—The inner layers of a helmet are usually made of closed-cell foam, some form of cradle, or a mixture of both. The main advantage of cradles is that they can be adjusted to fit more than one size head. They are also cooler in hot climates.

Closed-cell foam absorbs energy efficiently and leaves few spaces for water to fill if you capsize. Providing it is the right size, it is more comfortable to wear, and in cold water environments, it keeps your head warmer.

A few people wear full-face motorcycle helmets on whitewater. The lining used in these helmets absorbs water. This makes them very heavy once they get wet and increases the risk of neck injuries. They are not recommended.

▶ **FIT**—The front of a helmet should come well down over the wearer's forehead and protrude sufficiently to provide protection to the area around the wearer's eyes. There are many helmets available that either don't cover this area, or ride up and expose it.

The rear should come down far enough to cover the whole of the back of the cranium and the sides of the helmet should protect the temple and ear. Blows to any of these areas can lead to brain damage. There are many helmets on the market that are designed to look good or comply with minimum standards to satisfy competition rules. They do not provide adequate protection for serious whitewater use. If a helmet meets the above requirements and fits well, it will stay on with only a minimum of help from the chin strap.

HELMETS THAT ARE MARKETED FOR OTHER SPORTS OFTEN CONTAIN FITTINGS AND FASTENINGS THAT CORRODE IN WATER. THEY MAY BE A LITTLE CHEAPER BUT THEY ARE NOT A BARGAIN.

▶ **FACE GUARDS**—If you train yourself so that on capsizing you tuck into a screw roll position, with your face touching the front deck of your boat, your face will be well protected. This is because only the back of your helmet is exposed to the river bed. For this reason, and the fact that face guards inhibit vision and look very aggressive, few paddlers wear them.

If boaters feel the need for facial protection, then it is important that they wear a helmet with a good face guard that has been designed for the job. One quite often sees paddlers wearing canoe-polo face guards. While these are perfectly adequate for keeping paddle blades out of your face in a swimming pool environment, the manufacturers stress that they are not designed for whitewater situations. Their cage-like construction means that they could easily be snagged and the lack of quick release means that this could lead to a broken neck.

Personal Flotation Devices (PFDs)

When trying to evaluate a PFD, I ask myself the following questions:

1 Is it comfortable to wear?

2 Does it contain sufficient buoyancy to do its job if I go for a swim?

3 Does it allow sufficient freedom of movement so as not to inhibit good paddling technique?

4 Does it provide good body protection?

5 Is there somewhere to stow a knife and a spare karabiner?

6 Is it as "clean" as possible? In other words are there any unnecessary attachments or pockets that inhibit movement or increase the risk of getting snagged?

▶ **BUOYANCY**—The minimum buoyancy that a PFD may contain is now regulated by law. In the United States, PFDs are regulated by the Coast Guard. In Europe, the regulations come under The European Community Directive on Personal Protective Equipment.

In Europe PFDs come under one of two categories:

▶ **CEN 50N**—The British Canoe Union recommends this as the minimum standard for all canoeing and kayaking activities. 50 N stands for 50 newtons, which is a measurement of force. Put simply, this means that a 50 N PFD should be able to support a 12 lb. (5.5 kg) lead weight. This is for a person weighing 154 lb. (70 kg) or more. The table below shows the sliding scale used to determine the minimum buoyancy needed for a given weight.

▶ **CEN 100N**—Buoyancy aids that meet this standard must contain a minimum of 100 newtons of buoyancy for a person weighing 154 lb. or more. They must also have a flotation collar which makes them impractical for canoeing and kayaking. However on high volume runs some raft companies prefer these for inexperienced customers.

Figure 12-2 table showing CEN minimum and advertised buoyancy for a range of actual products.

Item Size	Weight (lb.)	Chest Size (in)	Buoyancy (N)
CEN 50 (European Standard)			
	66–88	—	35
	88–110	—	40
	110–132	—	40
	133–154	—	45
	>154	—	50
Fusion (Palm)			
XS/S	66–110	30–35	>60
M/L	110–154	35–43	>60
XL/XXL	>154	43–53	>60
Extreme II River Vest (Palm)			
XS/S	66–110	30–35	>70*
M/L	110–132	35–43	>70*
XL/XXL	132–154+	43–53	>70*

*optional foam pad in front pocket increases total buoyancy by 10 N

▶ **RIB AND SLAB**—Most whitewater PFDs are now made of large slabs of foam rather than lots of thin ribs of foam. Slab buoyancy has several advantages:

Less wetted surface area means that the foam degrades more slowly. There is more actual foam for a given surface area which allows manufacturers to make shorter garments that are more suited to boaters. Slab buoyancy also makes for a more effective body armor.

▶ **VESTS AND JACKETS**—There are two basic designs available. The way they are cut, the accessories they have and their color may vary immensely, but they are all variations on a theme.

Jackets consist of a rear piece and two front sections of foam encased in a nylon-based material. When worn the jacket is kept in place by a full length front zip and some sort of draw-cord or tape at the waist.

The main advantage of this design is that it is easier to put on and remove than a vest.

Figure 12-3 (left) jacket style, Palm RT Whitewater PFD. (right) vest style, Palm Axis Extreme PFD.

Vests have only two slabs of foam, (one front and one rear). The material is sewn to form a one piece vest and when worn it is held in place by two or more cinch straps on each side.

There are a number of advantages to the vest type of design:

- **The lack of a zip dividing the front buoyancy means that room doesn't have to be found elsewhere for the missing buoyancy. This means that there is more scope to cut the vest in such a way that your freedom of movement is less restricted.**

- **The use of a number of cinch straps to secure the garment means that it is easier to adjust the fit to your body shape.**

- **Although awkward to put on and take off, they are usually more comfortable to paddle in.**

▶ **AGING**—Paddlers should be aware that the foam used in buoyancy aids does degrade. Manufacturers deliberately put more foam than is needed in a new garment to allow for this. At the rate they expect it to degrade in normal use, it should remain within the design specification buoyancy for three years. However, in certain circumstances, such as when used in polluted water, the foam can deteriorate a good deal quicker.

If there are any doubts, the buoyancy should be tank tested, by seeing if it will float with the appropriate amount of weight tied to it.

Spraydecks

As cockpits have become larger, so the amount of tension required to keep the spraydeck in place has increased. This is achieved by using very stretchy neoprene material and holding the deck on the cockpit rim by using either:

1 A bungee cord sewn around the edge of the spraydeck skirt

2 A flat band, which can be made of solid or hollow tube rubber sewn in the same place

The bungee type is harder to put on when you are sitting in your boat but is relatively easy to remove. This makes it better for use by less experienced whitewater paddlers.

The flat band type is easier to put on and sticks so firmly that it is almost impossible to remove it accidentally. This has had the unfortunate side effect of ruining the classic post-swim excuse: "Honest . . . my spraydeck imploded!"

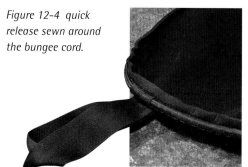

Figure 12-4 quick release sewn around the bungee cord.

▶ **QUICK RELEASES**—The other effect this has had is to make it imperative that the quick release fitting cannot become detached. In the past a length of nylon tape was sewn directly onto the rim at the front of the spray deck. Most manufacturers now sew the tape as a loop that goes right around the rubber band. This ensures that even if the stitching that secures the tape to the band should fail, the loop of tape would still enable you to release the spraydeck.

On some decks there is a back up system in the form of a tape sewn to both edges of the spraydeck. This is adjustable so that it is just in tension when the spraydeck is fitted. The idea is that if a paddler is unable to use his hands to release the spraydeck, he can release it by pushing his knee against the tensioned tape.

Thermal Layer

The layers of clothing worn under a waterproof outer shell have one purpose, to keep you warm; in cold climates that means in the boat and, if necessary, if you go for a swim. In many countries the air temperature is high but the water, being provided by melting snow or glaciers, is freezing. This means that paddlers need a combination that will not cause them to be too hot in their boat, yet will prevent them from succumbing to hypothermia should they go for a prolonged swim.

WETSUIT AND THERMALS—When paddling on a river with a warm air/ice cold water combination a "Long John" wetsuit with a thin thermal top is a good combination. Wetsuits are designed to work in the water. They work by warming a thin layer of water and retaining it close to your skin. This means that if a paddler has a long swim the wetsuit works very efficiently. If a paddler only has a short swim, as soon as he gets out of the water the thin layer of warm water drains away and he cools down.

The other advantage of a wetsuit is that it offers a paddler's legs and bottom some protection against the battering they can receive in a swim down a rocky river. For this reason this is probably still the best combination for use by novices and people who swim a lot, supplemented in cold climates by a fleece top and thermal under-trousers.

▶ **NO WETSUIT—**If you don't swim very often or you wear a drysuit, a combination of layers of thermal underwear and fleece garments may be more efficient. By adding or removing layers it is possible to cope with any conditions. In addition, this type of clothing is a lot more comfortable if worn for several hours or even days.

HEALTH WARNING

IF YOU'RE USED TO DRESSING LIGHTLY, EVEN IN THE WINTER, THINK CAREFULLY WHEN UNDERTAKING A LONGER TRIP ON A WILD RIVER AS SUCH CLOTHING MAY NOT BE ADEQUATE.

Figure 12-5 different combinations of clothing.

1 *shorts and short sleeve lightweight waterproof parka dry cag and thermal vest for warm air/warm water.*

2 *3/4 wetsuit trousers, lightweight waterproof parka and thermals for warm air/ cold water.*

3 *drysuit thermals and fleeces for cold air /cold water.*

Shell Clothing

Figure 12-6
venting a drysuit.

A wind and waterproof outer layer is essential to keep the paddler warm and dry. Good spraydecks and lightweight waterproof parkas, with their latex wrist and neck seals, keep virtually all the water out while the paddler remains in the boat. Overtrousers are needed to keep your legs warm and dry when out of the boat. In warmer climates a lightweight waterproof parka, with neoprene cuffs and a neoprene adjustable neck fastening, or even a short-sleeved one, may be more appropriate.

In very cold conditions it may be worth considering a drysuit. It is essential, when wearing a drysuit, to vent all the air out of the suit before getting on the water. This is achieved by pulling the neck seal away from your neck with your finger while at the same time forcing the air in the suit upwards by crouching in a fetal position. If this precaution is not taken and you capsize, the water pressure forces all the air into the legs of the suit. If you were then to come out of your boat you would float with your head down and your legs in the air! Should this happen a paddler would have to rip the latex ankle seals to allow the air to escape from the suit.

Footwear

When choosing footwear for whitewater one would expect it to:

1 **Provide a good grip when moving over greasy rocks or muddy banks.**

2 **Have a thick enough sole to protect feet from broken glass or sharp rocks.**

3 **Protect the bony protrusions on your ankles from knocks.**

4 **Keep your feet warm when it's cold and wet.**

5 **Help to keep your feet cool when it's hot.**

The truth is that no item of footwear can meet all of these criteria. Sports sandals are comfortable in warm weather, wetsuit bootees in very cold weather. Extreme boots are appropriate on rivers where there are committing gorge sections, difficult portages or where there is likely to be a great deal of bank protection needed.

A good compromise is to buy a pair of sports sandals and a pair of neoprene socks to wear with them in cold weather.

Figure 12-7
a selection of footwear.

 1 *wetsuit booties*   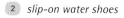 2 *slip-on water shoes*    3 *extreme whitewater boots*   4 *sports sandals*

Paddles

In the eighties and early nineties the trend towards paddling rocky technical rivers led to a demand for extremely strong paddles that wouldn't break at a critical moment and literally leave you "up the creek without a paddle." We got our strong paddles but paid for them in terms of their weight. If you were built like Arnold Schwarzenegger they were fine. For most of us there was a considerable loss in our ability to feel the water through the blade, and for smaller paddlers they were a disaster.

The advent of playboating and rodeo has meant that there has been a lot of crossover between competition and recreational paddlers. There are now a whole host of paddles made in carbon-fiber and thermoplastics to choose from. This means that we can have paddles that are strong and light!

▶ **SPARE PADDLES**—Canoeists, rafters and kayakers should carry at least one spare in the group in case of loss or damage. The spare should be as good as your main paddles.

Kayakers need to carry split paddles. Few kayaks are long enough for traditional two-part splits and four-part splits are easier to stow. The *paddlelock*™ system developed by Lendal is a really effective method of locking the paddles back together.

Figure 12-8 Lendal's split paddle system.

HEALTH WARNING

STIFF SHAFTS AND LARGE BLADE AREAS CAN LEAD TO TENDONITIS IN THE ELBOWS. I WOULD ADVISE MOST PADDLERS TO BUY A FLEXIBLE SHAFT WITH A MEDIUM OR SMALL BLADE AREA. (FLEXIBLE 'CARBON' SHAFTS ARE NORMALLY MADE FROM A COMBINATION OF ORDINARY GLASS AND CARBON-FIBER).

Kayaks

There are three questions we should ask when looking at a kayak from a whitewater safety point of view:

1 Does it have the whitewater safety features that you would expect to find in any design of whitewater kayak?

2 Is it the right size for its occupant?

3 Is its design suitable for the kind of whitewater paddling it is going to be used for?

Kayak Safety Features

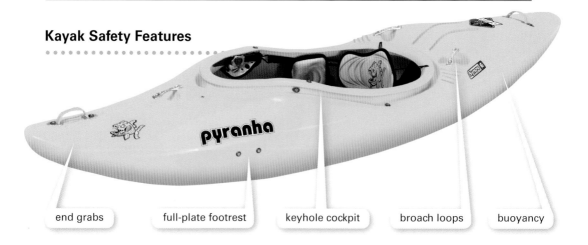

| end grabs | full-plate footrest | keyhole cockpit | broach loops | buoyancy |

Figure 12-9 safety features of a white-water kayak Photo: www.pyranha.com

▶ **KEYHOLE COCKPIT**—When the very first plastic boats came on the market, the materials used in the manufacture of spraydecks were not very stretchy. As a result cockpits were made as small as possible to minimize the chances of a wave collapsing the spraydeck. Boats made in ordinary glass-fiber tended to break up if they were badly broached, giving the paddler a chance to fight his way out. With plastic and diolen/carbon fiber combinations, this no longer happens; therefore cockpits must be designed in such a way as to make it possible to exit the boat even if the deck is collapsing.

Figure 12-10 the keyhole cockpit's size and shape ensures the leg can be released from the thigh braces with room to raise a knee and push out from the boat.

This is achieved by making the cockpit much larger and by making it a keyhole shape. When the paddler's knees are splayed out, they grip the thigh braces and when the knees are brought together, they are no longer held in.

An easy way to test the effectiveness of your boat's cockpit is to get some friends to stand your boat up against a wall with you in it to simulate a vertical pin. If you can get out unaided it's fine; if you can't, get another boat.

▶ **FULL-PLATE FOOTREST**—This is essential in a whitewater boat because, if a paddler hits a hard surface, they spread forces involved over the whole of the soles of both feet. This and the shock absorbing properties of the foam pad reduce the risk of ankle and lower limb injuries.

Figure 12-11 a full-plate footrest system.

In low volume play-boats there is not enough space for a full-plate footrest. Therefore the manufacturers supply foam shapes that can be used to fill the space in the bow and act as a solid yet shock absorbing footrest.

▶ **BUOYANCY**—The foam buoyancy that is used to strengthen most boats and provide a minimum of buoyancy is not sufficient for whitewater use. Paddlers should supplement this with airbags so that any space not filled by the paddler or equipment is buoyancy. This has two benefits:

Figure 12-12 cutaway showing an inflated airbag with the central (grey) foam buoyancy behind.

Tests carried out in the late seventies at Plas y Brenin provided confirming evidence of this effect.

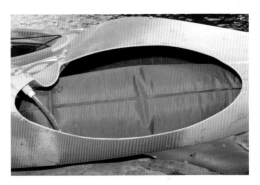

1 **The boat is far easier to recover as it contains less water and therefore weighs less.**

2 **Because a boat filled with buoyancy floats much higher in the water, it is less likely to fold if broached.**

▶ **ATTACHMENT POINTS**—Have two principal safety functions:

• **To give the swimmer something to keep hold of the boat with**

• **To provide a strong attachment point for boat recovery purposes**

Figure 12-13 end grab in the form of a continuous loop of tape. Should one of the anchor points at either end break, the connection will not be lost.

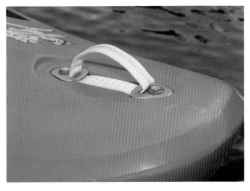

▶ **END GRABS -**
These need to be capable of being used as attachment points, so most manufacturers now make them strong enough to withstand a static load of at least 1100 lb. (500 kg). Swimmers may also use them as grab points, so they need to be made in such a way that it is impossible for a swimmer's hands or fingers to become trapped or injured.

*Figure 12-14
a broach loop securely
bolted in place with
large washers to
spread the load.*

▶ **BROACH LOOPS—**
These are increasingly common in specialist river running and creek boats. When present they are situated near the middle of the boat, just in front of the cockpit, or just behind it, or both. They are intended purely as attachment points for equipment recovery purposes.

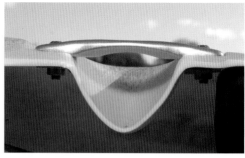

▶ **STREAMERS—**A streamer is a piece of nylon tape about 3 feet (1 m) long that is attached to the rear grab handle so that it "streams" behind the boat. It has two main uses:

*Some boaters attach
streamers to bow
and stern, which
can help in boat to
swimmer rescues.*

1 In a very short boat, by the time a paddler has exited his capsized boat, the boat may have floated far enough away that the grab handle is out of reach. The swimmer can grab the streamer instead.

2 Even with a keyhole cockpit, a long legged paddler in a vertically pinned kayak will find it easier if he can pull on the streamer. In this situation the streamer hangs down the length of the rear deck.

It is essential that the streamer is fitted in such a way that it does not form a loop or have any knots that could get snagged.

▶ **SIZE—**Every boat will perform best for paddlers within a certain body weight range. Therefore a boat that performs well for a paddler who weighs 110 lb. (50 kg), will wallow hopelessly if paddled by a 220 lb. (100 kg) paddler. Equally, if a 110 lb. paddler tries to paddle a boat that suits a 220 lb. paddler, he will be unable to edge, accelerate or maneuver effectively. That is assuming he hasn't already injured himself trying to pick the boat up!

Many manufacturers now sell two or three different sizes of the same model. So make sure you get the right one for you.

*Figure 12-15
customizable boat
outfitting, with a
highly repositionable
backrest, hip-pads
and seat position.*

▶ **FITTING—**We all come in different shapes and sizes, therefore kayak designs must fit the largest person intended for it. Good kayak control demands that your kayak fits like a glove. To this end, boaters should invest some time and effort

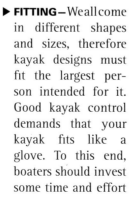
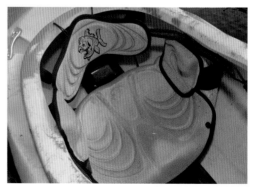

in customizing their boat. Some manufacturers now provide fittings that can be easily adjusted and kits to fine tune the fit.

▶ **HIP PADS**—Pieces of minicell foam can be cut to size, shaped with a rasp and then glued to the side of the seat. This ensures that any movement of the hips is transmitted to the boat, improving edge control and the ability to roll in rough water. Some manufacturers now provide these.

▶ **THIGH GRIPS**—Some modern kayak designs have adjustable thigh grips, which are a real bonus for people with nonstandard leg length. It is well worth spending some time finding the ideal position for comfort and effectiveness. Any thigh grip can be further improved by gluing on pieces of the closed cell foam used in camper mats. This improves the comfort and one's ability to grip. On non-adjustable thigh grips it is possible, by experimenting with different layers of foam, to improve the fit.

Kayak Designs

While it is true that, if a boater is good enough, he can paddle any kind of boat on any kind of river, it is also true that certain types of boats perform better on certain types of water.

Squirt boats are extremely specialized, being designed to spend as much time underwater as they do upon it, I will leave them to the specialist books. To make the distinction, all other kayaks that are used on whitewater are sometimes referred to as "float boats."

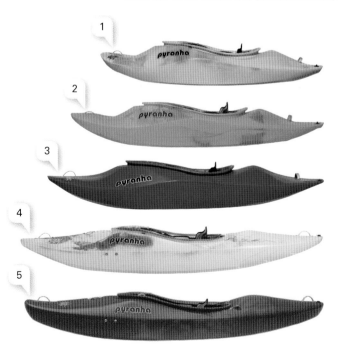

At the time of writing these can be split into five broad categories:

1 **Freestyle boats**

2 **Play boats**

3 **Fun river boats**

4 **River running boats**

5 **Creek boats**

Figure 12-16 profiles of examples of the five styles of kayak and their proportions. The plan template and hull features of each type differ significantly too. Photos: www.pyranha.com

▶ **FREESTYLE**—These are out-and-out freestyle boats where all other considerations are sacrificed for 3D performance. They are low volume, hard edged, flat bottomed and often under 6.5 feet (2 m) in length. Brilliant for cartwheeling or surfing on waves but very slow off them. Great for competition or "park and play," very uncomfortable and unforgiving on whitewater.

▶ **PLAY BOATS**—These are essentially less extreme freestyle boats. They are a little over 6.5 feet long, a little more voluminous and comfortable but still capable of all the freestyle moves. A good boat for playing around while running easier rivers that are well within your comfort zone.

▶ **FUN RIVER BOATS**—These boats have softer edges, extra length (7–8 feet or 2.1-2.5m) and enough volume for river running. They are faster, more forgiving but still low volume enough to surf playholes and do cartwheels on suitable water features.

▶ **RIVER RUNNING BOATS**—These are boats that are designed to maximize your control on serious whitewater. 3D performance is sacrificed for 2D control and forward speed. They are longer, around 8 feet, and faster. They are high volume and though many are still flat bottomed to increase performance on waves, they are not completely flat. This allows the edges to be softer and decreases the risk of catching an edge when sliding down rock slabs.

▶ **CREEK BOATS**—These are similar to river running boats except that they are a little shorter, have curved profile hulls, softer edges and increased rocker. These design features mean that they sacrifice performance on waves and forward speed in favor of less chance of catching edges on rock slabs and steep rocky rivers. Increased volume in the ends also decreases the likelihood of vertical pins.

There are of course kayaks that don't fit neatly into these categories. If we use our eyes and our brains it won't be too difficult to work out what kind of whitewater they best suit.

Traditional Open Boats

An open boat that is used on whitewater needs to be thoughtfully outfitted. Pole, spare paddle, bailer, rucksacks all have the potential to entangle the boater in the event of an upset. Simple and tidy is the answer.

▶ **END LOOPS**—A small loop of ($3/8$ inch/9 or 10mm) rope at each end of the canoe, threaded through holes drilled through the hull about 1.5 inches (4cm) below the gunwale, provides a secure attachment point in any recovery. The carrying handles on the deck that are usually provided are not secured to a strong enough attachment point.

▶ **ATTACHMENT POINTS ALONG THE SIDE**—There are two systems in common usage:

Eyelets—This involves pop riveting (metal gunwale), or screwing (wooden gunwale) a series of eyelets into the gunwale.

Figure 12-17 spare paddle and pole secured but to hand.

Drill & Lace—A series of holes are drilled about 1.5 inches below the gunwale and about 4 inches (10 cm) apart. These are then threaded with 0.2 inches (5mm) rope creating a series of attachment points inside the canoe; with a tight fit there is no perceptible leakage. As an extra, you can run shock cord down the inside of the boat by twisting it through the interior loops of the threaded rope; this enables you to quickly secure items such as a sponge or the end of a spare paddle, and yet have them readily to hand. Putting more shock cord under the seats allows spare paddles to be secured at the blade end.

Figure 12-18 painter, swim line and end buoyancy.

▶ **BUOYANCY**—All canoes used on whitewater should be fitted with extra buoyancy. I favor small buoyancy bags at each end of the canoe. By attaching a short rope to the end of the bag, then threading it through the end loop where it loops through the boat, the air bag can be secured to the end of the canoe. A thin rope criss-crossed through the interior side ties or eyelets of the canoe and over the air bag hold it down. To complete the system, a D-ring is glued to the floor and a strap run up over the bag to hold it into the canoe. Do not rely solely on the bag's own tie-in points as these can rip off.

▶ **FASTENING KIT INTO THE BOAT**—There are two distinct systems for fastening barrel, kit bags, etc. into the canoe; both have their advantages.

Leashed—One is to attach the kit via a long leash. The leash should be no longer than half the length of the canoe, and tied to the central thwart. The great advantage, particularly when paddling solo, is the ease with which the load can be moved around to adjust the trim. For most situations the canoe is paddled with the bow just a little lighter than the stern. However, in some windy conditions or while doing reverse moves on the river, it can be better to be bow heavy. The trim is altered by moving the load or the paddlers.

Tied in—The other system is to lash everything into the canoe using a series of lashings from side to side. As extra security, D-rings in the floor can be used to run a strap over the load lengthways, so as to stop any kit movement in the event of a swamping. The D-rings can be used to strap in extra buoyancy if you are not carrying kit. The kit bags now act as extra buoyancy bags enabling you to paddle the boat fully swamped and effect your own rescue. With a heavy load the canoe remains remarkably stable.

The disadvantage is the difficulty of changing the trim of the boat; none the less, in serious conditions I tend to lash everything.

Figure 12-19 kit lashed in, note D-rings.

D-ring

▶ **BAILER**—This can either be attached via a very short cord to a kara-biner and clipped to the boat, or a ring of old car inner tube can be whipped to a seat and the bailer simply pushed into the rubber.

▶ **RECOVERY / SWIM LINES**—The basic idea is simple. A throw line or swim line is attached to the boat in advance. Upon capsizing, you grab the rope, swim for the bank, and then quickly run the rope around the nearest rock or tree.

Some people attach the throw line to the side of one of the seats. This system works well on some boats by flipping them on their side and emptying them of water as the tension comes on. However it can be difficult to find the rope.

Alternately a throw line can be secured to the end loop and kept in place on the deck with a couple of pieces of shock cord. It only takes a moment to locate and free the rope. Some people attach a throw line to both ends of the canoe to make finding a rope even easier; 65 feet (20 m) of rope is usual but on wide rivers some people use 98 to 131 feet (30 to 40 m) of swim line.

Whitewater Open Boats

▶ **OUTFITTING**—Good control of a whitewater canoe requires an effective system of saddle, thigh straps and foot brace. It is possible to buy a canoe fitted out by the supplier but this is often a compromise as it may well be done with a range of different sizes and body shapes in mind. The type of water that you intend to paddle may demand a different approach to outfitting; big volume rivers, creeks, and rodeo/play will change your method of outfitting your boat.

▶ **SADDLE**—The saddle, or pedestal, is generally placed so that the canoe has a neutral trim. When the canoe is swamped, the saddle needs to be small enough to allow water to flow freely across the bottom of the boat, so that stability is not upset by water being trapped on one side of the boat.

► **THIGH STRAPS**—A strap system needs to do two things, in order of priority:

1. **Have a 100 percent effective and simple release mechanism**.

2. **Hold your knees in contact with the hull and your butt on the saddle even when upside down**.

Figure 12-20 thigh strap system with quick release handle attached to both buckles.

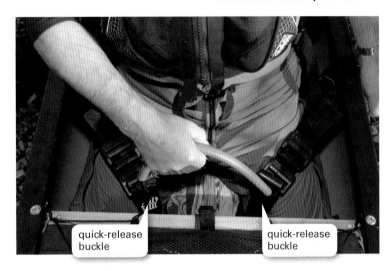

quick-release buckle

quick-release buckle

When starting from scratch, I have found it better to position the rest of the straps and D-rings by using the release system as a reference point. If for one reason or other the straps can't be released, you still need to be able to get out. It may be possible to remove your feet from the foot brace and slide out backward or build in a second point of release. Flap *Faster* type buckles on the D-rings work well.

► **FOOT BRACES**—Foot braces or toe blocks are an integral part of the system as they enable you to push forward and lock into the straps. My personal preference is for a *Keeper* style foot brace fixed to the saddle. This suits me because I prefer to paddle with my feet flat; it also enables me to slide my feet out easily. Alternatively, a range of toe-blocks that can be glued to the bottom of the hull are available.

Figure 12-21 specialist WW open canoe (OC1) fittings with adjustable foot braces.

foot-peg footrest

Figure 12-22
OC1 stern airbag.

▶ **AIR BAGS**—Air bags come in a range of sizes and which ones you choose depends on the style of paddling you use. Generally the stern bag will fill as much space as possible although you might want to leave room for some kit behind the saddle.

The bow bag for a predominant play paddler would be as big as possible so as to exclude the maximum amount of water from the boat. When paddling on a river, a shorter bag has the advantage of allowing room to bail while on the water. In sticky situations, upside down on a shallow rapid, you will have space to duck forward and escape a trashing, your back being protected by your buoyancy aid and your head safely inside the canoe.

▶ **RESCUE CONSIDERATIONS**—A whitewater open canoe doesn't make the best of rescue tools so be prepared to rely on a good repertoire of self-rescue techniques. How you set your boat up can save a lot of time and effort.

▶ **PAINTERS**—Short lengths of line attached to each end of the canoe which are normally used for tethering the boat while you inspect a rapid. Painters can also act as short recovery lines to pull the boat off a pin. The length of the lines should be just over half the length of the boat. They should be tied to each end loop and brought back to the thwarts behind and in front of the seat, and tied with a quick release hitch for quick access. Too long a line will result in loose rope flopping around in the bottom of the canoe.

▶ **RECOVERY/SWIM LINES**—The most common method of creating a recovery line is to attach the bag end of a throw bag to somewhere secure at one or both ends of the canoe. Remember that any potential load on this attachment may well be huge, so do not use the handle on the deck-plate as they tend to pull off. The bag can be secured with elastic, with the end of the rope free, ready to be pulled out in an emergency.

In the event of a swim this line can be pulled out and taken to the bank, thus swinging the boat in. Do not, under any circumstances, attach yourself to this line. The same technique can be used in a pin or a broach situation. In a risky situation the line can be thrown to the shore or released into the water and picked up downstream of the pin. When recovering an open canoe from a pin, it is usually better to try to roll the boat as it is pulled off, to spill the water and reduce the load that is being pulled (see Chapter 25).

▶ **CHASE BOATING**—A whitewater open canoe is not a great deal of use as a chase boat, apart from giving emotional support to the swimmer. Generally open boats are too slow to give an effective tow and too unstable to carry a swimmer. Therefore the importance of being self-sufficient and confident with self-rescue is, if anything, more important to canoeists than to our kayaking buddies.

Rafts

Figure 12-23 paddle raft on the Gore Canyon, Upper Colorado. Photo: Geraint Rowlands

▶ **RAFT TYPES**—The wide selection of whitewater rafts on the market is daunting and ranges from 10-foot (3 m) paddle rafts which are very unstable on large volume rivers right up to 37-foot (11 m) "J"-Rigs that have huge outboard motors and are used for ploughing through 15-foot (4.6 m) wave trains in the Grand Canyon; therefore a need exists to select the right raft for the conditions you will be facing.

The following is an outline of the non-motorized rafts available.

▶ **PADDLE RAFTS**—Paddle rafts are powered by a crew using single bladed, canoe style paddles. All paddlers sit on an inflated tube that forms the perimeter of the raft. Steering and the co-ordination of the crew's efforts is carried out by the raft guide who normally sits in the stern of the raft.

Originally, this style of raft had a membrane floor and was called a "bucket boat," as a bucket was required to bail out water that came over the top of the inflated outer tube. In May of 1983 SOTAR, an American raft building company, produced the first production self-bailing raft. Instead of a membrane floor the self-bailing raft has an inflated floor with a series of drainage holes along the floor's perimeter. Water entering the raft over the top of the outside tube is forced out of the drainage holes as the inflated floor rises back to the surface due to its inherent buoyancy. Bucket boats are still used today on calmer stretches of water, and on large volume non-technical rivers as they are less likely to flip once swamped with water compared to a modern self-bailing raft. However bucket boats are notoriously difficult to control once full of water and take a period of time to bail out in order to make them maneuverable; taking these factors into consideration it is easy to see why self-bailing rafts have revolutionized river running on technical, steep, grade 4/5 whitewater.

Figure 12-24 oar rig on the Colorado. Photo: Geraint Rowlands

▶ **OAR RIGS**—Any paddle raft can be transformed into an oar rig by attaching an oar frame. This specialist metal frame will provide a seat for the oarsman and allow for the attachment of oars.

Stern mounts or paddle-assisted rafts have a frame lashed to the stern of the raft; crew are located in front of the frame and respond to paddling commands in the same way as they would in a paddle raft. The high position of the seat, right at the stern, in a paddle assisted raft means that the guide is susceptible to being launched forward if the raft stalls, e.g. when hitting a rock or stopper bow first. Therefore the seat of a stern mount is often lovingly referred to as the "launch pad" and many guides choose to wear a quick release lap belt to keep them in position.

Crew members on a center-mounted oar rig are trained so that they are able to aggressively shift their weight around the raft should the need arise, e.g. during a broach, or when the raft is stuck surfing sideways in a stopper.

More commonly, the guide is centrally mounted in an oar rig and either transports equipment (gear boat) or non-paddling clients. Gear boats are predominantly used for multi-day raft trips. Frames used for gear boats consist of a series of spaces that dry boxes or cooler boxes can be slotted into, and the guide generally uses one of these boxes as a seat. It is important that all equipment that is stored on a gear boat is tightly lashed to the raft or frame so that it does not move in the event of a flip. When rigging a gear boat, your aim is to minimize potential entrapment hazards by ensuring that all webbing lies as close as possible to any baggage and ensuring that there are no exposed sharp edges. The increased weight associated with a gear boat makes this type of craft less maneuverable and only suitable for a very skilled guide when paddling tight technical whitewater.

▶ **CATARAFTS**—A Cataraft (or "cat") consists of two inflatable pontoons, sat side by side, linked by a centrally located frame that gives the craft its structural rigidity. Padded metal saddles placed on each pontoon make it possible for a cataraft to be paddled by two people using single bladed paddles; this type of craft is called a "paddle cat." A frame with a centrally mounted seat and the provision for oar mounts enable a guide to oar a cataraft; this type of craft is called an "oar cat." Catarafts have many advantages over conventional rafts in that they are faster, partly due to their small bow and stern profiles, and are more maneuverable, which relates to the large amounts of redundant buoyancy in the pontoons. Note however that catarafts don't offer you anywhere near the same amount of protection as being crouched and braced, ready for impact, in a paddle raft.

Basic Paddle Raft Components

Figure 12-25 Avon Adventurer 14-inch (36 cm) paddle raft shown without rigging (perimeter line and bow/stern lines).
Photo: Avon Inflatables

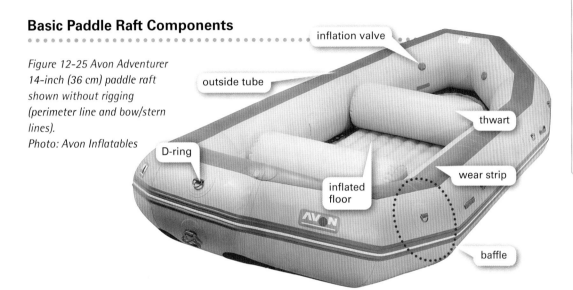

- ▶ **RAFT SIZE**—The amount of weight you wish to carry in a raft is going to be the main determining factor when selecting the raft size, be this people or equipment. Smaller rafts are more maneuverable, making them more effective on technical low-volume river sections. Larger rafts are less likely to flip and therefore perform well on powerful big-volume rivers.

- ▶ **OUTSIDE TUBE DIAMETER**—A tube diameter of 15–16 inches (38–40 cm) is as small as you will ever want to go and bigger is generally thought to be better. Rafts with larger diameter tubes sit higher in the water, which aids their maneuverability. Large diameter tubes are also more resistant to flips, which can be appreciated when you consider that it is harder for large tubes to be forced under the surface of the water. However, very large outside tube diameters do have their limitations. They can make it difficult to climb back into the raft, and can also make it difficult for crew members to reach the water with their paddles. Outside tube diameter generally increases with raft size.

- ▶ **RISE OR KICK**—Identical to the concept of a kayak's rocker, a raft has rise or kick, i.e. the bow and the stern will be slightly raised.

This rise in the bow will help the raft crest waves, plough over holes and land flatter when negotiating steep drops. The rise in the tail will assist any maneuveres performed backward such as a reverse ferry. Too much rocker however can result in a lower running speed and cause the raft to stall when it hits large holes.

▶ **MATERIALS**—Rafts are predominantly made of *Hypalon* or PVC. Rafts made of *Hypalon* seem to have the advantage of being more resistant to abrasion. PVC rafts have the advantage of being lighter and tend to slide over rocks easier. It is essential to carry a material specific repair kit on any raft trip.

▶ **THWARTS**—The main function of these inflated cross tubes is to add a large amount of structural integrity to a raft. In a paddle raft, crew will brace their feet under a thwart in order to decrease the chance of them falling out. It is possible to force your feet too far under a thwart and for this to become an entrapment hazard. Such an entrapment can damage joints and tendons of the lower limbs should the upper body be thrown around by the movements of the raft in whitewater. Thwarts are often removable and are taken out to make room for equipment in a gear raft.

▶ **MULTIPLE CHAMBERS**—The outside tube of a raft is usually made up of four separate compartments separated by internally glued circular diaphragms called baffles. The floor and each thwart also act as independent air chambers. The concept here is that you will still be able to paddle the raft to safety, should you puncture one of these compartments, and that the whole raft will not deflate. Valves for these chambers are placed on the inside of the raft generally so that they will not break should the raft strike a rock. The floor is often fitted with a special release valve as floors can be subjected to a high amount of internal damage if they are over-inflated.

▶ **D-RINGS**—Metal D-rings are threaded with webbing, and individually sewn onto patches, which are then glued onto the surface of the raft. These D-rings act as attachment points for the perimeter, bow, and stern line as well as attachment points for any rescue lines should a raft become broached. It is important to note that D-rings can fail in a load-bearing situation in that the glued patch comes away from the raft; therefore in rescue situations loads should always be distributed between more than one D-ring.

▶ **PERIMETER LINE**—The perimeter line acts as a handrail for the crew and the guide and is often grasped to improve one's chances of staying in the raft. Raft guides can use the perimeter line to pull themselves back into the raft if they should fall out. Raft crew members, thrown into the water, and in the immediate proximity of the raft, grasp the perimeter line to prevent being washed away; from this position it is relatively straightforward to pull the crew member back into the raft.

This perimeter line is secured via the D-rings to the outside tube of the raft and circles the entire perimeter, allowing for no spaces.

Figure 12-26 securing the bow/stern line.

1. *pass the coiled bow line under the perimeter line, leaving a good 24 inches (60 cm) tail free.*

2. *fold the bow line coil over the perimeter line and hold in place.*

3. *wrap the free tail around the coil and secure by placing a bite through the middle of the coil and jamming the wraps above down onto the bite.*

Ideally this line should consist of two lengths of rope starting at the stern, finishing at the bow, or vice versa, and running down either side of the raft. A larks foot is normally tied at each D-ring. The aforementioned measures are in place so that, in the event of the perimeter line accidentally being cut, numerous sections of the line will still be intact and will function as intended. A perimeter line should ideally be no less than $3/8$ inch (10 mm) thick and can also be sheathed in garden hose to allow for a good grip. Ensure that the perimeter line is sufficiently taut so as not to constitute an entrapment hazard. The perimeter line is a safety feature, and should not be used instead of the carrying handles to maneuver the raft on dry land.

▶ **BOW/STERN LINE**—The primary function of these lines is to tie off the raft when mooring. These lines should be attached to D-rings at the front and back of the raft and made of floating line no thinner than $5/16$ inch (9 mm). The lines should be twice the length of the raft so that they can be used to rig an internal "Z" drag in the event of a broach. The bow and stern line can also be used as an improvised flip line by passing the bow or stern line through a D-ring midway between the bow and stern and then throwing it over the top of the upturned raft. Bow and stern lines should be secured to the raft so that they do not pose an entrapment hazard.

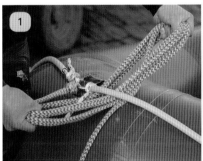  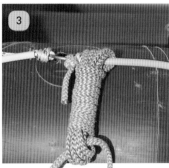

A neatly tied bow/stern line, close to the D-ring will be less of a snagging hazard and will release with a swift pull on the free end of the line.
Photos: Geraint Rowlands

▶ **FOOT CUPS/FOOT STRAPS**—Foot cups are foot-shaped pouches that are glued onto the floor of the raft. Raft guides and crew can slide their feet into these as an aid to securing themselves into the raft. Foot straps perform the same function as foot cups but differ in that they consist of a strap of material that forms a loop when glued in place. Foot cups are seen as being superior to foot straps as the nature of a pouch prevents you from pushing your foot in too far which, in the same way as forcing your foot too far under a thwart, can lead to an entrapment and subsequent injury. Trying to secure yourself in the raft by using either foot cups, foot straps, or thwarts may increase the risk of injury particularly to the knees and ankles but this needs to be balanced against the injuries associated with falling out of the raft in whitewater!

CHAPTER 13

Basic Rescue Equipment

Rescue is what happens when preventative measures have failed and we need to retrieve the situation. It is about safeguarding or saving people. In rescue situations involving water the time available is often limited to a few minutes. In such situations use of equipment should be kept to a minimum, as solutions need to be simple and quick. On the other hand, it is imperative that we become thoroughly practiced and competent in the use of the equipment that we do need to use.

If the following items are carried by every member of the team, they will have the tools needed to deal with almost any situation:

- **Throw bag**
- **Nylon tape sling**
- **Knife**
- **Two karabiners**

Any person prepared to contemplate entering the water during a rescue should also possess:

- **A whitewater chest harness**

In committing technical gorges or waterfalls, specialist equipment and techniques may be required in order that rescuers can get into a position to protect difficult sections. These techniques are dealt with in Section Four: Access and Recovery.

Raft guides, river guides and instructors who may be working with people who will not have their own rescue equipment will obviously have to carry enough to make up the shortfall.

The Throw Bag

The main use of the throw bag is to get a line to a swimmer in order to help him reach safety. It can also be used to ensure the safety of rescuers, recover equipment, or rig a tarpaulin.

Where difficult recoveries are envisaged, and ropes are likely to be needed for access purposes, it may be necessary to carry different types of ropes (see Chapter 23).

With the above uses in mind, the following features should be considered when choosing a throw bag.

Figure 13-1 typical throw bags.

▶ **THE LINE OR ROPE**—The line should be made of a floating material. A line that floats is less likely to become snagged on the river bed. The material should be woven in such a way as to provide a soft comfortable grip and not damage a user's hands even when considerable forces are involved.

To meet these criteria throw lines are usually made of braided polypropelene rope of no less than $^5/_8$ inch (8 mm) in diameter. Any smaller is extremely dangerous in that it can slice through muscle and sinew like a cheese-wire. Ropes that flatten are more comfortable to hold when used as throw lines and round ropes are stronger, cause less friction and are therefore better for hauling and recovery.

LESS THAN $^5/_8$ INCH (8 MM) IN DIAMETER… CAN SLICE THROUGH MUSCLE AND SINEW LIKE A CHEESE-WIRE

Figure 13-2 (top) "round" rope. (bottom) "flat" rope.

It is now possible to get throw lines made with an outer sheath of polypropelene and a core of aramid fibres such as Kevlar, Spectra or Dyneema. These have the advantages of being twice as strong as conventional polypropelene and the disadvantages of being twice as expensive. With boaters, storage space is at a premium, so it may make sense to have a throw bag made with kevlar core line that can also be used for more specialist access and recovery situations.

▶ **LENGTH**—Most commercially available ropes come in lengths between 33 and 80 feet (10 and 25 m).

Short ropes of 33 feet or less are useful on narrow technical rivers or for use by raft guides to throw to customers who have fallen out of the raft. This is because in both cases the distances involved are small and it is more important to be able to repack the rope quickly than throw long distances.

Medium ropes of 49 to 65 feet (15 to 20 m) are the most useful as throw lines. It all depends on how much rope the individual concerned can throw accurately.

Long ropes of over 65 feet are difficult to throw and are usually used for recovery or protecting and positioning rescuers. For this reason they are often made out of stronger, thicker diameter rope (³⁄₈ inch [10 mm] or more).

▶ **COLOR**—Both the bag and the rope should be constructed of highly visible materials. Bright primary colours such as yellow or orange are best. "Day-glow" colors are great when new; unfortunately they tend to fade very quickly. If carrying more than one rope it is a good idea to have different colored ropes.

▶ **SHAPE**—From the point of view of being easy to throw and easy to repack, a roughly cylindrical, or "bucket" shape is best. Ideally, it should taper so that it is narrower at the leading end and wider at the end that the rope comes out of.

▶ **PRINCIPLE OF THE CLEAN PROFILE**—Although the throw line is one of the most basic and most useful rescue tools, it can, through misuse or misfortune become a hazard in itself. Moving water and ropes are a bad mix.

MOVING WATER AND ROPES ARE A BAD MIX

If the situation arises where the rope is worsening the situation, and the victim is unwilling or unable to let go of the rope, the rescuer's only option is to let go of his end of the rope. In order to minimize the risk of the rope snagging in such a situation, it is best to remove any handles or knots from the thrower's end, permanently! If your brand new throw bag comes complete with a handle at the thrower's end, cut it off! In the unusual event of the rescuer needing a handle, it takes less than a second to tie an overhand knot on a bight.

Figure 13-3 packing a throw line.

The other advantage is that if the force of the water is such that rescuers are unable to hold the rope without the aid of a knot or handle, it will almost certainly pull them into the water, and they are better off letting go of the rope.

▶ **PACKING A THROW LINE**—It is vital that the line is fed down into the bag and not shoved in handfuls or, even worse, coils. This is the only way to guarantee that the lie will run smoothly and not snag.

If you pass the rope over your shoulder, gravity will help rather than hinder the action of feeding the line into the bag.

Figure 13-4 line coiled for drying and storage.

▶ **CARE AND MAINTENANCE**—During use, rescuers should take care not to tread on the rope as this pushes grit in between the fibers. The grit can then abrade and damage the rope from the inside.

After use, ropes should be rinsed in clean water to remove mud, sand and grit, dried and inspected, both visually and by running them through one's hands for any sign of damage. If a rope is obviously damaged, retire it. If you are in doubt, retire it. A rope that doesn't inspire confidence may or may not be physically safe but it is by definition bad for morale.

Ropes should be stored out of direct sunlight as they are weakened by prolonged exposure to UV rays. They must also be stored well away from any petroleum products, as any contamination will weaken them and may go unnoticed.

It also a good idea to store throw lines coiled and out of their bags. This ensures that they are inspected and correctly packed before use, by the person who is going to use them.

Figure 13-5 throw bags carried on a belt are favored by raft guides. Some kayakers use them but many find that they inhibit paddling.

▶ **STOWAGE**—Some people like to carry their throw bag on their PFD and others prefer to clip it to a strong point in the raft/open boat or behind the backrest of their kayak. A bag stowed on the rescuer's body has the advantages of being instantly accessible and impossible to leave behind during bank inspections. The disadvantage is that it impedes a paddler's freedom of movement.

Knives

Paddlers who carry or use a throw line should carry a safety knife. If the rescuer or victim become entangled it may be necessary to cut the rope immediately.

A safety knife designed for use on whitewater should be securely retained when not in use, yet easy to get hold of with one hand and easy to release or open. Most boaters and raft guides use small sheath knives or lock knives that have been specifically designed for the purpose.

Large, "Rambo" style knives are awkward to carry, likely to snag and present an aggressive image that many people find offensive or threatening. They are also illegal in some countries. I would therefore suggest that they have no place on the river.

*Figure 13-6
a selection of river
knives. Photo:
www.surf-lines.co.uk*

▶ **SHEATH KNIVES**—In the case of a sheath knife there must be some mechanism that holds the knife securely in the sheath when not in use. The rescuer must be able to remove it from the sheath one handed, so it must be possible to operate the release mechanism one handed and with either hand. It will also be necessary to attach the sheath to your PFD in such a way that it is accessible to either hand.

▶ **LOCK KNIVES**—Lock knives have the advantage of being more discreet and virtually impossible to snag. However, they must be designed so that they can be opened one handed and with either hand. Care should also be taken to select a PFD that has a suitably positioned knife pocket.

▶ **OTHER DESIGN FEATURES**—Many knives have serrated edges which are specifically designed for cutting ropes.

There is some debate as to whether a sharp point or a blunt end is best on a knife. The blunt ended knives are designed so that they can be used to cut but not to stab, which means that the risk of accidental injury to a person or damage to a raft is considerably reduced. The down side is that there are some extreme situations where it might be desirable to deliberately puncture a raft.

▶ **LANYARDS**—Some people attach their knife to their PFD by means of a thin piece of line, so as not to lose it if they let go of it. I would suggest that this is not good practice, as a razor sharp knife flailing around in a strong current could do the rescuer considerable damage.

Saws

*Figure 13-7
a folding saw.*

Small folding saws were very popular in the days of small cockpit kayaks. Modern keyhole cockpits make the prospect of needing to cut somebody out of a boat very unlikely. However it is certainly worth having one in the group as it may have other uses, such as the preventative removal of strainers.

Tape or Sling

An 8-foot (2.4 m) sewn sling of tubular nylon tape (Spectra) can be used for a whole variety of purposes: to quickly create an anchor point, to fasten a rescued boat to the bank, to fasten your own boat while you clamber onto a rock in midstream, to name but a few. It should be kept in a pocket so you can get at it quickly. Shortening it with an overhand knot and wearing it clipped around the waist using a karabiner is not a good idea. This is because it forms a potential snag loop that will take a 5,500-lb. (2,500 kg) load before breaking.

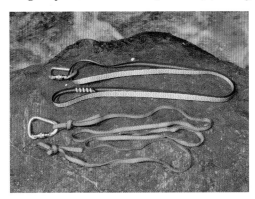

Figure 13-8 (top) sewn sling, (bottom) snake sling.

Otherwise, a "snake sling" can be used and carried in a similar way. For raft guides this is a better choice, as it doubles up as a flip-line (used to right upturned rafts). The length of the sling will depend on the size of the guide and raft.

Karabiners

Figure 13-9 (left) pear-shaped snaplink, (middle) pear-shaped screwgate, (right) D-shaped screwgate.

There are two shapes of karabiner: D-shaped and pear-shaped, which come in two types: snap-link and screwgate.

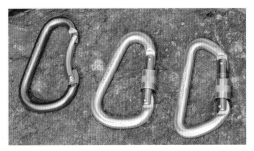

▶ **SHAPE**—D-shaped karabiners are lighter but are designed to be strong only at key points where the karabiner feeds the ropes.

Pear-shaped (or HMS) karabiners are engineered to take the strain over a much greater area of the karabiner. This makes them much more versatile as they can safely take more than one rope and can be used with a greater variety of knots and hitches.

I would therefore recommend that if paddlers are only going to carry a couple of karabiners, they should be pear-shaped ones.

▶ **SNAPLINK VERSUS SCREWGATE**—Snaplinks are lighter and quicker to use. Screwgates are stronger and, providing you remember to screw the gate shut, more difficult to accidentally become detached from. Professional rescue teams only use screwgates. However they usually only get involved in situations which are relatively stable, such as people stranded on a rock in midstream, or to recover bodies.

A WINDOW OF OPPORTUNITY . . .

Figure 13-10 an improvised detachable paddle hook.

Boaters or rafters involved in an incident have a window of opportunity, a period of about four to seventy seconds after an incident starts, during which time prompt action can sort out a situation before it develops into a major problem. This is why many of them prefer to use snaplinks for water-based incidents. A compromise is to use a snaplink to secure your throw bag and a screwgate on your tape sling.

Improvised Paddle Hook

A paddle hook is used to attach a line to a victim or piece of equipment that is out of reach. By using some surgical strapping tape from a first aid kit, or some gaffer tape from a repair kit, a paddle hook can be made using a snaplink karabiner with a curved gate designed to make it easy to clip to ropes. The karabiner is securely taped to the end of a paddle, or better still a long pole and the minimum amount of tape necessary is used to hold the gate open. Once the karabiner is hooked, a sharp tug is usually enough to detach the paddle, which might otherwise get in the way.

Whitewater Chest Harness

Figure 13-11 releasing from a chest harness.

1. *swimmer on line surfed to the surface.*
2. *still able to breathe under plume of water signals that he has decided to release.*
3. *quick release pulled—separation from line.*

Chest harnesses designed for use in whitewater rescue have only one function. They are designed as a safer way of attaching a swimmer to a line in fast flowing water. To achieve that simple objective they have to meet the following criteria:

1 **They must reliably release under a relatively light load right through to extreme loading.**

2 **They must self-release before pressures can reach levels which would result in chest injuries.**

3 **It should be difficult, if not impossible, to release them accidentally.**

4 **The attachment point of the line should be high enough up the centre line of the rescuer's back so as to ensure that rescuers are held in such a way that fast flowing water will surf them to the surface and maintain them in a stable position that ensures that they can breathe.**

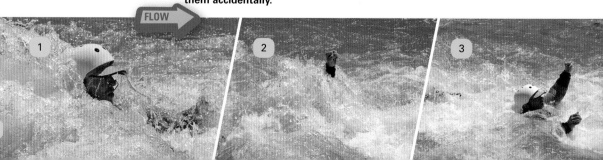

▶ **DESIGN**—Although the actual detail may vary, all the designs currently available tend to be similar. The design criteria are met by:

1 Integrating the design into a PFD. This means that the whole system is more stable and less likely to let the attachment point move from its optimum place than a separate harness.

2 Using purpose built release buckles that are designed to break or allow the belt of the harness to slide, if the loading reaches an injury threatening level.

It is important to realize that considerable time, money and experimental models are involved before manufacturers come up with their final product. These are not the sort of items that lend themselves to being improvised or home-made. It is also important to read the manufacturer's instructions or seek professional guidance on a safety and rescue course, to ensure that they are used correctly.

▶ **RELEASE BUCKLES**—The problem of having a release mechanism that will release or not release in different situations has led some manufacturers to add a friction plate that the paddler threads the belt through prior to fastening the quick release buckle itself. The plate is threaded in situations where it is essential that the harness does not allow the belt to slide, even under quite high loads, such as when being used to anchor a belayer to the river bank. It is not threaded when the rescuer may wish to release the harness under much smaller loads, as is the case in most swimming situations.

However, some systems are designed in such a way that it is the manufacturer's intention that the plate should always be threaded. If this is the case I would advise to check, through cautious experimentation in safe locations, whether the buckle will release under the lower pressures sometimes encountered in swimming situations.

Figure 13-12

release buckle with friction plate. There are two modes for threading the belt through the friction plate before securing with the buckle:

1 *friction plate threaded for water situations.*

2 *friction plate threaded for use with high loads.*

3 *released by pulling the toggle or the end of the tape.*

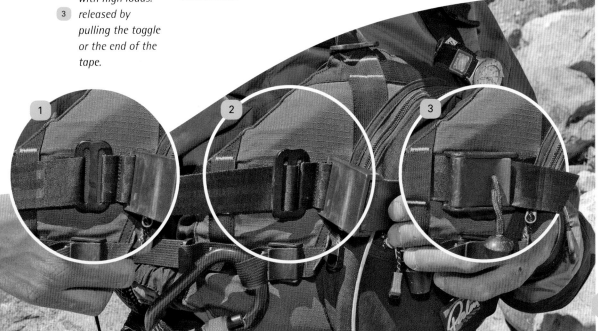

▶ **COWS' TAILS**—Cows' tails act as an extension, so that the rescuer doesn't have to get someone else to clip the line into the attachment point, or perform contortions to do it himself. When not in use the end that would clip into a line is clipped to a quick release point on the front of the buoyancy aid, so that the cow's tail fits snugly against the rescuer's chest. They are very convenient but some paddlers prefer to do without them. This is because, if they are worn loose they can snag an obstruction, whereas if they are worn tight they reduce mobility. Elasticized cow's tails go some way towards reducing these concerns.

In most situations where a chest harness is used, a buddy will be controlling the line from the bank, so a cow's tail is not necessary as the line can be attached by the buddy. However, if a stranded or pinned boater wishes to attach a line that has been thrown to them, a cow's tail makes the task much easier.

Figure 13-13 attached to a line via a cow's tail.

Figure 13-14 attached directly to a line.

WHEN ATTACHING A LINE DIRECTLY TO THE CHEST HARNESS **A SCREWGATE SHOULD ALWAYS BE USED.** SNAPLINKS CAN WORK THEMSELVES INTO THE RETAINING STRAPS SO THAT THE LINE MAY NOT BE RELEASED.

Figure 13-15 Never attach a line to chest harness with a snaplink as it can work its way into the retaining straps so that the line may not be released.

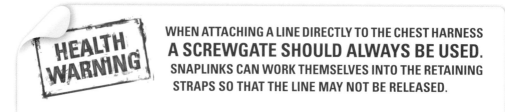

CHAPTER 14

Swimmers, Boats, and Paddles

A boater failing to roll, a rafter catapulted into the water; these are common occurrences on a whitewater trip. The first priority is obviously to get the swimmer out of the water, but the abandoned boats and paddles also need to be dealt with. Strictly speaking, I should deal with these items in the part of the book that deals with recovery. However, the techniques used for dealing with swimmers or items of equipment that are floating in the current are so similar that I have chosen to deal with them in the same chapter.

HEALTH WARNING

WE CAN NEVER JUSTIFY A HIGH LEVEL OF RISK TAKING WHEN ATTEMPTING TO RECOVER DRIFTING EQUIPMENT. IF IN DOUBT, LEAVE IT AND WAIT UNTIL A MORE FAVORABLE SITUATION DEVELOPS.

Figure 14-1 an everyday occurrence. Photo: www.swift waterrescue.at

Self Rescue

A POSITIVE MENTAL ATTITUDE

Self rescue is by far the most reliable form of rescue. The main requirement is a positive mental attitude.

Two people swimming on the same stretch of water who have a different mental approach are in two completely different situations! One a helpless victim, the other is a paddler in temporary difficulty.

Figure 14-2 kayakers should develop a bomb-proof roll. Photo: from Kayak Rolling by Loel Collins

As soon as a swimmer's head breaks the surface he should shake the water from his eyes and ears, and look around. Information needs to be gathered and conscious decisions need to be made:

1 Where is the nearest point of safety, and how to get to it? (In a rafter's case, this is normally the raft. However, there will be times when it will be easier and safer to make for the shore.)

2 Is anyone in a position to effect a rescue and if so, how can the swimmer best cooperate?

3 Whether to hang on to one's equipment or whether to ditch it so as to be able to swim more effectively?

Having gathered the information and decided on a course of action, the swimmer will need to be aware of, and preferably have practiced, good whitewater swimming techniques.

Swimming in Whitewater

When swimming in fast flowing water the greatest danger is getting a foot or hand caught between two boulders, or trapped in some other obstruction on the river bed. This would result in the swimmer being forced to the bottom by the current and drowned.

Figure 14-3 the basic swimming position allows the swimmer to fend off with his feet rather than his head!

Figure 14-4 progress to the side is made by ferry gliding

Figure 14-5 (left) good technique for shallow water—head back and hands and feet on surface. (right) if you lift your head up, your bottom is lowered and you will bump it hard on the rocks.

▶ **BASIC POSITION**—By swimming on our backs and keeping our feet and hands on the surface we can avoid the risk of foot entrapment. By keeping our heads upstream and our feet downstream we gain the following advantages:

- We can see where we are going.
- Our head is protected from impacts.
- We can fend off boulders with our feet.

- If we do make contact with the bottom, the knocks are taken on the back of the PFD or our buttocks, which means bruises rather than fractures.

Progress is made around hazards or obstacles and towards safety by swimming at a ferry angle, (i.e. about 45° to the main flow).

▶ **SHALLOW WATER**—In shallow water it is even more important to keep hands and feet on the surface. Keeping your head back helps keep your body flat and hips on the surface.

▶ **DEEP OR SLOW MOVING WATER**—If the water is deep or slow moving, we can use front crawl or breast stroke.

▶ **PASSIVE OR AGGRESSIVE**—Swimming in cold turbulent water is an exhausting business. Unlike in normal swimming, the swimmer has to have a reserve of oxygen in his blood and air in his lungs to survive periods when forced below the surface. These factors mean that it is not a good idea to swim flat-out for more than about 33 feet (10 m).

On narrow creeks the distances involved are so short that the only sensible option is to swim aggressively to the shore. Anyone falling out of a raft will usually be within a few feet of the raft. If they act quickly and swim aggressively they will regain contact with the raft within seconds.

If the distance to safety is too great, the swimmer should husband his strength. He should swim steadily towards safety but not so fast that he becomes short of breath. It may be better to stay in midstream and float passively to within striking distance of safety than to immediately strike out aggressively for the bank, only to be swept into a strainer or some other hazard.

The swimmer should plan ahead, swim passively towards safety and use short bursts of aggressive swimming to avoid obstacles and to make it those last few metres to safety. Above all he must remain calm and never give up.

Figure 14-6
the swimmer saves energy by swimming passively and ferry gliding for position. When in range of the eddy he turns on his front and swims aggressively into the eddy.

▶ **EDDIES**—Getting across an eddy line and into the eddy can be very difficult, simply because a swimmer moves comparatively slowly. There are two ways to approach this maneuver:

▶ **ATTACK**—The swimmer maneuvers himself to a point a little upstream of the eddy, then turns onto his front facing downstream and aggressively swims across the eddy line ("eddy fence"), at a 45°angle. This is essentially a swimmer's version of an eddy-in. The eddy-in can be further helped if the swimmer makes a high overarm stroke with his outside arm just as he crosses the eddy. This lowers his inside shoulder so that his body "carves" the turn into the eddy, and ensures that the stroke is planted deep in the eddy so as to anchor the turn.

reach into eddy

roll into eddy

▶ **ROTATE**—The speed of the current or shallow water may force a swimmer to maintain a ferry angle all the way into the eddy. This is what an open boater calls "setting in." The swimmer can help get himself across the eddy line by rolling over and over into the eddy.

▶ **WAVES**—When swimming through a series of waves, a swimmer's head will be on the surface in the troughs and under water in the peaks. The danger is that the swimmer instinctively only tries to breathe in and ends up with lungs bursting with stale air. What he should do is to consciously and deliberately breathe out as he goes through the peaks, (i.e. when his head is under water), so that he can get a lung full of clean air in the troughs.

Figure 14-7 (top) attacking the eddy line.

Figure 14-8 (left) rolling over the eddy line.

Figure 14-9 (bottom) swimming through a wave train.

breathe in   breathe out   breathe in

1 2 3

Figure 14-10 swimming over an obstacle/ potential strainer.

▶ **STRAINERS**—Strainers should be avoided at all costs. However if there is no avoiding a strainer, the only hope is to roll onto your front facing downstream and swim over the obstacle.

If you allow your legs to be swept under the obstacle, it is unlikely that you will be able to get back unaided. If the obstacle is a strainer under the water this is a potentially fatal situation.

Figure 14-11 a bad outcome with a strainer.

AVOIDANCE IS BETTER THAN CURE

Equipment during a Swim

The decision on whether to hang on to the boat and paddle, saving everyone a lot of trouble, or ditch them and concentrate on surviving the swim, should be just that: a conscious decision, not a panic reaction.

If a paddler is at the bottom of a rapid and is faced with a straight-forward swim to the shore or back to the raft, it makes sense for him to hang on to his equipment. On the other hand if he is at the start of a rapid, he should throw his paddle towards the shore and concentrate on getting himself to the side.

Figure 14-12 using a swim line.

▶ **KAYAKERS**—In the kayaker's case, the kayak should be kept downstream so that he can't find himself trapped between "a rock and a hard place." Ideally the paddle should be held in the same hand that is holding the boat so that the other arm can be used to swim with.

▶ **OPEN BOATERS**—The open boater can use the above approach where the prospect of a long swim is not too daunting. If however he has fitted out his open boat as shown in Chapter 12, he can grab the free end of the bow or stern throw line, swim to the shore unencumbered and then use the line to swing the boat into the shore.

IT IS PARTICULARLY IMPORTANT THAT OPEN BOATERS KEEP THEIR BOAT DOWNSTREAM WHEN SWIMMING WITH IT. IF THE BOAT IS BROACHED THE PRESSURES ARE IMMENSE. NOT ONLY CAN A SWIMMER BECOME TRAPPED BETWEEN THE BOAT AND A ROCK, BUT IT IS ALSO POSSIBLE FOR THE BOAT TO FOLD AROUND THE SWIMMER. THIS IS KNOWN IN OPEN BOAT CIRCLES AS BEING "BEAR-TRAPPED."

▶ **RAFTERS**—More often than not, it will be best if the swimmer can keep hold of his paddle. Nonetheless, there will be occasions when being able to swim unhindered makes the difference between getting back to the raft and a nasty swim.

Rescue

T	**R**	**T**	**T**	**G**
Talk	Reach	Throw	Tow	Go

The principle is that rescuers should go for the low risk options first. For the sake of clarity, I have broken this section down into the following areas:

1 **Victim Behavior**

2 **Talk Rescues**

3 **Reaching and Throwing Rescues**

4 **Bank-based Contact Rescues**

5 **Chase Boating for Swimmers**

6 **Chase Boating for Equipment**

7 **Swimmer Rescues**

This sequence follows the TRTTG principle in that I would regard bank-based contact rescues as less hazardous than chase boating, and both of these as much less hazardous than swimmer rescues.

8 **Dealing with a Flipped Raft**

This is dealt with at the end as it can involve a number of the previously discussed techniques.

Window of Opportunity

Time can place constraints on the TRTTG principle. Because speed is essential and it is often better to deal with a moving situation such as a swim quickly, it is often the case that chase boating may be our first resort. If a chase boater can nip the situation in the bud, it may well be that in that particular situation, chase boating is the safest option.

Victim Behavior

Which rescue technique is appropriate in a given situation will depend on, among other things, a victim's behavior. An unconscious or totally unresponsive victim will not be able to hold on to a thrown line, and it would be suicidal for a rescuer to swim out to and make contact with a panic-stricken victim.

A victim's behavior in a water-based rescue situation will depend on his state of mind. This can be divided into two broad categories: in control or out of control.

▶ **IN CONTROL**—A person may be totally in control of his faculties and yet behave in an inappropriate way, so we can divide the types of behavior we might come across into three types:

In Control/Competent—This person is in control, and because he is experienced, and/or well trained, is behaving in a way that is appropriate. Swimming purposefully towards safety or shouting for a throw line are good signs. This is the person who is unlikely to put your life at risk.

In Control/Incompetent—Rescuers should realize that behavior that might seem inappropriate to a trained boater or rescuer, such as swimming towards a strainer, may be the result of ignorance rather than a loss of control. This person may be doing all the wrong things but is switched on and will probably respond well if given clear instructions.

In Control/Lucky—Even a person who is untrained and inexperienced can make the right decisions and take the right course of action. Whether he is guided by instinct, or is just plain lucky, matters not, just as long as he keeps doing the right things and makes the rescuer's job easier.

▶ **OUT OF CONTROL**—People who have lost control of their minds are the ones who pose a very real risk to rescuers. At best they are no assistance and at worst they may actively cause the rescuer harm. In a water-based situation, people who lose control may do so in three different ways:

Panic—This is where victims are overwhelmed by anxiety and react aggressively and energetically. Reason goes out of the window as victims try to blindly fight their way out of trouble. Victims may be screaming, thrashing around and wasting valuable time and energy because their efforts lack direction or purpose.

Victims who are panicking pose by far the greatest threat to rescuers. Contact rescues should be avoided. It may be possible to calm the victim down by talking to them and behaving in a calm, authoritative manner.

Counter Panic—This type of behavior occurs when victims are overwhelmed by anxiety but react by withdrawing into themselves and becoming totally passive. They are unable to help themselves and do not react to instructions.

Although not actively endangering a rescuer, their inability to assist the rescuer in any way can hinder rescuers' efforts and force rescuers to use contact rescues. Both of these factors increase the risks involved. Victims of counter panic can sometimes be roused from their withdrawn state. Physically shaking victims and talking loudly to them, calling out their name, may have the desired effect.

Instinctive Drowning Response—Sometimes referred to as Passive Drowning. This will normally only affect victims who are not wearing PFDs. The victim who is unable to swim or float will hold his arms out to the side and try to push down on the water to try and keep his mouth and nose above water. While doing this the victim will be unable to scream or shout as all the effort is going into breathing. An adult will probably last only 60 seconds in this position before going under and drowning, a child only 20 seconds.

>> IDR victims regard a rescuer as simply a floating object that they can climb onto in order to get out of the water. Such victims are beyond reason and neither know nor care that their actions may drown a rescuer. The best way to deal with such victims is to give them a buoyant object to hold onto. Once they realize that they are not going under and are able to restore a normal breathing pattern they will probably regain control.

Talk Rescues

Figure 14-13 the rescuer shouts and signals to the swimmer to draw closer.

Sometimes it is possible to talk a cooperative victim into taking an action that will enable them to rescue themselves. A swimmer who is panicking may swim towards you if you can attract their attention.

Reaching & Throwing Rescues

These rescues involve little if any risk to the rescuer. They work best with a cooperative victim and may work with a panicked or IDR victim.

▶ **REACHING RESCUES**—Rescuers must first of all ensure their own safety by getting a firm hold of the bank, raft or another rescuer before reaching out to the victim. When holding on to another rescuer, it is best to get a firm grip of each other's wrist.

The length of a rescuer's reach can be extended by using a paddle. If using a single-bladed paddle it is best to offer the T-grip to the victim. It is easier to get hold of and less likely to injure the victim. If the swimmer is also holding a single bladed paddle, the reach can be further extended by hooking the two T-grips together.

Figure 14-14 reaching rescue, rescuer supported.

*Figure 14-15
it is better to hold
each other's wrists
than to grasp hands
when offering support
in this manner.*

▶ **GETTING A VICTIM BACK IN A RAFT**—The simplest way is to grasp the swimmer by the shoulder straps of his PFD, push him down into the water, and then pull him into the raft. The victim's own buoyancy helps to pop him out of the water. As you don't want the swimmer to think that the rescuer is trying to drown him, it is important to make clear during the safety briefing that this is normal procedure!

▶ **THROW LINE TO SWIMMER RESCUES**—This is probably the most common form of bank-based rescue. The secret of success is regular practice. The technique usually involves throwing the line to a swimmer from such an angle that, when the line becomes tight, the swimmer is pendulumed into a safe eddy or the slower helical flow. There are some notable exceptions which will be covered later.

*Figure 14-16
the rescuer uses an
underarm throw and a
standing brace, and the
swimmer is pendulumed
into the eddy.*

▶ POSITIONING—It is worse than useless for a rescuer to throw a rope without giving some thought as to where is the best place to throw a rope from. Such an action would violate two fundamental principles: Looking to your own safety and ensuring that nothing you do makes the victim worse off.

Experienced rescuers are able to make such assessments in a fraction of a second. They may also make a decision in a situation which a less experienced rescuer might find too close to call. Such marginal calls require experience and fine judgment. If in doubt, back off.

Figure 14-17 two ways of safeguarding a rescuer on steep or slippery banks. (left) Tied off to waist line. (right) Tied off to chest harness.

▶ RESCUER'S SAFETY—If the bank is very slippery and the rescuer is likely to end up in the water, it would make far more sense to move to a place with a better footing, even if this means that the victim will have a slightly longer swim.

If the only suitable place does pose this risk, the rescuer will have to be tied off to a suitable anchor. The rescuer must be tied off with a separate line, so that he retains the option of letting go of the end of the throw line should this become necessary.

▶ VICTIM'S SAFETY—The rescuer must also be sure that when the victim grabs the rope he will be swung into a place of safety and not into somewhere that is even more dangerous than the middle of the river, such as a strainer or undercut bank.

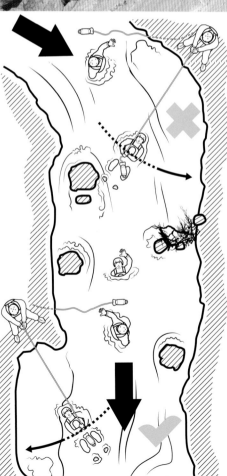

Figure 14-18 throw line positioning.

▶ **GAINING ATTENTION**—The rescuer needs to be far enough downstream from the obstacle that is likely to cause a swim, or any waves that will submerge the swimmer, for the swimmer to have come to the surface and recovered his senses enough to see the line. There is no point throwing a line if the swimmer doesn't see it and therefore doesn't hang on to it.

The rescuer should hold the line and bag clearly above his head, shout, "*Rope! Rope!*" and gain eye contact with the swimmer before throwing the line.

▶ **TECHNIQUE**—Throwing a line is a hand-eye coordination skill, combined with the ability to track a moving target. In other words it takes a great deal of practice to develop an accurate and reliable throw.

Different circumstances require different techniques. If you have waded out into an eddy and the water is thigh deep you will have to throw overarm, either with an action like like throwing a football or underarm with a bowling action. If you have to throw under overhanging branches you will have to throw underarm. A side-arm throw is difficult to master but can be useful when distance rather than accuracy is the issue.

Figure 14-19 rescuer attracts the swimmer's attention and then uses overarm throw.

Figure 14-20
underarm throw.

In all the above the following are useful guidelines:

1 Stand with the opposite foot to your throwing arm forward, i.e. if you are right-handed lead with your left foot.

2 Keep your eye on the target the whole time.

3 Follow through, i.e. as you release the bag your hand should be pointing at the target.

4 Do not forget to hold on to your end of the rope but do not wrap the rope around your hand, in case you need to let go in a hurry.

5 Aim to land the rope directly on the swimmer, as in practice you will find that whichever way you aim off will be the wrong way!

6 Try and achieve a low trajectory. This minimizes the chances of fouling tree branches or slalom lines and of the wind deflecting the line.

Holding the Line

Figure 14-21
standing brace.

If the current is not too powerful it is possible for the rescuer to brace against the pull on the line by adopting a stance that will allow him to absorb the shock as the line comes tight.

▶ **STANDING BRACE**—This involves:

- Turning side on to the direction of pull.
- Standing with feet apart.
- Keeping knees bent to absorb energy and lower the centre of gravity.
- Keeping elbows bent to absorb energy.
- Holding the loaded line.

Figure 14-22 underarm set up for quick waist belay.

▶ **SITTING BRACE**—This involves:

- **Facing the direction of pull.**
- **Sitting down as soon as the swimmer grabs the line and before the line becomes tight.**
- **Sitting with feet apart and braced against a boulder or similar obstruction.**
- **If possible wedging one's bottom against a boulder.**
- **Keeping knees bent to absorb energy.**
- **Keeping elbows bent to absorb energy.**
- **Holding the loaded line.**

Figure 14-23 from the setup above, the thrower is quickly seated into a waist belay.

▶ **QUICK WAIST BELAY**—If the current is very powerful, some form of belay may be necessary. This involves partially wrapping the line around one's body in such a way that the friction makes it easier to hold onto the line, while at the same time allowing you to pay out or let go if necessary.

This involves:

- **Taking a few feet of line out of the bag.**
- **Holding the bag in the throwing hand.**
- **Wrapping the line around your back at waist height so that the clean end is held in the other hand.**
- **Holding the line so that the clean end of the line comes into the hands from the thumb end.**

Important Points:

- Note that in this situation there is no need to complicate matters by wrapping the clean end around your arm.
- As your body is not tied off and you can turn to keep facing the direction of pull, you don't need to worry about whether the live rope is upstream or downstream. It is far more important that you hit the target, so throw the bag with your good hand.

Figure 14-24
underarm throw set
up for shoulder belay.

▶ **SHOULDER BELAY**—The advantage of the shoulder belay over other methods is that the line is wrapped around the belayer's body, in such a way that it doesn't interfere with the throwing action.

This involves:

- Taking a few feet of line out of the bag.

- Holding the bag in the throwing hand.

Figure 14-25 (left)
sitting down and
braced, correct
shoulder belay.
(right) line held the
wrong way around,
live rope over
shoulder pulls the
rescuer off balance.

- Wrapping the line around your back so that it goes from the throwing hand, diagonally across the back, over the opposite shoulder and down to waist height where the clean end is held in the other hand.

- Holding the line so that the clean end of the line comes into the hands from the little finger end.

As soon as the swimmer grabs the line the belayer sits down, braces with his feet and bottom and takes the strain using the shoulder belay. If the initial strain is considerable, it can be further eased by deliberately paying out a little rope.

HEALTH WARNING

SIT DOWN QUICKLY BUT GENTLY OR YOU COULD END UP DOING YOURSELF A NASTY INJURY WITH A ROCK ENEMA! I FIND IT BEST TO FOLD MY KNEE AND GO DOWN ON THE SIDE OF ONE LEG FIRST.

Receiving the Line

As with any rescue, everything is considerably easier if the victim remains calm, is cooperative and knows what to do.

On seeing that the rescuer is ready to throw a line, the swimmer can indicate that he is ready to receive it and make a bigger target by facing the rescuer and spreading his arms out wide. If the rescuer narrowly misses the target, a short burst of aggressive swimming can retrieve the line.

Figure 14-26 (top) line over shoulder, looking at feet. (bottom) line held under armpit.

▶ **OVER THE SHOULDER—**On grabbing the line the swimmer should be on his back facing downstream. The line should be held in both hands and draped over the shoulder that is farthest away from the rescuer. This will assist the pendulum by setting the swimmer's body up in a ferry angle, considerably easing the extra strain that would otherwise be caused by the increased drag and water pressure.

On the other hand you've only got a second or two before the strain comes on so if you can't work it out any shoulder will do.

As the line tightens the swimmer looks at his feet which causes his back to curve in such a way that he planes to the surface. Any water that does rush over his head does so in such a way that a pocket of air is created, enabling him to breathe. At the same time there will be a brief moment of instability which he must fight by spreading his legs out wide and kicking out.

▶ **UNDER THE ARM—**Some people find it better to hold the rope under their armpit. If this suits your body shape it does keep you higher on the surface. However, many find the position unstable. Experiment to see which position best suits you.

Second Throws

The best solution to the problem is to practice so often that you don't miss with your first throw. There are two types of situation we may have to deal with:

- **Where the victim is static, i.e. stranded or held in a hydraulic.**

- **Where the victim is floating downstream and the rescuer has to run down the bank after him.**

▶ STATIC SECOND THROW -

1 Free both hands by standing on the end of the rope.

2 Take in the rope hand over hand and pile it at your feet.

3 Scoop water into the bag to weight it and throw again.

This section is written for a right-handed person. Left-handed people simply substitute left for right and vice-versa.

▶ THROWING FROM COILS -

1 With your left hand held palm upwards, take in the rope with your right hand laying the coils into your left hand. Deliberately drag the rope on the water or ground as this ensures that the coils lay neatly and don't tangle.

2 When you have taken in about half the rope, trap the coils by curling your little and ring fingers.

Take in the remaining rope laying the coils on your middle and index finger.

3 Separate the two sets of coils, holding the coils nearest the bag in your right hand and those nearest the clean end in your left.

4 Trap the clean end of the rope under your little finger.

CONTINUED . . .

Figure 14-27 sequence, preparing coils for throwing.

Figure 14-28 throwing a coiled rope.

. . . CONTINUED

5 **Run down the bank and get a little ahead of the swimmer.**

6 **Throw the coils, leading with the bag end. Keep the end trapped under your little finger.**

Non-pendulum Situations

There are four situations where the rescuer is not trying to pendulum the victim to the side:

1 **Still or slow moving water.**

2 **Where the rescuer is moving at the same speed as the victim, i.e. throwing a line from a raft.**

3 **Where the water is fast flowing all the way to the bank and there are no eddies or helical flow. (This situation is due to the river's bed and sides being very smooth, and would normally be found on a canalized section of river or in a flood drainage channel.)**

4 **Where the thrower is positioned, either by mistake or lack of choice, in such a way that he is parallel, rather than at an angle to the main flow, as is often the case on the outside of a bend. This will hold the swimmer in the current and will probably involve such forces that the thrower is unable to change his position without letting go of the rope.**

▶ **SITUATIONS ONE & TWO**—In the first two situations the rescuer simply pulls in the line hand over hand and brings the victim to them. Very little force is involved.

▶ **SITUATION THREE**—In this situation the water will be moving very fast and the main flow will continue uninterrupted right up to the bank. The forces involved if the swimmer is pendulumed towards the bank and the angles change will be such that either the swimmer or the rescuer will be forced to let go of the line.

Providing the bank is unobstructed, the rescuer can reduce the forces involved by running down the bank at the same speed at which the swimmer is floating and pull him in at right angles to the current.

Figure 14-29 changing the angle of pull.

1 – **3** *by hand*

1 – **3** *using a sling and karabiner*

▶ **SITUATION FOUR**—If the current isn't too powerful and the rescuer has used a standing brace, he can simply move down the bank and change the angles involved.

In the case of a powerful current requiring a sitting brace or a belay, a second rescuer can change the angle of pull by grabbing the line and moving down the bank or eddy, thus changing the angles and forces involved.

An alternative is to clip the throw line with his tape sling and karabiner, and then run down the bank.

SITUATION THREE & FOUR—(Bank obstructed) The following technique would normally be used if there is time to set up beforehand:

1 Rescuer B clips a second line to Rescuer A's line before it is thrown and moves into position as far downstream of the thrower (Rescuer A) as he can.

3 As soon as the swimmer has hold of the throw line, Rescuer B pulls his line in as quickly as he can.

Figure 14-30 pre-arranged safety to enable throw line rescue of swimmer upstream of strainer.

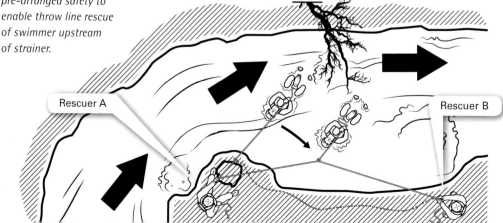

Rescuer A

Rescuer B

Bank-based Contact Rescues

All the methods illustrated so far depend on the victim being conscious and able to grab hold of a line or paddle. The following methods will also work for retrieving boats, paddles and unconscious or unresponsive swimmers who are drifting in the current.

RESCUERS MUST HAVE THOROUGHLY EVALUATED THE RISKS

All involve considerably more risk than reaching or throwing rescues as they involve a rescuer entering the water, therefore considerable judgment must be exercised. Rescuers must have thoroughly evaluated the risks involved, be well practiced in the use of these techniques and be confident of a successful outcome.

▶ **HANDRAIL**—The most important element of this technique is to read the river well. The rescuer needs to find a place downstream of the hazard that is being covered where the main current sets in close to a shallow eddy.

One end of a line is tied to a suitable anchor and a series of overhand knots on a bight are tied in the other end. The rescuer simply uses the knots to keep hold of the line. The line provides him with enough support to wade out to the edge of the current where he can reach out and grab hold of anything that floats past.

Figure 14-31 handrail. (inset left) tied off to anchor with a clove hitch.
(Inset right) with overhand knots on the bight down the length, tied so that fingers can't get caught in the loops.

Points to note:

1 The line must be anchored in such a position that, should the rescuer lose his footing, he would be pendulumed back into the eddy.

2 The line must be tied off so that only as much as is needed is in the water.

3 The overhand knots should be tied so that the bights are too small to put one's hand through them. The rescuer holds on by grasping the knot rather than by putting his hand through a loop, just in case he needs to let go.

4 Rescuers should only consider using this technique upstream of a stretch of water that they would be prepared to swim if necessary.

"Live Bait" Rescue

This is a two-person rescue. Rescuer A is in position ready to jump onto or swim after a victim or equipment and is attached, via a quick release chest harness, to a line which is waist-belayed by Rescuer B.

▶ **POSITIONING**—The rescue should be set up where the current will bring the victim or equipment as close as possible to the rescuers. Rescuer B, the belayer, must be positioned so that, when the line becomes tight, Rescuer A will be pendulumed out of the main flow and into a safe eddy. Ideally the rescue should be set up somewhere where the rescuer would be able to swim unaided to the shore should he become detached from the line.

Figure 14-32 full version of the waist belay. Note that the "dead" rope is wrapped around the forearm so that friction can be increased by folding the arm across your chest.

▶ **THE BELAYER**—In this situation, where the belayer can sit down with the rope already set up, a waist belay is the preferred method. The rope attached to the swimmer, known as the "live" rope, is held in the belayer's hand, passed around his back at waist level and held in the other hand (the dead rope) after it has been wrapped once around his forearm.

If you are unable to turn your body to follow the direction of pull of the rope as it changes, it is a good idea to ensure the live rope is in your upstream hand. This ensures that the rope wraps around your body, increasing rather than decreasing the friction.

The belayer is in a position to take rope in or feed it out as required by the swimmer. Practice is required to ensure that the belayer can do this without letting go of the dead rope at any time.

▶ **ENTRY**—Rescuer A, carrying a few loose coils of rope, jumps in when the target has floated as close as it is going to get. The aim is to achieve a low trajectory and a low angle of entry so as to achieve maximum distance and stay on the surface (a bit like skimming stones). He should hit the water with his belly, and with his hands, feet and head raised, so as to keep them on the surface.

Figure 14-33 jumping in for a "live bait" rescue.

If the target cannot be reached by the leap, the rescuer will have to use front crawl in order to swim fast enough to intercept the target. Therefore, when selecting a position to launch from, care will have to be taken to ensure that the water is deep enough.

With practice, it is possible to become more accurate swimming from an eddy to intercept than leaping. This is particularly the case if the rescuer is wearing swimming aids (see Chapter 26).

Figure 14-34 swim version of the live bait rescue.

▶ **CONTACT**—On reaching the victim, Rescuer A should turn him on his back and grab him by the shoulder straps of his PFD. By holding the victim tight against his chest and keeping the victim's head slightly lower than his own, he will ensure that they are both able to breathe when the line becomes tight and they plane to the surface and pendulum into the eddy.

Figure 14-35 live bait rescuer makes contact with the victim.

Although in the handrail and live bait rescues, contact could be made with a swimmer in a state of panic, the risk to rescuers posed by this factor is low. In the case of the handrail rescue, this is because the rescuer is in water that is no more than thigh deep. In the case of the live bait rescue it is because within a second or two, both the rescuer and the victim are swung into a safe eddy where the rescuer can be assisted by the belayer if necessary.

Chase Boating for Swimmers

Rescues of swimmers and their equipment are often made by other boaters, either as it happens, or on more difficult rapids by boaters pre-positioned to cover such eventualities. Rafters running more demanding rivers often use kayakers in this role as extra safety cover. Although less suited to chasing swimmers because of lack of speed and maneuverability, rafts do have the distinct advantage of providing a stable platform from which to effect a rescue once contact is made.

Chase boating is a high-risk activity. It requires top level boating skills and self-confidence, combined with the ability to make cool, rational decisions and snap judgments. It is vital that team members clearly identify who is prepared and able to take on this role, and who isn't.

▶ **ASSESSING VICTIM BEHAVIOR**—In boater to swimmer rescues, contact with a panic-stricken victim poses a very real threat to the rescuer's safety. The rescuer must keep his distance and assess the victim's state of mind by talking to him and observing his reactions before attempting to make physical contact.

THE ASSUMPTION MUST BE THAT HE IS A HOMICIDAL MANIAC WHOSE ONLY MISSION IN LIFE IS TO DROWN YOU!

*Principle of
Presumed Insanity*

Until the victim proves otherwise, the assumption must be that he is a homicidal maniac whose only mission in life is to drown you!

▶ **PANIC BEHAVIOR**—Physical contact with a panic-stricken victim should be avoided at all costs. The best a chase boater can do is to keep a safe distance and lure the victim towards safety.

▶ **COUNTER PANIC**—It may be possible, by talking to and physically shaking a victim, to shake him out of it, so he is able to offer some level of cooperation. If not he will need to be treated as an unconscious victim.

▶ **INSTINCTIVE DROWNING RESPONSE**—There are two possible outcomes if a boater allows somebody showing signs of IDR to get hold of the end of his boat:

1 The victim will hold on to the end of the boat, realize he can now float, and passively allow himself to be rescued.

2 The victim will grab hold of the boat and turn into a panicked victim. Therefore the chase boater should not make contact with such a victim unless he is prepared to leave his boat as a float for the victim to hang on to and swim to safety to avoid contact with the victim.

Escorting a Swimmer

Even if the victim's behavior is "normal," the chase boater may decide that the difficulty of the water is such that attempting to tow or carry a swimmer is too dangerous. By maintaining station close to a swimmer the chase boater can fulfill a number of useful functions:

▶ **PROVIDE MORAL SUPPORT**—The mere presence of another human being is reassuring, even if all he can do is cheer the swimmer on!

▶ **GIVE DIRECTIONS**—The chase boater is able to see and plan much further ahead and is therefore able to tell the swimmer which way to go to avoid hazards and reach safety.

▶ **GIVE WARNING**—If a hazard is unavoidable, the chase boater can give the swimmer more time to mentally and physically prepare.

▶ **ACT AS A MARKER**—The chase boater can help bank-based rescuers preparing a rescue by marking the position of the swimmer who might otherwise be hidden from them.

Contact Rescues

▶ **DRAG**—If the distance to safety is short, the swimmer can hold on to the rescuer's stern grab loop and be helped on his way. Progress is slow and exhausting due to the amount of drag to be overcome.

There is a victim mentality whereby, as soon as contact is made, the victim relaxes and allows things to happen rather than actively contributing to his own rescue. Therefore the rescuer will have to glance over his shoulder to ensure that the swimmer is still swimming vigorously.

Figure 14-36 ensure that the swimmer is helping.

▶ **PUSH—**This technique is best used in deep water that is not too rough. In rough or shallow water the victim risks being injured. It is particularly useful with exhausted or counter panicked victims who need to be kept under observation.

The swimmer holds on to the rescuer's bow, keeping it over one shoulder, so that he doesn't get a face full of plastic if the going gets rough. The swimmer's legs grip on either side of the boat and he is pushed to safety.

Figure 14-37 pushing allows the swimmer to be kept under observation.

▶ **CARRY—**Pros:

+ Less drag allows the rescue boat to move faster.

+ The paddling is less strenuous.

+ The victim is protected from being battered in shallow rapids.

Cons:

– Requires a high skill level on the part of the chase boater.

– Requires a cooperative swimmer.

– The chase boater's ability to maneuver is severely impeded.

Figure 14-38 during the carry keep talking to the swimmer.

▶ **INTERCEPTION—**If the chase boater is waiting in an eddy for the swimmer, has checked that the section downstream is no problem, and is sure that the swimmer is in control, it is quicker to intercept the swimmer by breaking out below them (i.e. from downstream). At all other times it is safer to approach a swimmer from upstream. This is because:

1 The chase boater is better able to back off if the swimmer turns out to be in a dangerous state of mind.

2 The chase boater has both the swimmer and his "future water" in view.

WHITEWATER SAFETY AND RESCUE

▶ **CONTACT**—The chase boater maneuvers so as to present the back of his boat to the swimmer, with the swimmer on the upstream side. The swimmer pulls himself up the back deck, holding on to the rear of the cockpit rim. He helps the boater by keeping his center of gravity as low as possible, keeping his head on the rear deck close to the boater's back and his legs trailing in the water to increase stability.

The untrained swimmer will instinctively try to see what is going on by raising his head and looking over the chase boater's shoulder. The chase boater can counter this by continually talking to the passenger about what is happening, and warning him at the approach of shallows, so that he can lift his legs just enough to avoid them being bumped and scraped.

Unconscious Victims

Dealing with an unconscious victim while chaseboating is both difficult and potentially extremely hazardous. Great care should be taken and if in doubt the rescuer should not attempt the rescue. There are in essence four possible strategies:

- **Attach throw line**
- **Long line**
- **Escort and swim**
- **Tow**

▶ **ATTACH THROW LINE**—This requires a team effort between a chase boater and a bank-based rescuer.

1 The chase boater paddles alongside the victim, until a bank-based rescuer can get into a position to throw him a line.

2 He then attaches the line to the victim's PFD shoulder strap, using a karabiner.

3 The bank based rescuer pulls or pendulums the victim to the shore.

▶ **LONG LINE**—For this to work the chase boater has to have a throw line to hand. The best way to carry it while approaching the victim is stuffed down the front of your PFD.

1 The chase boater comes alongside the victim and attaches the bag end of his throw line to the victim's PFD shoulder strap.

2 The chase boater paddles downstream of the victim, holding the end of the line in one hand, until the line is fully paid out.

3 The chase boater paddles into an

eddy, leaps out of his boat, and braces himself before the line comes tight.

4 The victim is pendulumed into the eddy.

▶ **TOW**—The victim is towed to the side using one of the methods described under "Chase Boating for Equipment."

▶ **ESCORT & SWIM**—The chase boater escorts the unconscious victim until he comes to a relatively safe section of river where he is prepared to get into the water, abandon his boat and perform a swimmer rescue. This is described later in this chapter.

HEALTH WARNING

THE CHASE BOATER SHOULD ONLY USE THE LAST TWO TECHNIQUES WHEN HE IS CERTAIN THAT THERE ARE NO DOWNSTREAM HAZARDS, AND THAT HE CAN TOW THE VICTIM TO THE SIDE BEFORE THE CURRENT CARRIES HIM OUT OF THIS ZONE OF RELATIVELY SAFE WATER.

Chase Boating for Equipment

The risks involved in chase boating for equipment are nearly as high as going for swimmers, but harder to justify. If in doubt, leave it!

IF IN DOUBT, LEAVE IT!

Paddles

If faced with both paddle and boat, it is probably best to deal with the paddle first. Firstly, they are much quicker to deal with and secondly, they are easier to lose sight of.

▶ **THE PICK-UP**—When collecting a paddle, it is best to aim to arrive alongside the paddle at one end and pick it up by a blade or the T grip. The classic mistake is for the chase boater to aim for the middle of the loom, run over the paddle and then struggle to retrieve the paddle from under his boat. Having retrieved the paddle, the chase boater can either throw or carry the paddle to the shore.

Figure 14-39 throwing the paddle.

▶ **THROWING**—When the paddle is being thrown towards the bank, it is best to throw it like a javelin.

Figure 14-40 throwing and catching a paddle.

If however the thrower is expecting someone to catch the paddle, it is best to throw it sideways, so that the catcher is presented with the loom.

▶ **PARALLEL CARRY**—This is simple enough in theory but requires some practice. The chase boater's own paddle is held as normally as possible and the recovered paddle is held parallel to and alongside it. People with small hands may not be able to use this technique.

Figure 14-41 carrying the paddles.

▶ **OPEN BOAT CARRY**—The paddle is stuffed under the bow buoyancy bag, so that it is securely wedged between the buoyancy bag and the hull, or between the buoyancy bag and the cord that holds the bag in place.

Boats

Getting a boat to shore is filled with danger. The chase boater must wait for a favorable stretch of water and be prepared to back off at any time.

Keeping a boat ashore is even harder. It is therefore essential that, on reaching the shore, the person who has lost his boat must run down the bank and offer assistance. Ideally, another member of the party would get out on the other shore and offer assistance should the boat be landed on the other bank.

If help is not immediately at hand, the chase boater may be able to use a tape sling to tether the boat to a convenient branch or exposed root until the boat's owner arrives.

Figure 14-42 nudging or "bulldozing" the boat to the shore. On low to medium volume, relatively narrow rivers, this is the technique to use.

There are three main ways of getting a boat to the shore:

▶ **NUDGE**—The chase boater pushes the boat towards the shore using the bow of his boat, keeping the abandoned boat at a ferry angle (45°) to the main flow.

The main advantage of this method is that the rescuer is not physically attached to a waterlogged boat that could drag him to his death, and is able to back off at any time.

▶ **FLIP & SHOVE**—If the current is going to take the boat within range of a large eddy, it can be flipped the right way up and given a good shove into the eddy (providing of course the boat is properly equipped with buoyancy bags).

Figure 14-43 flip and shove.

▶ **LONG LINE**—The above methods are ineffective when tackling open boats. The chase boater grabs the downstream swim line (as described in Chapter 12) or, if not fitted, clips a throw line to the downstream end of the boat. He then paddles off downstream to get ahead of the boat, holding the line in one hand. By paddling downstream he ensures that the line is not pulled tight. When the line is fully extended he maintains his distance from the boat until the current carries the convoy within range of a suitable eddy. At this point he breaks out ahead of the open canoe, leaps out of his boat and, as it drifts past him, uses the line to pendulum the boat into the eddy.

Towing

Towing a boat on fast moving or whitewater is a very hazardous activity. If the boat becomes snagged or is carried into a hazard and the chase boater is unable to immediately release the tow line, he will be dragged or pendulumed into the hazard. For this reason I would suggest the following guidelines:

1 **On creeks and narrow technical rivers, chase boaters should not tow at all. They should use other techniques or wait for the boat to become lodged on one of the many obstacles.**

2 **On high volume, wide rivers, chase boaters should only use towing systems that are fitted to the boat itself. That way, if the system fails to release, the rescuer can bail out and take his chances as an unattached swimmer. On very large rivers it is often best to wait for a calmer stretch and then do a deep water rescue and put the paddler back in his boat.**

▶ **BOAT-BASED TOW SYSTEMS**—These should be designed so that they are easy to attach and even easier to release. The release system must work whether the towline is being subjected to a massive load or a very gentle one. The length of the towline needs to be such that the bow of the boat being towed is close behind the stern of the boat that is towing.

▶ **PAINTER TOW**—With open boats an easily releasable, boat-based towing system can be improvised using one of the painters of the boat being recovered. The painter is wrapped around a thwart to create friction and then the boater simply kneels on the end of the rope. If it becomes necessary to release the tow, the boater simply unweights the relevant knee.

Figure 14-44 open boat quick release boat-based tow.

▶ **QUICK RELEASE HITCH**—Another alternative is to fasten the painter to a thwart using a quick release version of the clove hitch.

Figure 14-45
a quick release hitch
is another open boat
alternative.

▶ **IMPROVISED TOWS**—For all the reasons given above my advice is not to use these. There are a couple of systems that are occasionally used by some paddlers. Guidelines are precisely that, guidelines; "for the strict obedience of fools and the guidance of the wise." Providing the person using them is aware of the hazards involved and has judged the method to be suitable in that particular situation, exceptions can be made. The only justification for an improvised system is that it is rarely used. If you find yourself regularly using such a system, you should invest in a proper boat-mounted system.

▶ **SLING TOW**—The chase boater attaches a tape sling to the boat with a karabiner and drapes the sling over his arm so that it is held in the crook of his elbow.

Pros: Cons:

\+ **Easy to release**   – **Uncomfortable**   – **Interferes with paddling**

▶ **CHEST HARNESS TOW**—The boat is either attached directly to the cow's tail of the harness or, better still, a sling and karabiner are used to extend the tow to a more suitable distance.

Pros:

\+ **Quick to set up**   + **Doesn't interfere with paddling as much as a sling**

Cons:

– **A chest harness attaches high up on the boater's back. If there is a lot of resistance when towing, the boater will be pulled onto the rear deck of his boat making paddling difficult.**

– **Chest harnesses are designed to release under pressure. It may be that the towed boat provides enough resistance to slow the boater down, but not enough to release the chest harness. In these circumstances, the only way that the chase boater can be sure of the quick release working is if he pulls the toggle and then reaches behind his back and pulls the cow's tail hard enough to feed the belt through the system. Far too complex!**

Figure 14-46 (left)
tow using a sling.
(Right) tow using
a chest harness.

make contact

turn over into downstream position

recover to shore

Swimmer Rescues

Figure 14-47 (above) rescuing an unconscious swimmer.

Personally, I believe that it is hard for a boater or rafter to justify the risks involved in swimming out to rescue a victim unless:

1 The victims are either unconscious, counter panicked, exhausted or hypothermic, i.e. unable to help themselves or grab hold of a line.

2 The stretch of water is straightforward and there is ample time to get a victim to shore before the next set of rapids or hazards.

3 The rescuer is a very strong swimmer.

Making Contact

The rescuer should approach from upstream so that it is more difficult for the victim to rush him. The victim's type of behavior must be assessed and, if he is in a state of panic, contact must be avoided at all costs.

If the victim is conscious he should be instructed to turn onto his back facing downstream, i.e. away from the rescuer. If he complies, is unconscious or counter-panicked, the rescuer can grab hold of the PFD shoulder strap that is farthest from the shore he is headed towards (which sets the victim up in a ferry angle), and tow him in using back or sidestroke. If the victim is not wearing rafting or boating safety equipment, the rescuer will have to grab a collar, loose clothing, or a bunch of the victim's hair at the nape of the neck.

Defensive Tactics

▶ **AVOIDANCE**—The first line of defense is for the rescuer to swim, on his back, away from the victim. He needs to remain close enough to talk to the victim and try to calm him down, but far enough away to avoid being grabbed by the victim. If the struggling victim is

Figure 14-48 back away from the swimmer, luring him to the shore.

making any progress through the water in his efforts to grab the rescuer, the rescuer may be able to lure him towards safety.

▶ **FENDING OFF**—A panicking victim is trying desperately to grab hold of a floating object, any floating object; it is particularly serious if that object happens to be you! The victim will be totally unaware of anything below the water. By swimming on his back away from the victim, the rescuer has a second line of defense if the victim manages to close the gap. He can fend the victim off by placing a foot on the victim's chest and pushing him away.

Figure 14-49 fending off

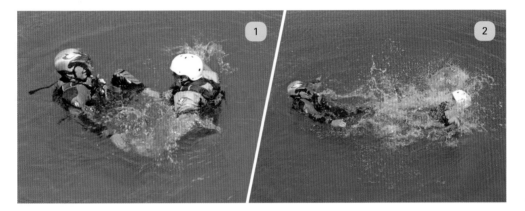

▶ **RELEASING A GRIP**—Despite the rescuer's best efforts, a panic-stricken victim may be able to get hold of him. There are a number of effective ways of releasing a grip. However, most of them require regular practice if they are to be remembered and used effectively under pressure. I will therefore only describe one method that is simple and easy to perform. The rescuer grabs hold of the victim's thumb and bends it back the way it shouldn't go!

Figure 14-50 releasing a grip.

Dealing with a Flipped Raft

Being the guide of a flipped raft can be an intense situation; you will have to act logically and with speed in order to minimize the risks associated with a whitewater environment.

There are a few definite outcomes of flipping a raft on whitewater: you will lose directional control over your raft for an often extended period of time; you and your entire crew will be committed to the water; you will have to rescue yourself first before you can assist your raft crew; the whole rafting flotilla and safety kayakers will be focused on locating, accessing, and transporting swimmers to safe locations, and you will have to decide when is the best moment to reflip your raft!

▶ **MAINTAIN CONTACT** — As a guide it is very important that you try and maintain contact with your raft during the course of the flip by holding onto the perimeter line. If you become detached you must make every effort to get back to your raft; you will not be able to play an active role in rescuing crew members if you lose contact. All guides and safety kayakers should make it their priority to get you back to your overturned raft in the event of you losing contact.

▶ **CLIMBING ONTO THE RAFT** — Assuming you have contact with your raft, reach up, and place your paddle on top of the raft, then climb onto the raft as quickly as you can. Climbing onto the raft is generally done by placing as many fingers as possible in the drainage holes along the floor and then using good technique combined with brute force to pull yourself up; trying to hook your heel up onto the raft as you climb helps. It is sometimes easier to use the bow or stern of the raft to climb up, as these areas sit low in the water when the raft is upside down. If you are using a raft for the first time, it is worth flipping it over on dry land and looking at the arrangement and position of the drainage holes; are they big enough to accommodate your fingers; are you going to be able to get enough fingers in drainage holds to pull yourself up? A pre-placed length of tape between two closely spaced drainage holes to form a small handle can be a useful climbing aid; this will also reduce the likelihood of you suffering a finger tendon injury.

Figure 14-51
while his crew are scattered, the guide climbs back onto the raft in preparation to reflip while the raft behind runs into the same difficulty. Photos: Geraint Rowlands

On larger volume rivers where snag hazards are practically non-existent, a permanently fixed line is sometimes tied across the raft, width ways, between two drainage holes. This permanent tensioned line allows the guide to climb up onto the raft, using a hand over hand technique. It is also possible to clip a flip-line to a D-ring along the side of the raft, tie the other end to the T-grip of your paddle, throw your paddle over the top of the raft, and then use this arrangement to help you climb up. Whichever technique is used, it needs to be practiced until it can be performed consistently, with speed, and in a variety of conditions.

▶ **COUNTING HEADS**—Once on top of the upturned raft, it is very important at this stage to count heads; getting a quick idea of where everyone is will enable you to plan the containment of the situation. Failing to complete this stage makes it possible to neglect a crew member that may be trapped under the raft! This worst-case scenario will be covered in the next section.

Making a Decision on Flipping a Raft

Rafts are generally flipped immediately after you've counted heads. However a guide may wait for a more appropriate moment, after taking the following factors into account:

1 How easy is it to reflip the raft?

2 How cold/rocky/fast/and shallow is the water?

3 How continuous is the river section; what is downstream?

4 Over what distance have the crew members been spread?

5 Is there anybody missing?

▶ **ASSISTANCE**—A raft loaded with multi-day equipment will require more than one person to reflip it. Often, there will only be a single oarsman on a gear boat; therefore the flotilla will have to mobilize a team effort quickly in order to reflip the raft.

Figure 14-52 a laden gear raft—quite a different proposition in the event of a flip. Photo: Geraint Rowlands

▶ **PADDLING AN OVERTURNED RAFT**—If a river section dictates that being in the water is hazardous, it may be appropriate to minimize these risk factors by pulling crew members onto the overturned raft. The raft can then be paddled, upside down, until a calmer, more appropriate section of water is reached before reflipping. Once on top of the raft you can brief crew members to assist you in pulling other swimmers up on top of the raft. Please note that the increased drag associated with paddling an overturned raft makes it feel sluggish during maneuvers, and staying on the raft is also made difficult without anything to brace against.

▶ **DOWNSTREAM HAZARDS**—If a rapid was very long and there would be little chance of riding it out on top of the raft, it may be appropriate to immediately reflip the raft should a suitable opportunity present itself. Likewise if there is a serious hazard looming downstream it may be more appropriate to reflip immediately in order to give you a chance of maneuvering around the hazard.

▶ **PROXIMITY OF CREW**—If crew members have been scattered over a large area, and there is very little additional safety cover in position, it may be more appropriate to flip the raft immediately as you will have to give chase; reflipping a raft makes it a lot faster than if you tried to paddle it upside down. Conversely if all of the crew members are in very close proximity to the raft after the flip, you could potentially reflip the raft onto a swimmer causing a neck injury; this is avoided by briefing crew members to move to the bow and stern of the raft and then momentarily letting go of the perimeter line on your command, thus enabling you to reflip; it is important that this is included in the safety brief.

▶ **TRAPPED CREW**—In an ideal world once the guide is on top of the flipped raft, he will look down and see every member of the raft crew holding onto the perimeter line and moving their way to the bow or stern to prepare for your reflip. Unfortunately this is seldom the case! If crew members find themselves underneath the raft this is not disastrous, as there are air pockets formed by the tubes, however there is an increased chance of impacting with underwater objects. Rafting crew need to be briefed not to remain under the raft for any reason, and that they should make their way out to the perimeter line; this can be achieved by using the direction of a thwart as a guide, and then ducking under the outside tube.

The guide's decision as regards what to do if they suspect a crew member is under the boat will depend on the rafting environment and on how long it will take to reflip the raft. Generally speaking if you are in a raft that you are able to reflip and conditions allow, I would argue that you should do so immediately. It is possible that a crew member trapped or holding onto the raft could prevent you from reflipping the raft. If so, try reattaching your flip line to the other side of the raft and flipping it in the other direction. If the situation dictates that you are unable to immediately flip the raft over because the raft is rigged with multi-day equipment or the river is shallow, rocky and fast moving, you must immediately try and get the raft to a location where you will be able to enter the water and check under the raft, such a location could be a safe eddy or a calm section of water. The raft may be paddled to such a location upside down by the raft crew, or a rescue line may be received from shore, and clipped to the raft; in skilled hands this line could then be used to pendulum the raft into an eddy.

Reflipping a Raft

As with climbing onto an upturned raft there are a number of methods of reflipping a raft depending on its size and whether it is loaded with multi-day equipment.

▶ **T-GRIP REFLIP**—Small narrow rafts can be flipped by the guide hooking the T-grip of his paddle under the outside line on the opposite side of the raft that he is standing on. Lean back and pull on the paddle while at the same time pushing down with your legs on the nearside tube.

▶ **FLIP-LINE REFLIP**—Perhaps the most standard method for reflipping unloaded rafts is for the guide to carry a flip-line approximately 6–9 feet (2-3 m) long with a snapgate karabiner on one end. This is clipped onto the permimeter line halfway along one side of the raft while the guide stands on the opposite side. Similar to the method above, the guide leans back on the line while pushing down with the legs and feet. If properly timed, waves on the river can be used to make the job much easier. A flip-line can be improvised by threading a bow or stern line through a D-ring halfway down one side of the raft and then making a right angle with the rope to take it across the width of the upturned floor.

Figure 14-53 using a flip-line. Photo: Geraint Rowlands

▶ **TEAM REFLIP**—Rafts loaded for multi-day journeys at best will require a number of people to reflip them. To aid this a length of rope is sometimes pre-attached between two D-rings on one side of the raft and then tied off in such a way to ensure that it is does not pose an entrapment hazard. Once flipped this can be released to form a U-shaped flip-line allowing for three or four people to get a hold and reflip the raft. If this is not possible then the raft may be paddled upside down to the shore/suitable eddy, where it is carefully unloaded before being reflipped.

Photo: www.swiftwaterrescue.at

CHAPTER 15

Stoppers

Figure 15-1 a huge hole the swimmers will be flushed out. The Bad Place, White Nile.

There are basically two stopper *(hole or hydraulic)* rescue situations:

1. A boater or a raft held in a hole, or surface stopper. This is not necessarily a serious situation because, more often than not, if the boater bails out or a rafter falls overboard, he will, being less buoyant than his craft, be flushed out by the undertow.

2. A swimmer held in a hydraulic, or deep recirculating stopper. This is by definition a serious matter.

Boaters

▶ **SELF RESCUE**—By spending a lot of time playing in tame holes, or stoppers, boaters develop the skills that will enable them to paddle their way out of trouble. More importantly, it will build up the experience that will enable them to judge whether a stopper is runnable or not.

When caught in a stopper, a boater will usually be turned sideways and held firmly in the slot. If the boater does nothing, the water flowing down the face of the wave will capsize him. In a powerful haudraulic the recirculating water will roll the boat and boater over and over like a roller blind.

▶ **STAYING UPRIGHT**—The boater prevents a capsize by lifting the upstream edge with his knee, so that the water flows under the hull of the boat and, if necessary, leaning onto his paddle for support on the downstream side, using a low or high brace. In some stoppers the best support will be found by placing the paddle on the surface of the boil line. On others the best support will be gained by reaching down into the less aerated water in the undertow.

How the boater stays upright is often dictated by the angle of the face of the stopper. The steeper the angle the more use will have to be made of the paddle.

▶ **FEEDING OUT**—As soon as control is regained the boater must gently unweight the paddle so that the boat is kept upright by a mixture of balance and edge control. Once the weight is off the paddle, the boater can slice it forward or backward so that he can put in a series of power strokes, to drive the boat along the stopper. By doing this he can reach a point where there is a weakness, some outflow (outwash), which will allow him to escape.

Figure 15-2 working along a stopper.

PROFICIENT ON BOTH SIDES

When moving forward the boater can use a low or high brace in between power strokes, depending on the shape of the stopper. However, the low brace sets the boater up for a more powerful forward power stroke. When reversing, he must use a low brace or he will be unable to use the powerful muscles in his trunk in the reverse power stroke.

The layout of the stopper will dictate which techniques are used and on which side strokes will need to be performed. It is therefore essential that we strive to become equally proficient on both sides.

In a "frowning" stopper that feeds towards the center, rather than out to the outflow at one or each end, it will be hard work to make it to the weakness. There are three ways to increase efficiency:

1 Make best use of edge control and balance so that all of the paddle power can go into moving the boat along the stopper rather than keeping the boat upright.

2 Deliberately move the boat in the opposite direction to the weakness you are trying to get to so that when you change direction you can get a run along the length of the stopper and build up enough speed to break through to the outflow.

3 Many stoppers pulse, that is to say that they change their shape and holding characteristics in a cyclical, predictable manner. By timing your run at the weakness to coincide with the best part of this cycle, you can maximize your chances of breaking free.

Not for big stoppers! ▶ **ENDERING OUT**—Though not an option in traditional open boats, this is an option for specialist whitewater open boats as well as closed deck C1s and kayaks.

If the boater hasn't quite made it clear of the stopper and it is clear that he is going to be sucked back in, he can deliberately drive the bow or stern deep into the face of the stopper. The boat can be made to literally stand on its end. The idea is to get the end of the boat down in the undertow so that it is pushed clean through the stopper and into the outflow.

If the stopper is too powerful or the boater's boat control inadequate, the boat may perform a complete loop (go end over end), and end up back in the slot again. The following techniques can help prevent this:

▶ **BOW ENDERS**—As the boat begins to stand on end, the boater stands upright on his footrest and leans back against the rear deck. This keeps his centre of gravity directly over the bow of the boat as opposed to having the weight of his own body overbalance him, so that he falls back into the slot.

▶ **STERN ENDERS**—(*tailies*) These only work on small stoppers.

1 As the stern digs in and the bow of the boat lifts towards the sky, the boater throws his weight forward so that his forehead is touching the deck. This will adjust his center of gravity.

2 At the same time he digs his paddle as deep as he can into the undertow and uses it to help pull him through the stopper. The support thus gained also enables him to apply pressure with the opposite knee to twist the boat through a few degrees and spill water off the back deck.

Boater to Boater Rescue

These rescues don't work in serious stoppers and are only likely to be used when guiding or coaching novices on easy rivers. They should only be attempted if the rescuer is considerably more skilled than the victim and is convinced that he can easily get himself out of the stopper concerned. If the length of the backwash is more than half a boat length they are definitely out of the question.

▶ **BUMPING OUT**—This technique involves another paddler deliberately positioning himself so that he is upstream and parallel to the victim who is stuck in the stopper. The rescuer then drops into the stopper and bumps the victim out. This is a dangerous technique that is far more likely to cause an injury than any stopper where it might work. Don't do it!

▶ **BOW RESCUE**—This rescue will work in any situation where bumping out will work and, as it involves far less risk of injury, should in my opinion be used instead.

The rescue boater approaches from downstream and, keeping most of his boat on the downstream side of the boil line, he positions his bow so that the victim can get hold of the grab loop. The victim can use the rescuer's bow for support while the rescuer reverse paddles out of the stopper.

In a weak stopper, the rescuer may be able to simply pull the victim and his boat over the boil line and out of the stopper. More often he will have to reverse paddle at a ferry angle to drag the victim along the stopper to a weakness where the outflow will push the victim out.

Bank-based Rescue

▶ **REACH**—It is sometimes the case that the weakness at the end of the stopper that the boater is trying to get out of is close to the bank or a rock that the rescuer can easily reach. The rescuer can simply get hold of the end grab loop and pull the boat and boater out of the stopper.

▶ **THROW**—If a boater is able to maintain a stable upright position but is unable to paddle out of the stopper, it is best to throw him a line before he subsequently bails out. (See swimmer rescues in this chapter for further details.)

Rafts

The big problem when a raft is held in a stopper is that if anyone falls in and is flushed out by the undertow, he rapidly loses contact with the raft. Though problematic enough for experienced rafters, it poses a much more serious problem for a commercial raft guide whose clients will have received a safety briefing but no real training.

▶ **SELF RESCUE**—Rafts rely primarily on their buoyancy to keep them upright and feed them out of a stopper but there is a considerable amount that can be done to help.

▶ **STAYING UPRIGHT**—A raft will flip in a big enough stopper so it is crucial to "high side," i.e. to get everyone onto the side that is lifting. In the case of a stopper, that is the downstream side away from the face of the stopper. The weight of the crew will then act as a counterbalance to counteract the weight of the water trying to push the downstream side of the raft down into the undertow.

▶ **FEEDING OUT**—The raft can be encouraged towards the outflow of a stopper in two ways:

▶ **TRIMMING**—By high siding, the balance of the boat is maintained. The trim of the raft can be changed by shifting some of the crew forward or backward. If the weight is shifted towards the back, the raft will tend to move forward and vice versa.

▶ **PADDLING**—If the raft is not being thrown around too violently, the raft guide and selected members of the crew can paddle the raft along the stopper.

▶ **LINE RESCUES**—A line is thrown to the raft, either from the bank or from another raft. Depending on circumstances, the raft can either be pulled directly downstream over the boil line or along the slot to the end where it is most likely to be fed out by the outflow.

▶ **RAFT HELD IN SWIMMER RETENTIVE STOPPER**—The raft will end up positioned sideways in the stopper and the upstream edge will be violently pushed under the water by the green flow entering the stopper. This can result in the raft flipping in upstream and swimmers recirculating with a flipped raft on top of them.

Guides have avoided catastrophic outcomes in this situation by having pre-placed live bait rescuers to access the stopper and latch onto the perimeter line, pulling the raft out of the stopper. Swimmers should make every effort to get out from underneath the raft and would ideally hold onto the perimeter line on the downstream tube. Holding on between the slot and the upstream tube is the worst location to be in. Holding onto the downstream tube can effectively keep you away from the slot while you await a measured throw bag rescue or live bait. If a throw bag rescue and live bait are seen to be ineffective or inappropriate another option would be to use a four point tethered raft described later in this chapter.

Swimmer Rescues

Any swimmer caught in a hydraulic is in a life-threatening situation. Time is limited. Rescues will have to be set up and effected quickly. This means that the simpler they are, the better.

The chances of a successful rescue are further enhanced if the rescuers and the victim are already familiar with, and practiced in, a range of stopper rescue techniques. This means that while one method is being tried, other ones can be prepared by other members of the team.

▶ **SELF RESCUE**—Many stoppers can be coped with, and will allow the swimmer who remains calm and maintains a positive mental attitude to help himself. We should remember that a backwash that is flowing at only 2–3 mph (3–5 kmph) is going far faster than people can swim. Therefore, many hydraulics that will hold a swimmer are not necessarily very turbulent, but will still be powerful enough to put a swimmer through "the rinse cycle" (pushed down under the water by the undertow, floating up to the surface upstream of the boil line and being sucked back into the slot by the backtow). A panicked victim will waste precious oxygen and energy by trying to swim against the backtow, even after it should have become obvious that it is moving faster than he can swim.

▶ **WORKING ALONG TO THE OUTFLOW**—If an initial attempt to swim across the boil line has failed, the swimmer should swim at right angles to the towback so as to try and reach a bank or a break in the stopper where the current flows through and will flush him out.

As soon as the swimmer gets to the surface he needs to get some air, shake the water from his eyes and ears and get his bearings. He may only need to swim a few strokes to get to an outflow that will flush him clear of the stopper. A rescuer may be about to throw him a line. There may be an overhanging tree branch he can hold onto. Who knows? Not the victim, unless he is looking for the breaks.

Figure 15-3 surfed to the surface in a "freefall" position.

▶ **TURBULENCE & DISORIENTATION**—Some stoppers are so turbulent that a swimmer may become totally disorientated. Even in this situation he should try to remain calm and feel around. Something might turn up: a buoyant object that can be held onto, the river bed that can be kicked off from, a throw line to hold on to.

If he is totally disorientated he should adopt a star shape or "freefall" position. This will increase the chances of being flushed through or surfed to the surface.

▶ **GETTING DOWN**—An alternative way to try and get out of a hydraulic is for the swimmer to deliberately swim as far as possible into the face of the green water that is flowing into the slot. If he can penetrate deeply enough into the downward flowing water, he may be pushed along the bottom in the undertow, past the boil line and out of the clutches of the stopper. There is a risk of being snagged on some obstruction on the river bed, so it is best if the swimmer tucks up into a ball to minimize this risk.

Figure 15-4 catching the elevator to the bottom to exit a hydraulic.

The important thing here is not to try and duck-dive towards the river bed. The secret is to penetrate the down flowing water horizontally so that the swimmer is pushed to the bottom by the power of the water.

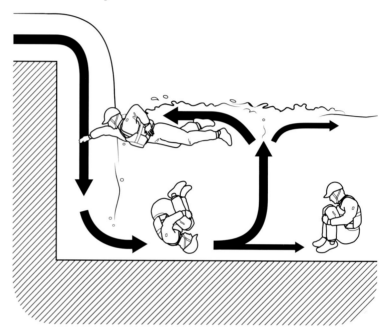

▶ **THE PFD CONTROVERSY**—There is a theory that a swimmer being recirculated in a stopper should, if all else fails, take off his PFD. The idea is that, being less buoyant, he may now be able to stay down in the undertow long enough to get past the boil line and be swept out of the stopper.

Most experts agree that this is not a good idea. It should only be considered if all other forms of self-rescue have failed and there is no prospect of being rescued by people on the bank. This is because:

1 If the swimmer has had time to consider this option, it is because he has survived this long by getting a breath of air each time he surfaces. If he takes his PFD off and isn't flushed out of the stopper, he may no longer have enough buoyancy to reach the surface and get a breath of air!

2 The only way to guarantee that a swimmer is no longer buoyant is to fill his lungs with water!

3 There is a high probability that an exhausted swimmer, swept out of a stopper minus his PFD, will drown in the rapids downstream.

Figure 15-5 body-surfing in a stopper.

▶ **BODY SURFING**—By holding his body in a position similar to that of a freefall parachutist, while facing upstream it is possible for a swimmer to body-surf a stopper and maintain a stable position. This means that, instead of being helplessly put through the rinse cycle, he is in a position to breathe and get his bearings. Even if a swimmer can't get out of the stopper, he can buy time for rescuers to set up and effect a rescue.

If he spots a break in the stopper where the water is flowing out, he can surf across to it by simply tilting and angling his body. If he tilts and angles to the right, he will move to his right (river left) and vice versa.

Bank-based Rescues

The following bank-based rescues have the advantage of involving little if any risk to the rescuers. They are listed in order of their simplicity and the speed with which they can be effected. A well trained team would organize themselves so that the more complex rescues were being set up at the same time as the simple ones were being tried. That way, by the time it became clear that one method wasn't going to work, other members of the team would be in position and ready to try another.

▶ **REACH**—On narrow creeks and boulder-choked rivers, stoppers may only be a few feet in width. The most effective rescue may be as simple as reaching out to the swimmer with a paddle or a canoe pole. The rescuer must ensure his own safety by keeping hold of something on the bank or holding onto another rescuer. When offering support it is best to grasp each other's wrist, rather than hold hands.

Figure 15-6 reaching rescue.

REMOVE ANY EXCESS ROPE BEFORE THROWING THE LINE

Figure 15-7 this photo shows the importance of downstream backup. While setting up the previous photo the swimmer was flushed out of the stopper before he could grab the proffered paddle.

▶ **THROW**—A well aimed throw line is another quick and simple rescue technique. However, when throwing a line to a recirculating swimmer, the following points should be borne in mind:

▶ **TIMING**—The temptation when throwing a line to a recirculating swimmer is to throw it the instant he bursts to the surface. The rescuer should remember that at that precise instant the swimmer's only concern is to get a breath of fresh air. The line needs to be thrown after the swimmer has had time to get his bearings but before he is fed back into the slot.

▶ **EXCESS ROPE**—A swimmer in a stopper may be tumbling violently when in the slot or under water. There is always a danger, in such a situation that the rope may become wrapped around the victim's neck. To reduce the chances of this happening the rescuer should estimate how much rope will be needed and remove any excess from the throw bag before throwing the line.

*Figure 15-8
throw line rescue.*

Figure 15-9 in this case the float-boat is fed along the slot of the stopper.

▶ **FLOAT-BOAT—** The rescuer clips the bag end of a throw line to one end of his boat and piles the line into the boat. While hanging on to the other end of the line he pushes the boat out into the current so that it is fed into the part of the stopper where the victim is recirculating. Depending on the geography of the location, this is sometimes best achieved by feeding the boat into the slot by pushing it out into the towback and sometimes by pushing it out into the current upstream of the stopper. When the swimmer grabs hold of the boat, the boat is dragged out of the stopper bringing the swimmer with it.

This method can be used by one rescuer but is a little easier if two are involved. One holds the line while the other pushes the boat out.

Pros + **The advantage of this method is that, even if a victim is panicking to the point where he neither sees nor reacts to a thrown line, a drowning person will instinctively cling to a large buoyant object.**

Cons − **The disadvantage is that in a turbulent stopper the boat may be thrown around violently. This introduces the possibility of the victim being injured. Therefore, in the case of a particularly violent, pulsing stopper, rescuers may have to rule out this form of rescue.**

▶ **TAG LINE—**This method requires a rescuer on each bank. Either two bags are clipped together to make a bright floating object, or even better, a spare PFD is tied to the rope. The rope is then tensioned so that the float is suspended above the water where the swimmer is expected to surface. As he surfaces the float is lowered right in front of his eyes.

When the swimmer grabs the float, either:

1 **Both rescuers move down the bank at the same speed and pull the victim over the boil line and out of the backwash. Or:**

2 **One rescuer pays out line while the other pulls the swimmer towards a weakness in the stopper which will flush him through.**

In either case neither rescuer should let go of the line. That way if the victim lets go the rescuers are already set up to try again.

Figure 15-10 tag line.

Pros:

+ **Difficult for swimmer to ignore the float**

+ **No risk of injury to rescuers or victim**

Cons:

– **Time consuming to set up**

– **Communication can be a major problem**

– **May not be practical if banks are heavily vegetated or too far apart**

▶ **TURN OFF THE WATER**—May take a little time but on many dam release rivers it can be arranged.

Contact Rescues

If victims are unconscious or counter panicked, they are not going to hold on to the line. Therefore someone will have to go out and make contact with them. Or will they? These techniques are potentially very risky and the topography and the hydrology of each stopper is different. The rescuers involved must carefully assess both the risks involved and the likelihood of a successful outcome before committing themselves to such a course of action.

At the risk of sounding callous, I must point out that there is no point in indulging in heroics if the victim has been in there so long that he is almost certainly dead. It may be that the role of the leader in this situation is to stop people following their hearts rather than their heads and risking a multiple tragedy.

The following are listed in order of increasing risk to the rescuer.

▶ **FOUR POINT TETHERED RAFT**—This rescue is simple in theory but difficult to control in practice. This is because it involves five groups of people, probably out of voice contact, working as a team.

One line is attached to each corner of the raft. The upstream lines are used to pull the raft over the boil line to where the swimmer is surfacing. The downstream lines are used to stop the raft being fed into the slot by the recirculating water. If person power is a problem, the leader should allocate more rescuers to the downstream lines than the upstream lines. All the lines must be kept taut at all times, so as to ensure that the raft doesn't build up any momentum and become hard to control.

This is the safest contact method and it will work in most weir, (low head dam), situations. It is not a viable option above grade 3.

Figure 15-11 four point tethered raft. It is best to have two rescuers in the raft, one to concentrate on dealing with the swimmer and one to fine tune the positioning of the raft with a paddle, and liaise with the teams controlling the lines.

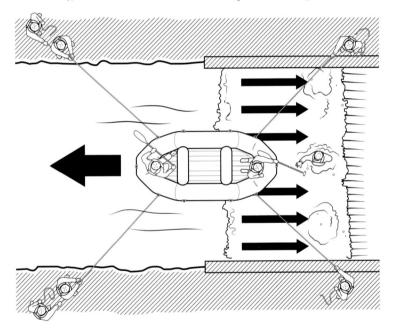

▶ **LIVE-BAIT**—This is essentially the same as the live bait rescue for swimmers. The difference is that, instead of one rescuer waist belaying, it is better to have two or more rescuers holding the rope tug-of-war fashion, ready to pull the swimmer/rescuer and victim out.

Moving water and ropes are always a dangerous mix. This is particularly true in a stopper where there is more potential for the line to get wrapped around some part of the rescuer's body. Those controlling the line will need to let out as little line as possible, and hold it as high as they can to keep as much of it out of the water as possible.

Pros **+ It is quick to set up and little coordination is needed.**

Cons **- It is a very high risk option for the rescuer and is only an option where the victim is close to the bank.**

▶ **TETHERED BOATER**—Other than deciding that a rescue is too risky, this is the only option left if:

1 The victim is unconscious or unresponsive.

2 The victim is being re-circulated too far from the bank for a live bait rescue.

3 There is no raft available.

4 There is still a reasonable possibility of a successful outcome.

The rescue boater is attached via a long line to a group of rescuers on the bank. Their task is to ensure that the rope is kept taut once he crosses the boil line so that he isn't sucked into the slot. As soon as contact is made, they pull the rescue boater and victim back across the boil line and into the shore.

▶ **LINE OR LINES?**—After considerable experimentation with this technique in Austria, it was found that it is best to attach a single line to the boater's chest harness. A line fed through the stern grab handle and attached to a quick-release towing system did make it easier to control the angle of the boat to the current. However, it was found that this was more than made up for by the extra time needed to set it up and the possibilities of entanglements and confusion.

Ray Goodwin, Lower Tryweryn, North Wales

"I was getting a new exhaust fitted to the car. From behind the garage came the scream, 'There's a child in the river.'

"I ran around behind the garage. The child was being cycled around in a deep recirculating stopper. He kept reappearing 4m downstream of the weir face before being towed back in. The river doubled in width below the weir and a powerful eddy fed back in from each side. The child was still conscious. I had no rescue kit with me.

"I yelled at the garage mechanic to get me a rope, anything! He returned minutes later with a hose-pipe. I went out on the concrete, coiling the hose for a throw. The child surfaced again but was now unconscious and not breathing. A throw was useless.

"A bowline secured the hose around my waist. My instructions to the people on the bank were simple; 'Once I dive on to the child, don't wait to see if I've got him, just pull me out!' The weir was a shallow V, so I could wade out along the lip above the stopper. My last thought before I dived in was a fervent hope that there was no plastic push joint in the hose.

"I clutched the child to my chest as we were slammed to the bottom. We were being pulled against the kick of the stopper. In a desperate attempt to reach air I let go of the child with one hand, and I have a vivid memory of him being pulled away from me, my other hand embedded in his tee shirt.

"We broke surface in the eddy. The pullers held me against the concrete apron while I put two breaths in him. Then on reaching the bank another six breaths and he started."

CHAPTER 16

Pins and Entrapments

*Figure 16-1
stranded rafters.
Photo: Spike Green*

This chapter deals with any situation where paddlers are trapped, in or out of a boat or raft. These include:

- Stranded victims
- Broaches
- Vertical pins
- Foot entrapments
- Strainers
- A swimmer trapped under a raft

Each entrapment situation that we may be confronted with will be different, but the way each of them is dealt with follows a basic pattern.

1 Assess the situation.

2 Stabilize the situation.

3 Extract the victim.

Only after the victim is extracted unharmed or he has been treated and evacuated to hospital would we then consider how to recover any equipment. (These elements are dealt with in Sections Three and Four).

Assessing the Situation

Time of day will also affect the water level of glacier-fed rivers.

Rescuers need to ask themselves:

1 What hazard does the entrap-ment pose for rescuers?

2 Is the situation stable or unstable?

3 Are the water levels rising, falling, or stable?

4 What time of day is it? The onset of darkness will make rescues more difficult and hazardous.

5 Are there any dangers down-stream that the victims or rescuers need to be aware of/protected from?

6 What is the quickest and accept-ably safe way of getting into a position to be able to rescue the victim?

▶ **DANGER TO RESCUERS**—An assessment of the potential dangers faced by rescuers is something that should be done in any rescue situation. It may only take a few seconds but it must be done.

▶ **STABLE OR UNSTABLE?**—Any situation where victims are trapped in cold water or in an exposed position will have to be dealt with reasonably quickly because of the onset of hypothermia. However, if victims are in a situation where they have no difficulty breathing, rescuers can afford to take more time to plan the rescue.

In many cases, the victim may have already decided that the situation he is in is relatively stable. A victim stranded on a rock or a boater held in a vertical pin may decide that it is far safer to wait to be rescued than to bail out and swim for it.

On the other hand, a victim who is unable to breathe or having difficulty breathing needs to be dealt with in a matter of minutes.

▶ **DOWNSTREAM HAZARDS**—It is vital to consider these and arrange some protection or back-up. It is no use freeing a trapped victim, only to see him carried by the current into an even worse hazard. Even if there are no significant hazards downstream a means of getting the freed victim to the side must be in place as the victim will probably be exhausted and unable to swim effectively.

▶ **ACCESS TECHNIQUES**—Boating, rafting, swimming, wading, noth-ing should be ruled out. If the victim is unable to breathe, the quickest method will be the best. However, in most situations the technique used should be the one that involves the least risk to the rescuers. The following approaches are listed in order of priority:

- Self rescue
- Access from the bank
- Access by boat
- Access by wading
- Access by swimming

Chapter 26 explores a variety of alternative or more complex tech-niques that may need to be employed in situations where the above mentioned, quick and simple techniques are judged to be too haz-ardous or not practicable.

Stabilizing the Situation

The aim is to ensure that the victim can breathe and that the situation does not deteriorate further. The solution must be quick and simple. The fancier the rope tricks, the longer it takes, the more likely it is that you will be dealing with a body. It must be borne in mind that there are occasions where extracting the victim is so easy that it is the quickest and simplest method that stabilizes the situation.

Methods for stabilizing the situation fall into three groups:

- **Direct contact**
- **Line pulls**
- **Snag lines**

The solution must be quick and simple.

▶ **DIRECT CONTACT**—It is often the case that the very obstacle that has caused the problem, or the eddy that forms downstream of it, provides a means for rescuers to gain access to the victim. The victim's buddy can simply breakout behind the obstacle, climb on to it, grab a hold of the victim and support him so that he can keep his head above water.

▶ **LINE PULLS**—In a situation such as the one described above where it is difficult to maintain such a position, or the rescuer needs to be freed up to perform other duties, a line can be attached to the victim and tied off.

In many situations, where it is not possible to make direct contact with the victim, a line can be lowered, thrown or floated to him. The victim is then able to simply hold onto the line for support or clip it into a chest harness or shoulder strap. The victim will probably be holding onto something to keep his head above water. This means that he will have to attach the line one handed, so this is one situation where it may be a good idea to tie a loop in the end of the line and even have a karabiner already attached.

If a rescuer can get close to the victim it may be possible to attach a line to him directly, or by using an improvised paddle hook (see Chapter 13).

▶ **TAG LINES**—If a victim is trapped in midstream and is in need of support, a tag line may be the only viable option. A line is held across the river and dragged upstream until it catches across the victim's waist or across his chest and under his armpits. The line is then pulled tight enough to support the victim. If there are suitable anchor points available, one or both ends of the line can be tied off if the rescuers need to be freed up for the extraction phase.

A broached victim may be able to pass a loop of rope over his head and shoulders so that the rescuer can pull on both ends of the line and support the victim's upper body, allowing him to keep his head out of the water.

Extracting the Victim

The technique used to free a victim will depend on the exact circumstances of the entrapment. Stabilizing the situation may have bought some time but the rescuers will still need to come up with a solution quickly. Cold water, the force of the current and fear will be sapping the victim's energy reserves and morale.

This is definitely a time for lateral thinking. A victim may be freed by using one or a combination of the following approaches:

- Pulling the victim in the right direction
- Freeing the boat and in the process the victim
- Cutting any webbing or line that is holding the victim
- Cutting the boat or raft so as to relieve pressure or free the victim
- Removing the obstacle that is causing the problem

It is absolutely vital that rescuers have planned for what will happen once the victim is freed. It would be extremely bad if, freed from an entrapment, the victim was allowed to float into even more danger!

Stranded Victims

Figure 16-2 simple use of a throw line to return boat to stranded paddler.

By definition these are relatively stable situations. The victims are only stranded because they have decided that it is unnecessarily risky to swim or climb out of their predicament unaided.

▶ **BOAT TO SWIMMER**—In many situations the safest answer will be to return the boat and equipment to the stranded paddler.

Figure 16-3 stable situation, stranded person waits for throw line rather than attempting the swim and risking being swept into the next rapid.

▶ **CONTROLLED SWIMMER RESCUE**—The quickest and simplest solutions will involve the same techniques as used to rescue a swimmer, the difference being that everything can be set up before the victim is committed. A line can be gotten to the victims and set up for a pendulum before they enter the water. The victims can be fetched by a raft or chase boaters and climb on board in relative safety.

▶ **TENSIONED DIAGONAL**—This is a useful method for moving people across a fast current in a controlled and precise manner. It is particularly useful for getting a rescuer into the eddy behind an obstruction in a high risk environment where free swimming and boating are not an option. It is also particularly useful for evacuating a large number of people in a quick and controlled manner. As it has a large number of different applications it is discussed in detail in Chapter 26. In essence it consists of tensioning a line across a river at an angle of 45˚ or less to the main flow. The stranded paddlers then work their way along the rope to safety.

HEALTH WARNING

READ CHAPTER 26 AS THE TENSIONED DIAGONAL TECHNIQUE NEEDS TO BE THOROUGHLY UNDERSTOOD.

Figure 16-4 tensioned diagonal used to return the kayak to the stranded paddler.

Broaches

In a single point broach, where the boat or raft is caught sideways onto a single boulder it is often relatively easy for a rescuer to access the victim via the eddy that forms behind the obstruction. In a two point broach, where the boat is held at each end and the paddler is trapped in the middle it may well be quicker and simpler to lift one of the ends over the obstruction to free the boat and paddler. If the pressure is such that the rescuer is unable to do this, another option is to cut off the end of the boat or puncture the end tube of the raft to achieve the same effect.

Once the situation has been stabilized by whatever means, the victim needs to be extracted. Different craft will have different considerations.

▶ **OPEN BOATS** — When open boats are broached the pressures involved are enormous and often result in the boat being badly damaged. Therefore, moving the boat is seldom the quickest or easiest option. Fortunately, as there is no deck the boater is less likely to be trapped by the structure of the boat. He is much more likely to be caught up in webbing or line. If the boater is unable to cut the line himself, a rescuer will have to do the job for him.

▶ **RAFTS** — When rafts wrap themselves around an obstacle, the forces involved are even greater than in an open boat. If "high siding" the raft (see Chapter 2) has kept the raft upright but the raft is wrapped, the raft guide will need to evacuate the raft and account for all the crew. Although the obstacle itself and the eddy formed by it will provide temporary refuge, the crew will need to be evacuated to the shore. The options for doing this are as for dealing with stranded victims.

There are two possibilities for entrapment:

Either -

1 Someone gets a foot caught in a twisted foot strap or in the gutter wedged between the side and floor tube.

Or -

2 When trying to "high side" the raft, a crew member falls between the raft and the boulder.

In the first case, unless the raft can be moved quickly and easily, the best solution would be to try and find a way of cutting the footstrap. Depending on exactly how the raft is broached it may be possible to get at the strap from the eddy, by cutting a small hole through the floor of the raft.

If there is even the slightest suspicion that someone is caught between the raft and the obstruction, the raft guide will have no option but to cut a hole in the floor of the raft, or even cut the raft in half. Immediately!

▶ **KAYAKS—**If a kayaker lifts his upstream edge and leans onto the obstruction, he will probably be able to work his way off the broach unaided. If the upstream edge catches and the boat is rolled over so that the spraydeck is collapsed by the force of the water, it will wrap. Due to the development of the keyhole cockpit, the kayaker will still probably be able to exit the kayak providing he is quick about it.

Assuming that the victim is trapped and the situation stable or stabilized, there are several possibilities for extricating the victim. The simplest solution is often to pull the victim towards the rear of the kayak so that his body straightens out and he slides out of the cockpit. If this is done by attaching a line to the victim, the rescuers have already put in place the means to pendulum him to the shore.

Other solutions include cutting the boat up or freeing the boat by pulling or pushing it in the direction that the current favors. Great care must be taken that attempting this solution does not worsen the situation by increasing the pressure on the victim's legs, or cause the boat to lodge itself in a position that makes things even worse.

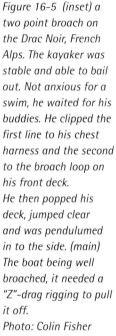

Figure 16-5 (inset) a two point broach on the Drac Noir, French Alps. The kayaker was stable and able to bail out. Not anxious for a swim, he waited for his buddies. He clipped the first line to his chest harness and the second to the broach loop on his front deck.
He then popped his deck, jumped clear and was pendulumed in to the side. (main) The boat being well broached, it needed a "Z"-drag rigging to pull it off.
Photo: Colin Fisher

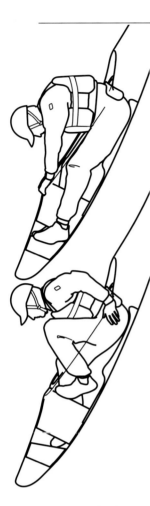

Vertical Pins

Vertical pins are almost exclusively the province of kayaks and closed deck C1s. With modern footrest designs and keyhole cockpits the boaters are rarely unable to exit the boat. They may bark their shins on the way out but they can almost always get out if they choose to. This is not true of older designs (see below!) and I have seen two cases (one involved me) where the victim was unable to exit unaided because a section of rock protruded over the front of the cockpit.

A boater who waits for rescue in this situation has usually decided that the swim is not an attractive option. The rescuer's main concern is to get a line to the boater so that he can reach the bank safely. If it is possible to set up a line in such a way that he can effect a more controlled exit so much the better.

In creek boating, the volume of water can be so low that it is possible to thread the clean end of a line through the stern end grab. The rescuers then pull on the doubled line and, when the boat is free, let go of the clean end. The end of the line feeds back through the end grab and the boater is free to continue his run.

Figure 16-6 (top) bracing off the cockpit rim for support and to help create an air pocket. (bottom) Using the keyhole cockpit to clear a knee and step up off the central buoyancy.

Figure 16-7 (right) a dummy has been set up in this exercise scenario. The assumption is that the victim is unable or unwilling to exit unaided. Victims are often (not always) able to breathe in this position as the water flows over them creating an air pocket. A snagline (weighted with two karabiners) is used to support the victim with his head above the flow. In this position he is able to catch a line and attach it to his chest harness so that he can be pulled out of the cockpit backward. Alternatively a cinch line could be used. Photo: Loel Collins

Figure 16-8 Conwy Falls, North Wales.

Learning River Safety the Hard Way—Conwy Falls, North Wales, By Chris Wheeler

"It was decision time. I did not want to die like this, an undignified, self-inflicted death, crucified in my boat in front of my helpless friends, on a damp miserable day in North Wales. My thighs pinned painfully against the cockpit rim, with freezing cold water falling down onto my back, doubling me up, I could see no way out. I knew that time was running out—after close on five minutes, my strength was steadily being sapped by the cold and the effort of staying up out of the water. My friends' efforts with throw lines had failed and they couldn't reach me. I was on my own. I was surprisingly calm and rational—I had one final plan—I was trapped in the boat by my legs so I would use the power of the water to break my legs. So I made a decisive heave forward and to the left, into the current. I was free. I shot off downstream towards the next drop. Thankfully my friend Fred was in the right place at the right time and plucked me out of the water. Grappled and pulled up the rocks, I slumped down and gasped for air. It was only then that we realized the price I had paid for my close escape—no broken bones but it was worse than that, my knees were bent the wrong way, both knees had been dislocated and I could no longer walk.

"After three months I stood up for the first time without plaster casts, feeling my way uncertainly, like a young Bambi. One month later I was back in a boat, squirt boating and surfing. Tedious daily physiotherapy went on for 10 months, as I worked hard to build up my leg muscles, to ensure that they would be stable without any cruciate ligaments. I had a 'drop foot' too, caused by damage to the nerves and I needed a splint to hold my foot up to enable me to walk normally. The advice was that it could take 18 months (at an inch per month) for the nerve to grow back. I was lucky, the movement and feeling miraculously returned as I kept trying to push my foot down but not until 4-5 months later. Life went on. I couldn't fully straighten my right leg and OK, I gave up squash and skiing, but otherwise, life returned to normal; after all, my legs were stable and I could walk normally. It wasn't long before I was back on Grade 4-5 and over the last 14 years I've paddled here, there and everywhere and my knees have coped with everything from 3 mile walk-ins, to portages from hell. I've been lucky.

"How has it affected my paddling? At first glance to many people I may still seem fairly gung ho, keen to take on Grade 4/5 and spate creek boating. However, I have clear personal boundaries. I will not paddle drops where there is a high risk of a vertical pin, I will not touch waterfalls higher than 10m and I hate disappearing down into slots where there is any element of randomness about the outcome. In other words, I avoid drops with a high risk but low skill factor. I have learnt to say no and walk even when others run the drop, and when I do run the drop, I don't have to run the drop first, not when the younger guys are volunteering to act as 'probes'! Why rush? What have I got to prove? I am also now, belatedly, evangelical about creek boats and keyhole cockpits! The fact that I've survived another 14 years of creek boating suggests I must have learnt something."

Foot Entrapments

Foot entrapments are extremely dangerous. People who lose their footing when wading or find themselves swimming in fast shallow water must swim on their back and keep their feet and hands on the surface!

MOST PEOPLE WHO SURVIVE FOOT ENTRAPMENTS ARE IN RELATIVELY WEAK FLOWS WHERE THEY ARE ABLE TO KEEP THEIR HEADS ABOVE WATER. THE FOLLOWING TECHNIQUES ARE OFFERED AS POSSIBLE RATHER THAN PROBABLE SOLUTIONS. THE REAL ANSWER IS, IF YOU START TO LOSE YOUR FOOTING, **FEET AND HANDS ON THE SURFACE AND SWIM.**

Foot Entrapments—Two Bank Access

If the river is narrow enough to allow access from both banks the following techniques might be attempted.

▶ **TAG LINE**—More usually, the only way to stabilize the victim will be by using a tag line. Once the victim is tagged, it may be possible to free him by simply using the line to pull him upstream.

Figure 16-9 tag line.

▶ **RESCUE SWIMMER**—If the tag line isn't sufficient to free the trapped victim, it does at least provide him with support. If one end of the line is tied off, a rescuer, who should be a strong swimmer, can use the line as a tensioned diagonal (see Chapter 26) to gain access to the victim. Once in position, the rescuer can use the eddy created by the victim and support from the line to try and get into a position to help the victim free his trapped limb. This rescue should only be attempted if the stretch of water downstream of the entrapment is a straightforward swim, or sufficient safety cover is in place to collect the victim and the rescuer.

Figure 16-10 rescuer using the tag line as a tensioned diagonal.

▶ **SNAG LINE**—If the current is too powerful for a rescue swimmer then a snag line may be the answer. A heavy weight is attached to the middle of a line and dragged upstream along the river bed. The idea is to run the line under the victim until it snags his ankle. Pressure can then be applied as close as possible to the trapped limb and the foot freed.

Figure 16-11 snag line with (inset) weighted bag in center.

sunken snag line

▶ **TWO LINE PULL**—With this method it is possible to either simply change the direction of pull that can be applied with a tag line, and a greater force applied by creating leverage on the tensioned rope (see Chapter 24), or the tag line can be cinched around the victim's body.

1 The victim is stabilized with a tag line.

2 A second line is thrown across the river, upstream of the victim and clipped to the tag line.

3 The line is pulled at a 90° angle to the tag line to change the direction of pull.

4 As a last resort, the line is pulled at a shallower angle so that the tag line is cinched around the victim's body and pulled towards the bank.

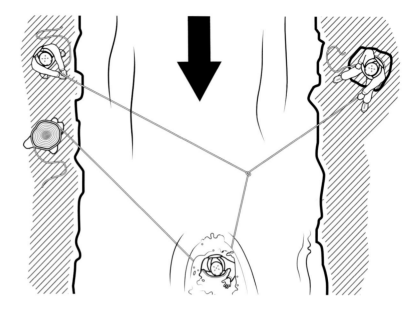

Figure 16-12 two line pull. Second line used to create a vector pull.

If, having completed stage three, the victim is in an unstable position and is in the process of drowning, I would move on to stage four. However, if the victim is in a relatively stable position and there is time to reorganize I would advise using the Two Line Cinch instead.

▶ **TWO LINE CINCH**—This is an ingenious method of getting a rescue line securely around a trapped paddler's waist in such a way that a more directional pull may be attempted without the risk of losing contact with the victim. It gives the rescuers a greater degree of control than a Two Line Pull.

Figure 16-13 positioning a cinch line. Note that in the drawing the victim is already stabilized with a tag line.

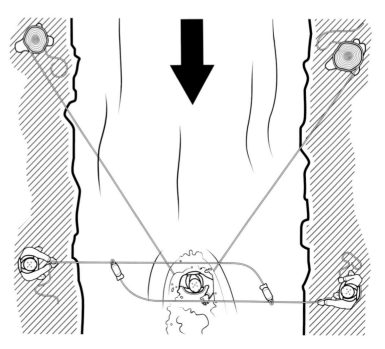

It works best with throw bags that have a fairly firm layer of foam sewn into the body of the bag, so that the bag is relatively stiff. If foam padded bags are used, the bag limits how tight the cinch can become and acts as a padded waist belt, affording the victim a greater degree of comfort and safety.

1 Throw two lines across the river; one from each side, one upstream and one downstream of the victim.

2 The bags are then either clipped to the other rope using a karabiner, or better still, the clean end is threaded through the handle of the other line.

3 The lines are then pulled tight forming an enclosed loop around the victim's body.

4 If necessary, one of the lines can be thrown to the other bank so that both lines can pull in the same direction.

▶ **TWO POINT TETHERED RESCUER**—This rescue, sometimes known as a V lower, involves holding a rescuer in the current using one line from each bank. The rescuer is attached via a chest harness.

By creating an eddy with his own body, the rescuer takes some of the pressure off the victim. Once in place just upstream of the victim the rescuer may also be able to help the victim remove the foot or hand from the entrapment.

▶ **SIGNALS**—It is vital to establish a set of signals to ensure that the tethered rescuer's (A) wishes are clearly understood. If possible, it is a good idea to have a rescuer (B) stand downstream of the rescuer A so that he can see his face and keep eye contact. This rescuer then relays the signals to the rescuers (C and D) who are handling the lines.

Figure 16-14 a two point tethered lower. In this example an Italian friction hitch is used by each belayer to control the rate at which the ropes are let out. See Chapter 24.

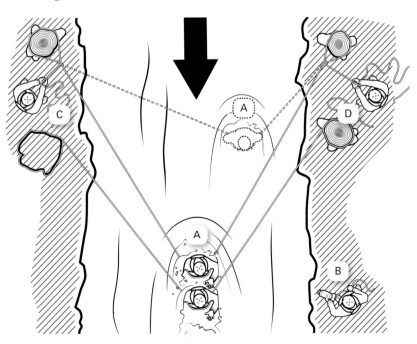

In a small team where the leader has to become physically involved in the rescue, this is the best job for him to take on. This is because he is in the best position to see everything and is the least physically involved in the rescue.

▶ **TWO POINT TETHERED RAFT** — Similar to the rescue described above except that a raft is lowered with a team of rescuers in it. The advantage over the tethered rescuer is that the rescuers can work from a stable platform and do not need to enter the water. The disadvantage is that the raft doesn't form a deep eddy and therefore most of the force of the current is still pressing on the victim.

▶ **RAFT TEAM** — Ideally the team would consist of three rescuers, two to assist the victim and one to use a paddle to fine tune the raft's position and coordinate with the team on the bank.

Foot Entrapments — One Bank Access

▶ **HANDRAIL** — If a foot entrapment occurs fairly close to the bank and the current is not too powerful, a rescuer may be able to use a handrail (see Chapter 14) to gain enough support to stay on his feet and wade out to the victim. Once contact is made, the victim will be able to use the tensioned line to support himself while the rescuer frees the trapped limb.

▶ **ONE BANK TAG OR CINCH LINES** — There are two methods whereby a swimmer can be used to loop a tag or snag line around a victim who can only be reached from one bank. The first is quicker and more reliable; the second involves less risk to the rescuer. If a swim is relatively safe use the first; if not, use the second method.

Figure 16-15 (opposite page) single bank strong swimmer cinch rescue.

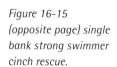

▶ **STRONG SWIMMER METHOD** — A swimmer has a line attached to his chest harness. He enters the water upstream of the victim while his buddy pays out the line. He swims around the victim and then receives a throw bag which pendulums him back into a downstream eddy. The line that is now looped around the victim is taken upstream and both ends are pulled to form a tag line.

By clipping the swimmer's end of the line to the upstream part of the line and pulling on the buddy's end a cinch line can be formed.

See Figure 16-16 (page 202) securing a single bank cinch using the live bait method.

▶ **LIVE BAIT METHOD** — A throw bag is thrown in upstream of the victim and allowed to float past him. It is retrieved by a live bait rescuer and then pulled upstream to form either a tag or a cinch line (see page 202)

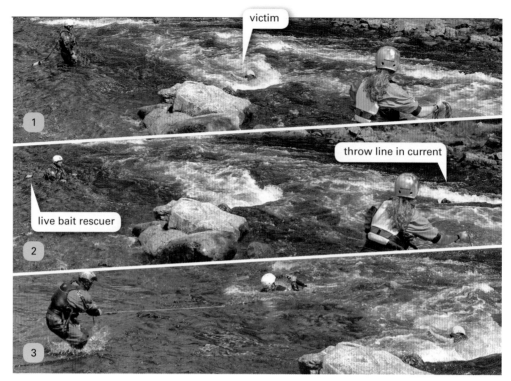

Figure 16-16 single bank cinch, live bait method.

Labels in image: victim · throw line in current · live bait rescuer · 1 · 2 · 3

Strainers

The techniques described for foot entrapments can be used in strainer rescues. However it should be borne in mind that any technique that involves rescuers being upstream of the strainer puts the rescuer at extreme risk. If at all possible it is far better for rescuers to approach the victim from the downstream side of the strainer, either climbing over the obstruction or cutting their way through it.

▶ **TWO POINT TETHERED RAFT**—Correctly trimmed, the shallow draft of a raft allows it to be easily positioned in the eddy below an obstruction. This makes it a very useful technique for getting at a victim from the downstream side of a strainer. If an approach from upstream is the only solution, a tethered raft offers a stable platform and, if it's properly controlled, the least dangerous solution.

Swimmer Trapped under Raft

It sometime happens that a rafter, having fallen out of the raft, can then be swept under it. Clients are instructed during the safety brief to push away from the raft and kick their legs so that they propel themselves in one direction, out from underneath the raft.

If the swimmer doesn't immediately pop out from underneath the raft, get the crew to paddle in an upstream direction. This should result in the swimmer being swept by the flow of the river to the front of the raft where a reach rescue can be made. Floating along at the same speed as the water is conversely the worst course of action.

handrail

River Guil, France. Photo: Dino Heald

CHAPTER 17

Protecting a Rapid

*Figure 17-1
using a handrail
to cover a hazard.*

If, on inspecting a rapid, it becomes obvious that there is a reasonable possibility of members of the group blowing their line, it makes sense to have the means of effecting a rescue in place before the event. On easier rapids this may be necessary to protect less skilful or experienced members of the party. On harder rapids it is part and parcel of running the river. In Chapters 6 and 7 we looked at how to scout a rapid, and how to identify hazards and assess the risks involved. In this chapter we need to look at how best to lessen the consequences of mistakes and consequently lower the risk.

Guidelines

When deciding how best to deploy the person power we have available, one should bear in mind the following guidelines:

- **Provide a back-up wherever possible**
- **Try not to rely on one method**
- **Have the means available to cover both banks**
- **Stay flexible**
- **The Principle of Most Usefulness**

▶ **BACK-UP**—If someone goes for a swim, and the swim is serious enough to warrant protection, we have to allow for human error. If the rescuer misses with a throw line we need to have another rescuer in a position to take over.

▶ **MULTIPLE METHODS**—Whenever possible it makes sense to cover a potential rescue situation with more than one method of effecting a rescue. In the photo the hazard is a short steep rapid. The consequence of not tackling it correctly is a trashing followed by a long swim. The other members of the team are covering the situation by having two rescuers standing by with a throw line (back-up) and the other in position as a chase boater (back-up and different method).

Figure 17-2 this photo illustrates the use of back-up, multiple methods and covering both banks. Surprise Surprise, River Dart. Photo: Mark Rainsley

▶ **BOTH BANKS**—If one bank is inaccessible, the eddies are all on one side of the river or the line to be protected is on one side of the river, it is easy to end up with all the rescuers positioned on one side of the river. If something unforeseen happens on the other side of the river, there is no one in a position to deal with it. In the photo above, the chase boater could have positioned himself in a small eddy on river left but deliberately positioned himself in the eddy on river right. There are two reasons for doing this:

1 There is the possibility of getting tangled in the throw line if he breaks in (eddies out) from river left.

2 If anything should happen that requires a bank-based rescuer to be on river right, he can get out of his boat and deal with it.

▶ **FLEXIBILITY**—When planning a line down a rapid, making best use of the cover available can be built into the plan. In Figure 17-3 (opposite) Rescuer B is in position with a handrail to recover equipment or swimmers and is also able to quickly move upstream to help anyone who gets into trouble in the strainer.

Rescuer A is ready to throw a line to a swimmer but prepared to move up or downstream to assist as necessary.

The Rescue-boater C is positioned as far upstream as is useful. It is easy enough for a chase boater to move downstream to cover an incident but difficult if not impossible to quickly move upstream.

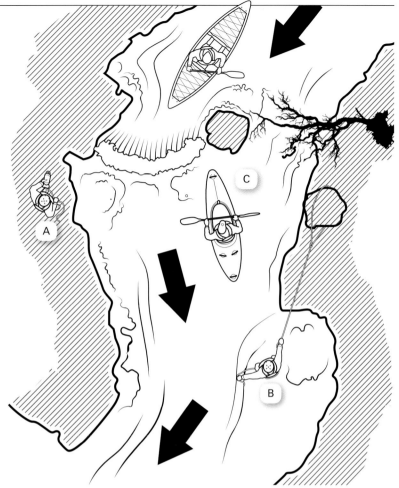

Figure 17-3 protecting a complex rapid.

▶ **USEFULNESS**—In accordance with the Principle of Most Usefulness, Rescuer B is positioned where he is most likely to be of use despite the fact that the strainer is a serious hazard. This is because the team has decided that this is an unlikely event given the line to be followed and the way the water is flowing. Nonetheless there is a contingency plan for Rescuer B to quickly get to the strainer should the unlikely event occur.

▶ **ORGANIZATION & COMMUNICATION**—It is vital that everyone knows who is coordinating the rescue cover and exactly what their job is. To avoid confusion, when inspecting a rapid and discussing a feature, or a hazard in midstream, it may help to throw a stone at it to ensure that everyone is talking about the same feature.

Good briefings, prior training and/or experience of working together, combined with clear effective signals can speed the process up. (See Chapters 9 and 10.) This is important. After all, we are there to paddle, not mess about on the bank longer than is necessary.

CHAPTER 18

Incident Management

When a mishap first occurs in a whitewater situation, either the victim or a nearby person will have to do something to retrieve or at least stabilize the situation. The situation is often retrieved so quickly that the only team organization needed is to recover the equipment. However, if the initial action is only able to stabilize the situation and buy time, the team will be faced with a rescue that will require effective management.

Figure 18-1 a dislocated shoulder and a bad swim (inset)—now to manage the evacuation. River Drac Noir, French Alps. Photos: Pete Knowles

Roles

It is essential that team members are clear as to what their roles are in the event of a rescue. Whether in a formally structured rescue team or an informal group of friends we can identify the following roles:

- **Leader**
- **Specialist**
- **Gofer**
- **Rescuers**

▶ **LEADER**—If at all possible leaders should take a "hands off" approach. They should literally take a step back, tuck their hands in their PFD, and see the whole picture. As soon as rescuers become physically involved in a rescue they, quite rightly, become "focused" on the task, or the individual they are helping. This means that they will probably not realize that there is no back-up downstream, or that no one has been sent to call an ambulance.

With small teams of boaters, the lack of numbers means that the leader has to be in on the action. In this case the leader should take on the task that requires the least involvement.

▶ **SPECIALIST**—Different people in the team will have different skills that may need to be identified. They may be trained first-aiders, have climbing and rope skills, or be particularly strong and confident swimmers, willing to be involved in "wet" rescues.

▶ **GOFER**—It is a good idea to appoint someone whose role is to try and make sure that the rescuers have all the equipment or people they need. If this person has no other specific task, he also has an overview, which enables him to anticipate rescuers' needs and make up the shortfall before it occurs. With complex rescues or recoveries, it makes sense to establish an equipment dump. All the spare equipment that rescuers have but don't anticipate using to complete their allotted task is left here for the gofer.

▶ **RESCUERS**—This should be everyone else in the team. Some will be less experienced, skilled or confident than others but anyone can help out by pulling a rope or keeping an eye out upstream for floating hazards or other paddlers.

Sequence of Events

Most rescues will involve a sequence of events that will be something like the one outlined below:

1 **Assess the situation.**

2 **Stabilize the situation.**

3 **Reassess the situation.**

4 **Decide on a plan of action.**

5 **Communicate plan to team.**

6 **Allocate tasks and ensure everyone is clear what their task involves.**

7 **Execute the plan.**

8 **Review incident to learn lessons and improve future performance.**

▶ **THE PLAN OF ACTION**—Typically broken into a number of phases. These are:

1 **Get victim safely to shore. If victim OK, carry on with trip.**

If not:

2 **If injured, administer first aid.**

3 **Evacuate injured.**

4 **Recover equipment.**

5 **Evacuate team members and equipment.**

If there are plenty of rescuers available, a team leader who is able to keep the whole picture in view will try and have more than one of these events happening at the same time.

A Scenario

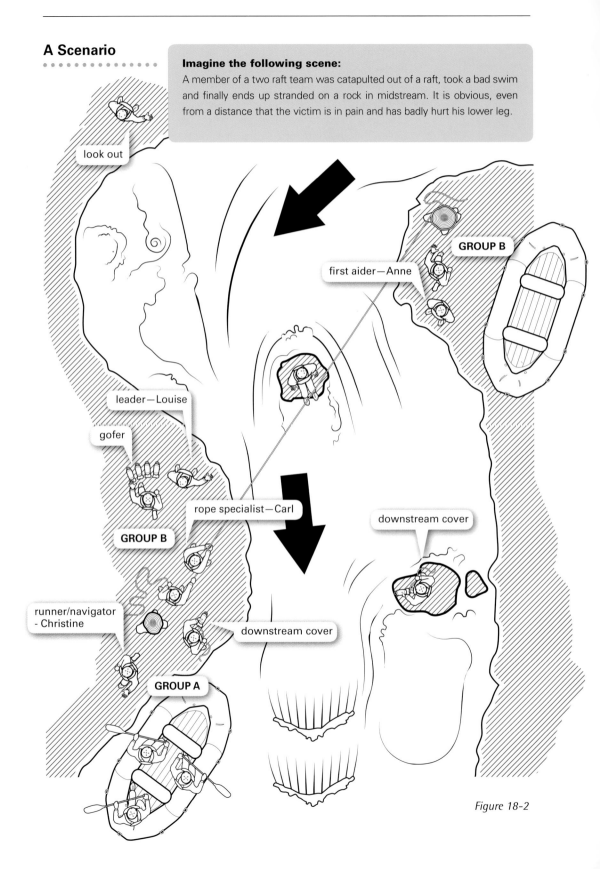

Imagine the following scene:

A member of a two raft team was catapulted out of a raft, took a bad swim and finally ends up stranded on a rock in midstream. It is obvious, even from a distance that the victim is in pain and has badly hurt his lower leg.

look out

GROUP B

first aider—Anne

leader—Louise

gofer

rope specialist—Carl

GROUP B

downstream cover

runner/navigator - Christine

downstream cover

GROUP A

Figure 18-2

▶ **PHASE ONE**—The leader, **Louise**, quickly assesses the situation, formulates a plan of action and delegates the following tasks to the fourteen people she has available.

Carl (specialist) the other raft guide, is tasked to set up a tensioned diagonal to access the boulder. Three rescuers are tasked to work under his direction.

Jane, who has quite a lot of rafting experience, is promoted to raft guide and is tasked to ferry rescuers back and forth across the quiet stretch of river below the rapid as required. She is allocated three other rescuers to crew the raft and is also charged with using the raft as a chase boat should anyone fall in during the rescue.

Pete is appointed gofer and establishes a central equipment dump.

Christine, who is a ranking orienteer (specialist), is sent to the nearest road to await the ambulance that she has already summoned by mobile phone.

Eric is posted as upstream lookout. His task is to warn any other paddlers that the rapid is obstructed with lines and that they should not run it till the rescue is complete.

The two remaining rescuers are positioned, one on each bank, below the scene of the rescue, ready to throw a line to anyone who might accidentally end up in the water.

Once everyone is briefed they get on with the first phase of the rescue plan.

▶ **PHASE TWO**—As soon as the tensioned diagonal is set up, Louise splits Carl's team in two.

Anne, who is a trained first-aider (specialist) is sent down the tensioned diagonal accompanied by one of the other rescuers. Her task is to treat the victim's injuries and evacuate him from the rock.

Eric and the other rescuer are now tasked with building a stretcher with which to carry the injured victim to the road.

▶ **PHASE THREE**—As soon as the victim is safely on the bank, Louise sends the two rescuers who were standing by with throw lines to dismantle the tensioned diagonal. This done, everyone is ferried to the same side of the river. The whole group help in the evacuation to the road. They take it in turns to carry the stretcher and change places frequently as it is a tiring job. Anne, the first aider, stays at the head of the stretcher and monitors the victim the whole time.

▶ **PHASE FOUR**—Once the casualty is handed over to the ambulance crew, Louise has to think about whether to evacuate the whole team by road or carry on with the trip.

If she had allowed herself to become an actively involved rescuer with a specific task, Louise would not have been able to be forward planning. There would probably have been oversights and mistakes.

There would certainly have been a great deal of time wasted when one step was completed before anyone thought about the next step.

With smaller teams the approach is still valid. However, there will obviously have to be compromises due to the lack of numbers.

Signals

Dealing with a rescue and coordinating rescuers requires different signals from those used when running a river. In addition, we may receive help from, or offer help to, other paddlers or even professional rescue teams. I therefore propose to introduce the standard signals that are taught on *Rescue Three International* Swift Water Technician courses. This is because these courses have become the de facto internationally recognized standard for rescue teams and raft guides.

▶ **HAND SIGNALS**—Signal with clear deliberate movements:

▶ NEED MEDIC KIT & HELP

both arms crossed in front of chest

Meaning: I need a first aider and/or a first aid kit.

▶ OKAY

two hands forming an "O" above head

Meaning: Affirmative, expression of agreement, or "I am OK."

▶ DISTRESS/NEED ASSISTANCE

one hand extended above head

Meaning: "I am in distress and require rescue and/or need first aid attention."

▶ MOVE, SWIM OR MOVE BOAT

two hands extending above head then pointing left/right.

Meaning: Directed at a person, "move yourself to the left/right" either in the general direction or to the location indicated.

▶ MAKE THAT EDDY

two hands extending above head, wave arms in a circular motion, then point left/right.

Meaning: Directed at a person, "move yourself to that eddy," pointing both arms at the indicated eddy.

▶ **WHISTLE SIGNALS** - Short, sharp blasts on the whistle.

▶ **STOP / ATTENTION** ✸ ....*one blast*

▶ **UPSTREAM** ✸ ✸ ....*two blasts*

▶ **DOWNSTREAM** ✸ ✸ ✸ ....*three blasts*

▶ **EMERGENCY** ✸ ✸ ✸ – ✸ ✸ ✸ ...*three blasts repeated*

CHAPTER 19

First Aid

> In my view, anyone who regularly participates in risk sports owes it to himself, and his friends, to regularly attend first aid training courses. If you haven't, get yourself into a first aid course ASAP!

That said, real first aid consists of keeping people breathing and stopping them bleeding. It's not rocket science.

*Figure 19-1
a fairly common
injury, especially
with cut down or
poorly fitting helmets.
Photo: Dave Burton*

REAL FIRST AID CONSISTS OF KEEPING PEOPLE BREATHING AND STOPPING THEM BLEEDING

The chapter is written on the assumption that the reader already has a basic knowledge of first aid. I would recommend the following two books:

First Aid Manual—The authorized manual of St. John's Ambulance, St. Andrew's Ambulance Association and The British Red Cross. (ISBN 0751337048)

Medicine for Mountaineering (and Other Wilderness Activities)—Particularly useful for those operating in remote locations. (ISBN 0898867991)

▶ **AIMS**—The aims of the chapter are as follows:

1 To suggest an accident procedure

2 To offer some guidelines aimed specifically at the water-based first aider

4 To look at how we can adapt our kit to improvise in a first aid situation

3 To discuss some issues that affect first aiders in a whitewater situation

Accident Procedure

When approaching an injured or distressed person it is important that the first aider remains calm and thinks logically. This may be easier said than done when the adrenaline is pumping, so it is important to have a system which will ensure that nothing is forgotten and that the priorities are taken care of in the right order.

If a first aider is suddenly confronted with a situation, he should physically take a step back to help trigger the ability to mentally step back. Given the luxury of some prior warning, the first aider should stop a short distance away from the victim, compose himself and survey the scene.

Rescue and Emergency Care suggest the following mnemonic to remember the sequence of priorities when dealing with an accident:

A	**B**	**C**	**D**	**E**
Assess	Breathing	Circulation	Deformity	Emotion

ASSESS	The situation
	Safety
	How to get medical assistance if necessary
	The level of consciousness of the victim
BREATHING	Check airway (see Issues)
	Assess normality of breathing
CIRCULATION	Check pulse
	Look for bleeding
DEFORMITY	Casualty examination
	Signs of fractures, shock, internal injuries
EMOTION	Reassurance and continuing care
	Emotional well-being of patient

If we work our way methodically through the sequence, we won't miss out anything vital. The sequence works in terms of both order and priority.

For example, the safety of the rescuer comes first, but unless he takes time to assess the situation he cannot make a judgment on safety. If a victim is clutching a badly bleeding arm and screaming for help, it is obvious that he is fully conscious and breathing. Therefore the fact that the rescuer is going to deal with the bleeding arm fits in nicely with our sequence of checks and priorities.

If at any time the first aider gets confused, he should finish off what he was doing and then start from the top again, A,B,C,D and E.

The Situation

Taking the time to survey the scene allows the first aider to try and work out how the accident happened. The history of the accident is an important factor in assessing safety and diagnosing possible injuries. If the victim fell 10 feet (3 m) onto his head, one can suspect head and neck injuries!

It is important to find out how many people were involved. There might be someone missing. Someone might have been swept downstream by the current or simply wandered off looking for help.

▶ **SAFETY**—The first aider needs to prevent a second accident. The priorities are as follows:

1 The first aider	**3 Bystanders**
2 Other rescuers	**4 The victim**

Our ability to help the victim will be seriously impaired if the first aider is injured or he ends up having to treat several other victims.

Whenever possible it is best to examine the casualty and treat injuries before moving him. If the casualty is in a dangerous position, it may be necessary to move him first.

How to Get Medical Assistance if Necessary

If someone is seriously hurt the first aider's task is to do his best to stabilize their condition and obtain specialist medical treatment as soon as possible. Therefore the question of how to get the victim to a hospital or paramedics to the victim should be considered right at the outset.

▶ **FIRST AID KITS**—Most first aid treatment of traumatic injuries is relatively simple:

- Bleeding is treated by applying a sterile dressing and pressure and elevation.
- Fractures are immobilized in the position that the victim finds most comfortable.
- Burns are treated by cooling with cold water for at least ten minutes and then covering with a sterile dressing.

There are obviously lots of complications and exceptions but everything else is basically a variation on the theme.

What most people call first aid kits can be divided into two parts:

Medicine Chest—Tender loving care and longer term treatment.

First Aid Kit—Immediate temporary care of traumatic injuries.

First aid kits need only contain the following items:

- Sterile dressings—for stopping bleeding
- Band aids for small wounds
- Non stick sterile dressings—burns or the first layer on a wound
- Triangular bandages—for bandaging or immobilizing fractures
- Conforming (crepe) bandages—bandaging or immobilizing fractures

There should be two kits in any party in case the boat that is lost is the one containing the first aid kit.

Figure 19-2 an extra large triangular bandage can be made by tracing the outline of an ordinary one on a sheet of polythene, allowing an extra 2 inches (5 cm) all round, and cutting it out. It won't mind getting wet.

Figure 19-3 kayakers can use their spray deck to make a comfortable and warm support sling.

Figure 19-4 duct tape used to immobilize a fractured arm in the position of most comfort.

▶ **IMPROVISATION**—Much of the materials and equipment used by whitewater paddlers can be adapted for first aid purposes.

▶ **DUCT TAPE**—Duct tape is found in most boaters' repair kits. It is great for immobilizing fractures or waterproofing dressings. In my opinion it is better than straps made for specific purposes.

▶ **ELECTRICAL TAPE**—Great for taping a broken finger to a sound one, covering rubbing points on fingers to prevent them blistering, and waterproofing small dressings.

▶ **FOAM**—The closed-cell foam in camping mats and PFDs can be used as padding, or by folding it, as a splint.

▶ **NECK BRACE**—If a person has sustained head injuries one should suspect neck injuries. The first aider should feel for any irregularities along the spine and try not to move the neck unnecessarily. If the patient must be moved it should be ideally on a rigid stretcher and with the neck immobilized by padding strapped on either side of the head. If the casualty has no choice but to walk or boat out a collar should be fitted. If necessary a collar can be improvised by removing the slab buoyancy from a PFD, carving it to the right shape, and taping it in place with some duct tape from the repair kit. The fit of the collar should be checked by trying it out on someone else who is of similar build to the casualty.

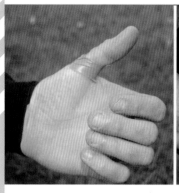 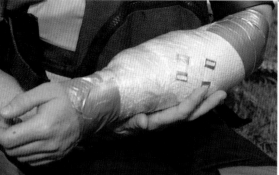 

Figure 19-5 (left) electical tape is great for covering plasters and small cuts or to stop a rub becoming a blister.

Figure 19-6 (middle) waterproofing a dressed and bandaged forearm.

Figure 19-7 (right) a length of the tape is folded back on itself so that both sides are non-sticky making it easier to pass the strap under the casualty's leg.

▶ **POLYTHENE BAGS**—Although not sterile, a clean sheet of polythene makes a good non-stick burn dressing. Plastic film, the stuff used to wrap sandwiches, is sterile if it is fresh off the roll. Polythene bags are also useful for waterproofing dressings.

▶ **DRIFTWOOD/SPARE PADDLES**—Driftwood can be cut into suitable lengths, padded with foam and used as rigid splints.

▶ **NYLON TAPE**—The tape slings and lengths carried for rescue and recovery purposes can be pressed into service as straps for immobilizing fractures.

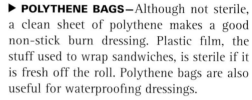

Figure 19-8 nylon tape, duct tape and a triangular bandage used to immobilize a fractured leg.

Guidelines for Outdoor First Aid

- **Do not rush**
- **Delegate if possible**
- **Never step over the casualty**
- **Treat from the downhill side**
- **Try to compose the casualty**
- **Keep talking, even if the casualty is unconscious**
- **Never leave the casualty— unless safety considerations require it, or you are the only person who can go for help**

- **Never lose body or eye contact with the casualty**
- **Prevent heat loss**
- **Take account of weather conditions**

► **DO NOT RUSH!** — A few seconds spent composing oneself, surveying the scene or deciding on the correct course of action is time well spent. Getting it right will more than make up for any time used up in this way.

► **DELEGATE IF POSSIBLE** — Ideally, the leader should not be directly involved in administering first aid as he needs to be coordinating all the other things that are going on.

Once contact has been made, whoever has been assigned the role of first aider needs to closely monitor the airway and vital signs, and reassure the casualty. Therefore the first aider should delegate as much of the treatment as possible to other rescuers so that he can remain at the casualty's head.

► **NEVER STEP OVER THE CASUALTY** — Rescuers should get in the habit of walking around the casualty. Time and time again one sees rescuers tread on an already painful injury.

► **TREAT FROM THE DOWNHILL SIDE** — It is disconcerting, to say the least, if a casualty rolls down the slope into the river.

► **TRY TO COMPOSE THE CASUALTY** — It is difficult to sufficiently stress the importance of the victim's morale when it comes to fighting the onset of shock and hypothermia. By not rushing and by appearing calm, the first aider can do a lot to reassure and calm a casualty. Speaking calmly, both to the victim and other rescuers, is important. Rescuers need to be very careful what they say within the casualty's hearing. Phrases like: "He's done for!" are generally considered to be unhelpful.

► **KEEP TALKING** — It is important to remember that even a totally unresponsive unconscious casualty may be able to hear what a rescuer is saying. Many casualties who have recovered from a deep coma report that one of the things that kept them going was the calm reassuring voice of the rescuer. If this voice suddenly stops, and it is the victim's only way of knowing that he is being looked after, it will be very distressing. Use the casualties name, if known.

► **NEVER LEAVE THE CASUALTY** — In a whitewater situation, it may be some time before help arrives or the casualty can be evacuated to the nearest road. The casualty will have formed a reassuring bond with whoever first started treating him. It is important that this person stays with the victim and monitors his progress even if another more experienced first aider takes over responsibility for the casualty's treatment. The casualty does not need the stress of losing someone he has come to trust, and having to rebuild a new relationship.

► **NEVER LOSE BODY OR EYE CONTACT** — Just as a calm friendly voice is reassuring, body and eye contact is important. Once the first aider first lays hands on the casualty, he should try not to lose physical contact. When treatment has been completed and the first aider is monitoring, he should hold the victim's hand, talk constantly and maintain eye contact throughout.

▶ **PREVENT HEAT LOSS**—In all but the warmest of climates hypothermia is a concern (see Chapter 3). Anyone who is injured is far more likely to succumb to hypothermia. This cannot be stressed enough!

▶ **TAKE ACCOUNT OF WEATHER CONDITIONS**—This is linked to the above point. Weather conditions and their effect on a casualty and the rest of the party will play a major role in deciding on a plan of action.

Issues

▶ **CERVICAL SPINE & AIRWAY**—If damage to the spine or neck (C or cervical spine) is suspected, every effort should be made to keep the spine and C spine in as straight a line as possible and avoid any unnecessary bending or twisting.

However, airway always takes precedence over cervical (neck) spine injuries. In other words, even if the first aider suspects neck injuries, if the victim is not breathing, the airway must be opened. Nonetheless, the first aider should quickly assess the possibility of C spine injuries before opening the airway.

If the history of the accident, signs such as bruising or swelling, or pain in that area suggests that C spine injuries are a possibility, care should be taken not to do any unnecessary damage. This is why first aiders are now taught to open the airway using two fingers on the forehead and the chin.

To check the airway—Open the casualty's mouth and look inside.

To open the airway—If there is no blood or debris in the mouth, ensure that the unconscious casualty's tongue does not block their airway by placing two fingers of one hand on the forehead and two fingers of the other under the point of the chin and tilting the head back. This ensures that the airway is opened with the minimum of force.

To clear the airway—Look inside the victim's mouth and remove any visible obstruction. If there is blood, vomit or debris in the mouth, turn the casualty on his side supporting the head and neck, open his mouth and allow it to drain. If necessary, use a finger to scoop out the debris.

Figure 19-9
1 *checking the airway*
2 *opening the airway.*

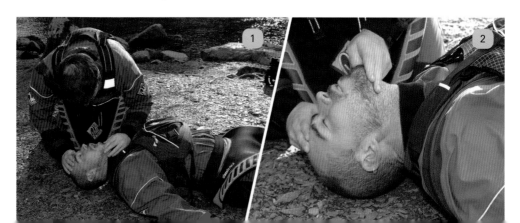

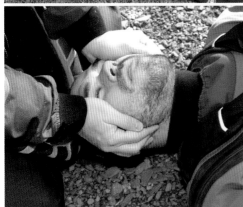

The first aider should also take care to stabilize the head and ensure that the C spine is only tilted back and not twisted, rotated, or moved from side to side. If the casualty needs to be placed on his side (to clear or protect the airway) pad his head so that the spine stays in as straight a line as possible.

▶ **JAW THRUST**—This is an alternative way of opening the airway of an unconscious casualty if the problem is the casualty's tongue rather than blood, vomit or debris. It keeps the head stable and can be used when C spine injuries are suspected.

1 Kneel at the casualty's head looking down the length of his body.

2 Place your thumbs on his chin and your fingers on the corner of his jawbone.

3 Gently but firmly lift his jaw up and forward.

▶ **HELMETS**—If there is no need to remove the helmet it is best left on to provide protection and warmth. However, if an airway needs to be established or resuscitation started it should be carefully removed.

Figure 19-10 (top) clearing the airway, note the use of padding to support the head and neck and keep the spine and C spine in as straight a line as possible.

Figure 19-11 (middle) a simple way to keep the C spine immobilized.

Figure 19-12 (bottom) jaw thrust.

▶ **CASUALTY'S DIGNITY**—It is important to remember that we are dealing with a sensitive human being and to consider feelings and dignity at all times. If the first aider needs to examine an injury in a potentially embarrassing location, there is no need for the rest of the team to stand there gawking (although it is a good idea to have a witness of the same sex as the casualty present).

We should try not to treat the casualty as a "body." It is far better to ask a casualty to move or adjust his clothing than to manhandle him unnecessarily.

▶ **CONSENT**—This is an important issue, both from the point of view of the casualty's dignity and in terms of possible legal repercussions. If a person tells a first aider not to touch them, then that is the end of the matter. To continue an examination or treatment would constitute assault.

The best way to address this issue is for the first aider to talk to the casualty the whole time and tell him what he is going to do next. If the casualty does not object, consent is implied.

Monitoring Vital Signs

If first aiders keep a record of the casualty's progress it can save vital time when he receives expert medical attention. This is because monitoring has already taken place and information on which to base decisions has already been gathered. An examination will give a doctor a great deal of information but a record of a series of checks tells us whether the patient is stable, deteriorating or improving.

If for example, a patient is going deeper into shock and the examination has revealed no obvious reason why this should happen, we must suspect internal injuries. A surgeon may be able to decide to prepare for an exploratory operation even before the casualty arrives at the hospital on the basis of the first aider's observations.

In order to help us diagnose what is abnormal, it is vital that we practice monitoring the vital signs of as many "normal" people as we can. We need to be confident in our ability to do this. The vital signs are:

- Level of Consciousness
- Breathing
- Pulse
- Temperature
- Color

(Blood pressure is also an important vital sign but most first aiders will not have the means to monitor this.)

A record card can be improvised, or better still, kept in the first aid kit. The vital signs should be monitored and recorded every five minutes.

▶ **LEVEL OF CONSCIOUSNESS—**

The acronym **AVPU** helps us remember the four levels that we can differentiate in a first aid situation.

ALERT	Normal behavior given the circumstances
VOCAL	The victim is less than fully conscious but responds to direct questions
PAIN	The victim is deeply unconscious but responds to pain
UNRESPONSIVE	The victim is totally unresponsive

▶ **BREATHING**—With an unconscious victim the airway should be checked, even if the victim is breathing. There may be debris or blood in the mouth that needs to be cleared. Very often, the act of checking and clearing the airway is all that is needed for an unconscious victim to start breathing unaided.

Even if a person is alert and is obviously breathing, it is important to check out how normal his breathing is. A normal range is 12–15 breaths a minute. This will help us diagnose other, possibly hidden injuries. Painful or irregular breathing could indicate chest injuries. A significantly faster breathing rate than usual (more than 20 breaths a minute) is one of the signs of shock.

We can listen, look and feel for breathing. Listen for sounds of breathing by putting your ear close to the victim's mouth. Look to see the chest or abdomen rise and fall. Feel the casualty's breath on your ear and put a hand on his abdomen to feel the movement of the upper belly/chest.

Figure 19-13 look, listen and feel for breathing.

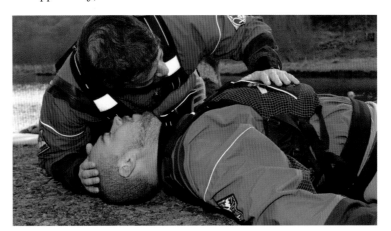

▶ **PULSE**—Cold, restrictive clothing and wrist seals can make a wrist pulse very difficult to detect. Therefore the best way to take a pulse in an outdoor situation is take the neck pulse. The tips of two or three fingers are placed on the Adam's Apple and then slid gently but firmly to the side, until they slide into a groove between the Adam's Apple and the first large set of neck muscles. Here the finger tips will push the artery against the large muscle and the first aider is able to feel the pulse. A normal adult pulse rate is between 60 and 100 beats a minute. If there is a pulse it can tell you a great deal:

- A fast weak pulse (over 100 beats a minute) is a sign of shock.

- A slow, bounding pulse is a sign of head injuries.

- A slow weak pulse is one of the signs of hypothermia.

▶ **TEMPERATURE**—In a windy, wet environment it is very difficult to accurately gauge someone's temperature. Normal thermometers don't work very well in these conditions and the use of a rectal thermometer is impractical. In such conditions the history of the accident and other signs will be of more use.

Sign: Probably indicates:

• Cold and Sweaty . . . . • Shock

• Hot and Sweaty . . . . • Fever, Infection

• Unusual Warmth . . . . • Heat Exhaustion

• Coolness . . . . • Hypothermia

COLOR—A healthy underlying skin tone is a sign that oxygen is reaching all parts of the body as it should. We should look for changes in skin color especially in the face. This is especially useful in detecting the onset of shock

Skin type: Changes to:

• Caucasian (White) . . . . • Pale, Ash Grey

• African/Asian (Black) . . . . • Dull Ash Grey

• East Asian . . . . • Pale Grey

We should also look at the inside of the lips and cheek for changes in the normal pink/red coloring. Blueness of the lips (cyanosis) is a serious sign which indicates a low level of oxygen in the blood. It indicates that attention to the airway and pulse is necessary or that hypothermia is setting in.

Treatment Issues

Being in a whitewater environment and dressed in outlandish garb raises a number of issues that affect treatment.

BREATHING—If a casualty's breathing has stopped or is impaired, it may help to remove his helmet and loosen or even remove his PFD. Tight fitting neck seals of dry tops may be cut for the same reasons.

However, I would advise trying not to do this unless it is really necessary. Apart from the issue of damaging a friend's expensive equipment, we must never forget the nature of the environment we are in. There are two issues here:

1 When the time comes to move a casualty he will need to be wearing personal protective equipment, just as the rescuers will. On or within 33 feet (10 m) of the water's edge this means helmets and PFDs.

2 Any injured person is far more susceptible to the onset of hypothermia. Removing or reducing the efficiency of clothing can only make this worse.

▶ **BLEEDING**—From a first aid point of view, the problem with clothing that is designed to keep water out is that it is very good at keeping blood in. This can hide major blood loss from a first aider. The blood will pool, and the first aider may be able to feel liquid, like water in a bag.

Running water will make it harder to stop wounds bleeding by washing away the blood that is clotting. Therefore it is important to keep casualties out of the water. If the wound is minor or it is decided that the easiest way to evacuate is by continuing the journey, the dressing should be waterproofed by using electricians' insulating tape or a combination of a piece of polythene and electrical or duct tape.

▶ **UNCONSCIOUSNESS**—People who are less than "Alert" on the **AVPU** scale are deemed to be unconscious in terms of treatment. The main worry is that they cannot protect their own airway due to the loss of their choking reflex.

They should be placed in the Safe Airway Position. From a medical standpoint, people who are less than completely conscious are in a state of unconsciousness. Forty percent of unconscious victims who die might have been saved if their airways had been protected. The SAP does this by putting casualties in a position that ensures they cannot swallow their own tongue and that any fluids drain out of their mouths rather than into the back of their throat.

Ideally, casualties should be monitored contantly and the first aider ready to intervene with resuscitation at any time. Heat loss from the casualty is even more of an issue with unconscious casualties.

See Figure 19-14, page 224.

▶ **SHOCK**—This is a condition where insufficient oxygen is reaching the vital tissues of the body, due to a lack of effective circulating blood volume. It is a serious sign that the body is not coping and can be thought of as the phase before death. Faced with more than one casualty, a first aider must decide who is in most urgent need of evacuation to expert attention; the casualty in shock is the priority.

Cause: The cause of shock is a loss of body fluids arising from:

- **External bleeding**
- **Internal bleeding**
- **Burns weeping**
- **Dehydration**
- **Diarrhea**
- **Septic shock, caused by severe infections**

Signs and Symptoms:

- **Cold, pale ("pale as death"), sweaty (clammy) skin**
- **Rising pulse, usually climbing to over 100 beats a minute**
- **Rising breathing rate, usually climbing to over 20 breaths a minute**
- **Fear, anxiety and restlessness**

Figure 19-14 SAP

(Safe Airway Position):

Treatment for shock

- **A,B,C (Assess, Airway, Breathing, Circulation)**
- **Treat injuries**
- **Reassure**
- **Monitor vital signs**
- **Raise legs to concentrate blood supply where it is needed**
- **Prevent heat loss**
- **Evacuate as quickly as possible**

If the casualty is not evacuated the outlook is bleak!

▶ **LIMITATIONS OF TREATMENT**—First aiders must always work within the limits of their training. In a situation where help is a long way off, it helps to remember that a casualty surgeon who does not have access to specialist equipment could do little more than a trained first aider in most situations.

First aiders should not be tempted to carry out medical or surgical procedures in which they have had no training. If they do, and a post-mortem indicates that the bungled procedure contributed to the casualty's death, they are in serious trouble.

▶ **REMOTE MEDICINE**—The exception to the above comment is if the first aider is told to carry out such a procedure under the direction of a medical practitioner. Due to the increased use of radios and mobile phones, specialist casualty surgeons are becoming increasingly adept at "remote medicine." The potential for remote treatment is another reason why it is important to become practiced in the monitoring of vital signs. The doctor will only have your observations to go on.

Remote Locations

. . . .

There are some issues that arise if evacuation to expert medical treatment will take several hours or even days.

▶ **PAIN RELIEF**—The general rule when expert medical help is close at hand is to relieve pain by treating the injury but not to give pain killing drugs (analgesics). This is because they will mask signs and symptoms and hinder diagnosis when the victim arrives at a hospital. However, the relief of pain is an important part of the treatment of shock. If help is a long way off there is no doubt that the use of suitable analgesics may improve the casualty's prospects.

There are also a number of legal problems involved with the administration of even mild analgesics. My advice is that when paddling in remote areas, people should carry their own analgesics. They should also consult their own personal physician as to which ones to take. (Not least because some analgesics cannot be safely taken in combination with other medicines. Paddlers should therefore seek advice on all the medicines that they may decide to take on such trips).

Analgesics can be divided into three types:

- **Mild** . . . . e.g. aspirin, ibuprofen
- **Moderate** . . . . e.g. codeine combined with acetaminophen
- **Strong** . . . . e.g. morphine and its derivatives

STRONG ANALGESICS HAVE A TENDENCY TO DEPRESS RESPIRATION AND SHOULD THEREFORE NOT BE TAKEN BY CASUALTIES WITH HEAD INJURIES.

ASPIRIN & IBUPROFEN SHOULD NOT BE TAKEN BY ANYONE SUFFERING FROM A STOMACH DISORDER.

ASTHMA CAN BE AGGRAVATED BY A NUMBER OF ANALGESICS (ESP. ASPIRIN). PEOPLE WHO ARE KNOWN TO HAVE ASTHMA SHOULD NOT BE GIVEN ASPIRIN-BASED PAIN KILLERS.

CERTAIN MIXTURES OF DRUGS CAN CAUSE SERIOUS COMPLICATIONS. THEREFORE IT IS ESSENTIAL TO KNOW IF A CASUALTY IS ALREADY ON MEDICATION AND THAT PERSON SHOULD ONLY USE DRUGS APPROVED BY HIS DOCTOR.

Vomiting is also a possible side effect of strong analgesics.

▶ **GIVING FLUIDS**—Once again the general advice is not to give fluids if expert medical attention is close at hand. For anyone who is less than fully conscious, first aiders need to be careful to safeguard their airway and allowing victims to drink may induce vomiting. If vomit gets into the lungs it can cause irreparable harm.

If help is a long way off the gains in terms of treating shock more than outweigh the risks. Casualties who are conscious enough should be encouraged to take small sips of water at body temperature, little and often.

People expeditioning in extremely remote locations should consider having a doctor join the team, or getting paramedic training, and carrying the equipment needed for giving fluids intravenously. However, there are great difficulties in terms of storage as the solutions used have to be pre-packed, sterile and kept within certain temperature ranges. Another option in remote locations is to administer fluids through the rectum. The advantages are:

1 The fluid is delivered directly to the part of the body at which fluids are absorbed.

2 Although the fluid used, (rehydration fluids or slightly salted water), should be as clean as possible, it doesn't have to be sterile.

▶ **REDUCING DISLOCATIONS**—Dislocated shoulders are one of the injuries we are likely to come across in a paddling situation. The general first aid advice is that if it doesn't pop back in of its own accord it should be immobilized and dealt with in hospital. This is because, although it is true that the sooner a dislocation is dealt with the easier it is to reduce it (put it back in its socket), if it is reduced badly, nerves can be trapped and long term damage done.

That said, in terms of outcome, a reduced joint is nearly always better than a long standing unreduced joint. On a remote trip where the only feasible way out is to carry on paddling, immobilization may not be an option. If this has occurred before and the casualty knows how to deal with it, the first aider can help reduce it under the casualty's direction. Whichever approach is used, it should be the casualty's decision whether to attempt to reduce the dislocation or not.

The principle of reducing a dislocation is to exert a very slow and continuous pull to tease out the muscle spasm. The following approach is the least risky:

1 If the decision is made, the sooner it is attempted the easier it will be.

2 The casualty should take the strongest painkiller available, preferably one that also acts as a muscle relaxant.

3 The casualty should lie down somewhere where his arm can hang down (a boulder or steep-edged river bank).

4 A helmet or bag is tied to the affected arm and stones loaded into it until it weighs about 4.4 lb. (2 kg), or 6.6 lb. (3 kg) for a large patient.

5 The weight is slowly increased to about double. If this causes pain the weight is reduced.

6 The casualty is left alone so that gravity can do the work as the casualty's muscles relax. The patient should feel a clunk as the shoulder relocates.

After the attempt, whether it is successful or not, the casualty's wrist pulse should be checked to ensure that no major blood vessels have been trapped. If no pulse can be found the arm will have to be moved till it can. Another important sign to look out for is a color change (this occurs very quickly). If the arm appears white and "dead" a major blood vessel has probably been trapped.

▶ **CONCLUSION**—All the publications on wilderness medicine that I have read agree that unless a hospital is reasonably close, a dislocation should be reduced. They go on to say that the chances of doing further harm are small. The advantages are:

- **Pain relief is usually dramatic.**
- **The risk of circulatory or neural damage is reduced.**
- **Immobilization of the joint is easier.**
- **Transportation of the victim is easier.**

After the reduction the joint should be immobilized. On return to civilization a doctor and a physiotherapist should be consulted.

CHAPTER 20

Resuscitation

The protocols taught by first aiders are put together by an international committee of physicians, whose advice is based on statistics. These show that the vast majority of incidents involving Basic Life Support concern heart attack victims in an urban situation. In any situation where the heart has stopped and full **CPR** (Cardiopulmonary Resuscitation) is needed there is very little chance of the first aider restarting the heart, and in the case of a diseased heart, none at all. The first aider acts as a machine that mechanically ventilates the lungs, and compresses the heart so as to pump oxygenated blood around the body. This keeps the vital tissues oxygenated until a defibrillator can be used to electrically stop the fibrillation (the fibers of the heart muscle contracting in an unsynchronized way), and electrically kick-start the heart. In most cases, by giving Basic Life Support, first aiders merely bridge the gap between someone collapsing and the arrival of expert medical attention.

Although the odds are still stacked against them, near drowning victims are often young, fit and have healthy hearts. Therefore, unlike with heart attack victims, resuscitation can occasionally succeed, even without a defibrillator.

Basic Life Support Protocol

As always the first priority is to assess for danger. That done the victim's level of consciousness is assessed. Anyone dealing with an unconscious casualty, whatever the cause, should clear and open the victim's airway and check for breathing. It is suggested that the first aider should look, listen and feel for no more than ten seconds before deciding that breathing is absent.

▶ **ONE RESCUER**—The protocol is complicated by the fact that there is a different procedure for victims of drowning than there is for suspected heart attack victims, (anyone who has stopped breathing for reasons other than drowning).

Unresponsive/not breathing
—drowning:

- **Give 5 rescue breaths**

Still not breathing

- **Give CPR for 1 minute**
- **Phone, radio, or go for help**
- **Return and reassess**

If we work methodically through the sequence, we won't miss out anything vital. The sequence works in both order and priority.

Unresponsive/not breathing—Other (suspect heart attack):

- **Phone, radio, or go for help**
- **Return and reassess**

▶ **MULTIPLE RESCUERS**—When there is more than one rescuer involved there is no need for decisions on when one should go for help. The first aider performs the resuscitation while someone else goes for help.

Unresponsive/not breathing —drowning

- **Give 5 rescue breaths**

still not breathing

- **Give CPR – 30 compressions, 2 breaths**
- **Carry on until victim starts breathing or help arrives**

Unresponsive/not breathing—Other (suspect heart attack)

- **Give CPR – 30 compressions, 2 breaths**
- **Continue until victim starts breathing or help arrives**

Rescue Breathing

When we breathe in and out at a normal rate we only use a small amount of the oxygen in each lung full of air. This leaves more than enough for the casualty's needs during rescue breathing. If the casualty does not start breathing after 5 rescue breaths, you should go on to CPR.

▶ **MOUTH TO MOUTH RESUSCITATION -**

1 With the casualty lying flat on his back, if possible look inside and remove any obvious obstructions from the casualty's mouth. Leave well fitting dentures in place but remove any that are broken or displaced.

2 Open the airway by placing two fingers under the casualty's chin and lifting the jaw, at the same time putting the fingers of the other hand on his forehead and tilting the head back. Take care to keep the neck in line if there is any reason to suspect injury to the cervical spine. See Figure 20-1 (1).

3 Close the casualty's nose by pinching it between your finger and thumb. Take a full breath and place your lips around his mouth, making a good seal. See Figure 20-1 (2).

4 Blow slowly and steadily into the casualty's mouth until you see his chest rise. It should take about one full second for a full inflation.

5 Remove your lips and allow the chest to fall fully.

*Figure 20-1
mouth to mouth
resuscitation.*

▶ **CHEST DOES NOT RISE**—If you cannot get breaths into the casualty's lungs, check that:

- **The casualty's head is tilted far enough back.**
- **You have remembered to pinch the casualty's nose**

- **You have a firm seal around the casualty's mouth**
- **The airway is not obstructed by blood, vomit or a foreign body**

▶ **CLEARING OBSTRUCTIONS**—These measures should only be taken if one is certain that there is an obstruction, because the other possible causes of the chest not rising have been eliminated.

- **Providing the jaw is relaxed, open the casualty's mouth and remove any visible obstruction.**
- **If there is blood or vomit, turn him on his side to allow it to drain and if necessary, carefully sweep a finger around inside the mouth to assist this.**

▶ **USE OF MASKS**—The risk of infection through performing rescue breathing is negligible and rescuers who do not have a mask or face shield should not hesitate to give help in this way. Nevertheless there are a number of advantages to using these devices.

Face Shields—These consist of a simple sheet of plastic with a valve through which the rescuer ventilates the casualty. The shield simply acts as a barrier. Although the risk of infection through contact with saliva is minute, contact with saliva, blood or vomit is far from pleasant. Though not as useful or effective as a proper mask, face shields pack so small that it is feasible to carry one in a pocket.

Masks—As well as being a more efficient barrier, a proper face mask makes it easier to make a seal around the casualty's mouth than a shield. This is particularly true if the casualty's mouth is damaged.

▶ **DAMAGED FACE**—Mouth to nose is just as efficient for getting air into a casualty's lungs. However, it can be more difficult for the air to be exhaled than in mouth to mouth. If a casualty's mouth is damaged and a mask is not available it will work well enough.

If a rescuer is unable to give rescue breaths it is recommended that he should give chest compressions alone.

Cardiopulmonary Resuscitation (CPR)

Cardiopulmonary Resuscitation consists of chest compressions combined with rescue breathing. The casualty is given thirty chest compressions to pump the oxygenated blood around the system so that it reaches the vital organs, followed by two breaths of air to re-oxygenate the blood.

▶ **CHEST COMPRESSION**—Although difficult, it is possible to perform rescue breathing with the casualty in a variety of positions. Chest compressions can only be performed effectively if the casualty is lying on his back on a firm surface. It is essential to remove the victim's PFD or it will absorb much of the pressure exerted by the rescuer. It can also make it difficult to achieve full release.

1 Kneel beside the casualty and place the heel of one hand in the center of the victim's chest. (Do not apply pressure to the upper abdomen or the bony sternum (breastbone.)

3 Place the heel of your first hand on top of the other hand and interlock the fingers. Keep the fingers off the chest so that the pressure is applied through the heel of the hand directly on the center of the chest.

4 Lean over the casualty, and with your arms straight press down vertically to depress the breastbone about 1.5–2 inches (4–5 cm). Release the pressure without removing your hands but ensuring that you allow the rib cage to fully expand (this allows the heart to expand, sucking in more blood).

5 Repeat for 30 compressions, aiming at a rate of about 100 compressions a minute.

Figure 20-2 chest compressions.

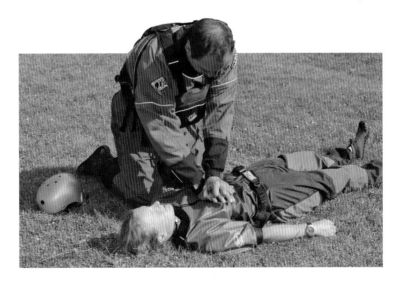

▶ **FULL CPR**—Combining chest compressions with rescue breathing:

1 Compressions and ventilations are combined at a ratio of 30 compressions to 2 breaths.

2 Stop only if the victim shows signs of breathing normally.

3 If more than one first aider is present, one should rest and one perform CPR, swapping every 2 minutes.

Cardiopulmonary Resuscitation consists of chest compressions combined with rescue breathing. The casualty is given thirty chest compressions to pump the oxygenated blood around the system so that it reaches the vital organs, followed by two breaths of air to re-oxygenate the blood.

Drowning

In a whitewater environment we are more likely to have to intervene in a drowning situation. To be technically correct, drowning is what occurs if the victim doesn't survive. If the victim does survive the medical term for what occurs is "near drowning." The reason why many people do survive near drownings is that the human body is capable of a number of remarkable reflexes.

▶ **DRY DROWNING**—The vast majority of both drowning and near drowning victims have little water in their lungs. In a last desperate attempt to survive, the human body will cause muscles in the throat to spasm and block the airway. The victims do not so much drown as suffocate. Blowing air into the victim's lungs (rescue breathing) will of itself open the casualty's air passage.

▶ **WATER IN THE STOMACH**—Due to the effects of dry drowning most of the water that the victim swallows goes into the stomach. During or after resuscitation, rescuers should not attempt to squeeze or in any other way force the water out. The danger is that this water is accidentally aspirated into the lungs.

▶ **MAMMALIAN DIVING REFLEX (MDR)**—This reflex usually occurs in very cold water and mostly affects children and fit young adults. As well as the throat constricting, the victim's heartbeat slows down to an imperceptible one beat a minute or less. The majority of the cardiovascular system is shut down and what oxygen there is in the bloodstream is diverted to the vital organs, particularly the brain.

Often referred to as the "golden hour"

The norm is that permanent brain damage occurs to the brain after the casualty has stopped breathing for four minutes. There have been rare instances of people who have been submerged in icy water for three hours, being resuscitated and making a complete recovery. The norm for rescue teams is to assume that a person submerged in cold water has a chance of survival for up to one hour.

▶ **SECONDARY DROWNING**—Anyone who has been the victim of a near drowning must be admitted to hospital for tests and observation as soon as possible. This is the case even if the victim feels fine and is convinced that he has fully recovered.

The human body deals with any water that does get into the lungs by absorbing it into the bloodstream. This leads to dangerous, often lethal, complications, chief among which are:

1 **Chemical imbalances in the bloodstream which can cause vital organs to malfunction**

2 **Water seeping back into the lungs (usually while the victim is asleep)**

3 **Swelling and subsequent blocking of the air passages caused by the lung tissue being irritated by water**

4 **The possibility of pneumonia developing extremely rapidly (it can happen in 2 hours!)**

Whitewater Issues

There are a number of factors that affect whitewater paddlers where resuscitation is involved, that are not tackled on standard first aid courses. These are:

- **The effect of the elements**
- **The effects of cold water immersion in a near drowning situation**
- **The decisions faced by rescuers who may be several hours or even days away from expert medical assistance**

▶ **VITAL SIGNS**—The effects of cold on a casualty's body and the effects of wind, rain or noise in a whitewater environment conspire to make checking for breathing and pulse more difficult. The guidelines suggest that we take no more than ten seconds to check for signs of breathing.

Trials suggest that most people are not very good at taking a pulse or looking for signs of circulation, which makes them unwilling to start CPR. For this reason the new protocols rely solely on the absence of breathing when it comes to deciding whether to start resuscitation. However in remote situations it will be helpful if you can take a pulse when deciding whether or not to stop giving CPR (see below).

▶ **DRY DROWNING**—Whereas it is not possible to carry out chest compressions until the victim can be laid out on a firm surface on the river bank, it is possible to perform rescue breathing while in a raft, an open canoe or wading in the shallows. In such a situation it will do no harm to open the airway, give up to five breaths and then head for the shore.

▶ **MAMMALIAN DIVING REFLEX**—Many people worry about starting CPR, when because of MDR the heart is still beating, albeit very slowly. However, the advice currently available is that if the casualty does not start breathing within five rescue breaths we commence CPR and that this will not have an adverse effect.

▶ **HYPOTHERMIA**—If you witness someone fall into a cold river and the person has stopped breathing when you pull him out, you should work on the assumption that he needs resuscitation, no matter how cold he is.

If someone has been in the water for many hours, for example if you found someone floating in the water and had no idea how long they had been there, they showed no signs of life and were very cold, you would assume they are deeply hypothermic.

If a casualty showed signs of hypothermia and then deteriorated to the point where they stopped breathing, you should assume that this is due to deep hypothermia.

In the case of deep hypothermia you do not start resuscitation as this will pump cold blood to the vital organs. Resuscitation should take place in a hospital as part of the rewarming process. Remember— they are only dead when they are warm and dead. Don't give up, get them to a hospital.

▶ **REMOTENESS**—In a first aid context, remoteness is defined as being more than thirty minutes from help.

If someone's heart stops beating it is extremely unlikely that it can be restarted without specialist medical attention. Anyone who has a cardiac arrest in a remote situation is unlikely to survive despite the best efforts of first aiders. This does not mean that we should not attempt basic life support. Rescue breathing is often successful and CPR may succeed. We might get lucky and help may arrive sooner than expected or from an unexpected quarter. It is also important to try for the future mental well-being of the rescuers.

The normal advice given to first aiders is to carry on performing CPR until expert medical help arrives or the first aider is too exhausted to continue. There are two reasons why a decision to stop CPR could be made:

1 **The safety of the rest of the party is threatened, e.g. by the onset of hypothermia or approaching darkness.**

2 **CPR is not keeping the victim alive.**

Legally, only a doctor of medicine can declare a person dead. However, as laymen we may have to make the reasonable assumption that someone is dead. It would be reasonable to assume death if:

1 **The victim has sustained injuries that are incompatible with life. To give an extreme example, if someone's head was severed it would be reasonable to assume that he was dead.**

Or:

2 **There was a complete absence of signs of life. This would mean:**

   • **No breathing—for a prolonged period**

   • **No pulse—for a prolonged period**

   • **Completely dilated pupils and "glassy" eyes**

   • **No reaction of the eyes to a light source**

In a wilderness situation where there is no prospect of help arriving within a reasonable time, most sources seem to agree that CPR should be stopped if there is no sign of life after thirty minutes.

Key Points

1 **Most victims who survive a near drowning still have a heart beat.**

2 **If the throat has constricted, the act of opening the airway by removing any debris, tilting the head back and giving the first breath or two of rescue breathing is the action that is most likely to save the casualty's life.**

If you are ever unlucky enough to come across a resuscitation situation, you must be mentally prepared for the fact that the odds are against the victim. This means that the odds are that the victim will die. If he does it will not be your fault! Anything you do will give the victim more of a chance than he would have otherwise had.

▶ **PRACTICE**—Like a good deal of first aid, it isn't what you know that saves lives, it's what you do. Rescue breathing and CPR are skills, and skills need to be practiced if they are to remain effective. Keep your resuscitation skills up to date and organize sessions using practice mannequins.

> ## KEEP YOUR RESUSCITATION SKILLS UP TO DATE

HEALTH WARNING

THESE BASIC LIFE SUPPORT PROTOCOLS ARE BASED ON THE GUIDELINES PROVIDED BY THE RESUSCITATION COUNCIL (UK) which are based on the document "*2005 International Consensus on Cardiopulmonary Resuscitation and Emergency Cardiovascular Care Science with Treatment Recommendations (CoSTR)*", published in November 2005.

The main changes are aimed at simplifying the protocols in the hope that they will be easier to remember and that people will be more likely to attempt. Because adults who suffer from a heart attack have plenty of oxygen in the blood stream for up to five minutes after cardiac arrest, the resuscitation sequence starts with compressions.

Although they acknowledge that drowning is different (ventilation being essential) and suggest a more appropriate protocol (used in this chapter), they recommend that in order not to confuse people "This modification should be taught only to those who have a specific duty of care to potential drowning victims (e.g. lifeguards)."

THIS MEANS THAT MANY FIRST AID PROVIDERS MAY NOT BE TEACHING THE BEST WAY TO DEAL WITH A NEAR DROWNING VICTIM! SO CHECK THE SYLLABUS BEFORE ENROLLING IN A COURSE.

CHAPTER 21
Moving Casualties

When deciding how and whether to evacuate or even move a casualty there are a number of important considerations:

1. Is it necessary to move the casualty at all?
2. What are the nature of the injuries?
3. What resources are available?
4. How far does the casualty have to be transported?
5. Over what sort of terrain?

Guidelines

The following guidelines may help:

- **Don't move the casualty without good reason.**
- **Unless in imminent danger— assess casualty first.**
- **Stop bleeding and immobilize fractures before moving.**
- **Use most efficient method time allows.**

- **Plan movement.**
- **Leadership/teamwork.**
- **Communication—with casualty—with team.**
- **Keep monitoring casualty.**
- **Involve the casualty as much as possible.**
- **Be gentle but firm.**

To Move or Not to Move

If the emergency services can get to and stabilize the casualty with their specialist equipment and skills, there may be no point moving the casualty at all.

DON'T MOVE THE CASUALTY WITHOUT GOOD REASON

Possible reasons for moving a casualty are:

▶ **IMMEDIATE DANGER**—The casualty is in immediate danger, e.g. of being washed away or sliding down a slippery bank. This is the one case in which it may be necessary to move a casualty before he has been examined.

▶ **SHELTER FROM THE ELEMENTS**—Except on remote rivers where the nearest road is some way off, or dense forest would make a helicopter evacuation dangerous, this is the most likely reason for moving a casualty. If a casualty's injuries have been treated and his condition is stable the greatest threat is posed by the onset of hypothermia. Therefore moving a casualty a short distance to a sheltered, comfortable spot is well worth the effort. In a hot climate you may need to move the casualty to a cool, shady spot.

 **IF A CASUALTY MUST BE MOVED,** UNLESS THERE IS IMMINENT DANGER HE SHOULD BE CHECKED FOR INJURIES AND THE INJURIES STABILIZED FIRST.

Casualty Assessment

Apart from the need to identify and treat injuries, a proper casualty examination will enable rescuers to make decisions about how to move the casualty. This is because we can divide serious injuries into two types:

1 Injuries which require urgent surgical intervention if the casualty is to survive. Speed of evacuation is the priority.

2 Injuries which have been stabilized or are by their nature stable but which could deteriorate if the casualty is badly handled. Careful casualty handling is the priority.

The question is whether we "stay and play, or load and go?"

SPEED—Injuries that would come into this category include:

- Serious head injuries
- Internal injuries
- Chest injuries where the lung or lungs are damaged
- Any injuries where the casualty is going deeper into shock

CARE—Injuries that would come into this category include:

- Spinal injuries (back), (suspected or diagnosed)
- Spinal injuries (neck), (suspected or diagnosed)
- Any major fracture, such as a pelvis or femur, including those where shock is present but not worsening

Stabilizing the Casualty

Any treatment that stops bleeding, prevents further damage occurring and relieves pain should be carried out before moving a casualty. The aim is to stabilize the casualty's condition so that he doesn't continue to deteriorate during transport.

Moving the Casualty

The details of how the casualty is moved will be dictated by the nature and location of the injuries, the number of rescuers available and the type of terrain. If the injury is to the spine, only a rigid stretcher is appropriate, even though this will entail waiting for one to arrive, or spending some time manufacturing one. If the injury does not involve the casualty's legs and speed is of the essence, it may be best if he walks out.

▶ **PLAN MOVEMENT**—Whoever is going to coordinate moving a casualty should take time out to plan while the casualty is being stabilized. This is true even if the distance involved is only a few feet. In the case of a full evacuation, rescuers should be delegated to scout and mark a route.

This is definitely a situation where most people, not least the patient, will be reassured by a decisive/formal leadership style.

▶ **LEADERSHIP/TEAMWORK**—When evacuating an injured person, it is essential that there is a plan and that everyone knows what it is. Once again, everyone must know:

1 **Who their boss is**.

2 **What their job is**.

If a long stretcher-carry is necessary, the leader must not allow any of the rescuers to perform heroics. If there are enough rescuers, the people performing the carry should change over frequently; alternatively the team should rest frequently.

▶ **COMMUNICATION**—Teamwork is only possible if the task is clearly understood and timing is coordinated. Instructions to other members of the team should be clear and concise. Team members should acknowledge that they have understood or make it clear that they have not understood.

It is equally important to communicate with the casualty. Apart from reassuring him and letting him know what is going on, it offers him the opportunity to be of assistance or provide valuable feedback.

▶ **MONITORING**—Whoever first established a rapport with the victim should stay at the victim's head and monitor his progress throughout the evacuation. With seriously injured people, vital signs should be monitored every five minutes. This is not as much of a nuisance as it sounds as the rescuers carrying the stretcher will need to rest frequently. Nonetheless, such frequent monitoring may not be practical. The first aider may have to settle for frequently monitoring the airway and recording the other signs regularly, but at greater intervals, perhaps every ten or fifteen minutes.

A combination approach is often best. The first aider may say to the casualty: "If I support your injured leg, do you think you can get yourself onto the stretcher?"

▶ **INVOLVE THE CASUALTY**—Casualties should be encouraged to do as much of the moving as possible for themselves. Why risk a back strain lifting a casualty onto a stretcher when he can get on it himself? Another reason is that the casualty can feel which is the least painful way to move.

> ▶ **HANDLING** — When handling the casualty the rescuers must be gentle but firm. The casualty will not be pleased if he is dropped because someone didn't get a good grip, even if it was because they were worried it might hurt him. Equally, his sense of well-being will not be enhanced if he believes himself to be at the mercy of a bunch of clumsy sadists.

Carrying Techniques

> **HEALTH WARNING**
>
> **ALL OF THE FOLLOWING TECHNIQUES COULD RESULT IN A BACK INJURY** TO THE RESCUER IF THEY ARE CARRIED OUT INCORRECTLY OR INAPPROPRIATELY. ANYONE WITH A HISTORY OF BACK INJURIES SHOULD INFORM THE LEADER SO THAT HE CAN BE DELEGATED TO PERFORM A TASK THAT DOES NOT INVOLVE LIFTING. SINGLE PERSON CARRIES SHOULD ONLY BE ATTEMPTED ON CASUALTIES THAT ARE LIGHTER THAN THE RESCUER. ALL LIFTS MUST BE COORDINATED & THE COORDINATOR MUST ENSURE THAT EVERYONE HAS **BENT KNEES & A STRAIGHT BACK BEFORE GIVING THE ORDER TO LIFT.**

> ▶ **WALKING WOUNDED** — Depending on the nature of the injuries it may be possible for casualties to walk. It is worth asking casualties if they think they can walk. Injured people will often fall prey to victim mentality and just do as they are told. It may not occur to them to offer to walk. A rescuer can be placed on either side of a victim, providing or ready to provide support if necessary.

> ▶ **DRAGGING** — If a rescuer or even a couple of rescuers need to move a heavy casualty, this may be their only option. That said, dragging a person carefully will cause him far less pain and damage than carrying him badly. Providing the ground is not too rough it supports the casualty and keeps the spine straight.

> ▶ **INLINE DRAG** — This is usually used as a way to protect a casualty's C spine (something to be wary of with unconscious victims) while moving them through the shallows to the bank. Although very hard work it can be used on dry land.

Figure 21-1 inline drag. The rescuer's hands pull on the PFD while his forearms keep the victim's helmet wedged tight, thus holding his head still and protecting his head.

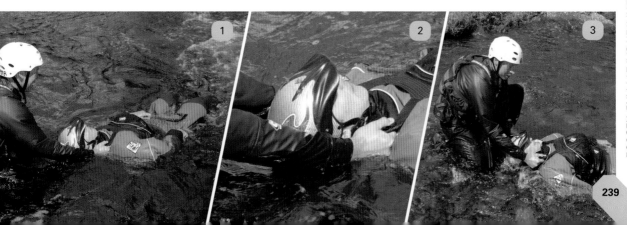

1   2   3

Figure 21-2
four hand seat.

▶ **THREE PERSON DRAG**—One rescuer supports and protects the neck. The other two grab a PFD shoulder strap each and pull evenly.

▶ **SEAT CARRIES**—These are particularly useful with conscious casualties who have lower limb injuries.

▶ **FOUR HAND SEAT**—Two rescuers grip each other's hands as shown in the photo to make a seat. The casualty sits on the seat with an arm over each of the rescuer's shoulders. Quick, simple, and suitable for a short carry.

▶ **BOSUN'S CHAIR**—A pole or paddle is supported by nylon tape slings supported over two rescuers' shoulders. This provides a sturdy seat leaving the rescuers' hands free to support the casualty. A better choice if longer distances are involved.

▶ **FIREMAN'S LIFT**—The fireman's lift is not particularly comfortable for the victim but is very effective. It is a good choice if the casualty needs to be moved urgently over terrain where dragging is not feasible or the injuries do not require careful handling. This technique does involve some risk to the rescuer and should not be attempted by anyone with a history of back injuries.

▶ **PIGGYBACK CARRY**—Useful for carrying a person with a lower leg injury over broken terrain.

Figure 21-3 (top)
bosun's chair.

Figure 21-4 (bottom
left) fireman's lift.

Figure 21-5 (bottom
right) piggyback.

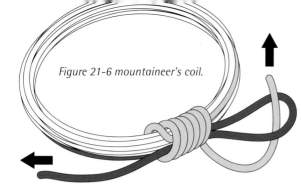

Figure 21-6 mountaineer's coil.

▶ **SPLIT ROPE CARRIES**—First of all, the rope used must be coiled using a method that mountaineers call a "classic coil." A full arm's span length of rope is measured and coiled. The action is repeated until all the rope is coiled. The coil is then tied off as shown in Figure 21-6. The size of coil thus formed is perfect for a single person carry. For a double person carry the coils are longer. The rope will have to be padded for the casualty's comfort.

▶ **SINGLE PERSON CARRY**—The coils of rope are split into two and the casualty puts one leg through each of the two sets of coils. The rescuer then carries the casualty using the coils as if they were rucksack straps.

▶ **TWO PERSON CARRY**—The coils are once again split into two. This time, each of the two rescuers wears one set of coils over one shoulder. The casualty is then carried as if he were sitting on a swing.

Figure 21-7 (left) single person split carry.

Figure 21-8 (right) two person split carry.

▶ **LITTERS**—Litters are quick and simple to make but do not provide the same splinting effect as a rigid stretcher. They would do for a hypothermia victim but would be useless for a victim with spinal injuries or a broken femur. Camping mats or PFDs should then be used to pad and insulate the litter.

▶ **BIVOUAC BAG LITTER**— Items required:
- **One 6.6 x 3.3-foot (2 x 1 m) polythene bivouac bag**
- **Six half-fist sized pebbles**
- **Six short pieces of cord**

Pebbles are inserted into the bag so that there is one in each corner and one half-way down each side of the bag. The pebbles are given a couple of twists so that the nearby polythene is wrapped around them. The string is used to tie the bag so that the pebbles remain in place, forming a kind of handle.

Figure 21-9 bivouac bag litter.

▶ **POLE & JACKET LITTER**—Items required to make this litter:

- **Two poles (the two halves of a sectioned open canoe pole are ideal)**
- **Four or five jackets or light-weight water-proof parkas**

The arms of the jackets are turned inside out so that they are inside the jacket and the poles fed through them.

▶ **RIGID STRETCHERS**—The best rigid stretchers are those that are specially made. However it is possible to make a rigid stretcher by constructing a framework of poles using "square lashings" to hold the structure together.

If carrying a casualty any distance on a stretcher, it is important to follow these guidelines:

1 **Ensure that the casualty is well padded and insulated.**

2 **Ensure that the casualty is securely fastened to the stretcher with a series of straps. The casualty should be so well secured that, if he were to vomit, it would be possible to protect his airway by turning the stretcher on its side without the casualty falling out of the stretcher.**

3 **Monitor the casualty at all times.**

▶ **UNCONSCIOUS CASUALTIES**—When paramedics prepare to evacuate an unconscious casualty, they may decide to intubate the patient, i.e. protect the casualty's airway by inserting a tube down it. This option is not available to first aiders who have not been specifically trained to do this.

The other approach is to load the casualty onto the stretcher in the Safe Airway Position (SAP). Plenty of padding (air bags can be useful here) and strapping will have to be used to keep the casualty securely in position.

Spinal Injuries

If spinal injuries are suspected it is best not to move the casualty at all if possible. However, if hazards or the presence of other life-threatening injuries dictate that movement is necessary, rescuers should not hesitate.

When moving a person with suspected spinal injuries the aim is to keep the whole of the spine, including the neck in a straight line. Bending or twisting must be avoided. Keep the casualty's nose in line with the center of his chest, in line with his groin.

Tilting the head far enough back to open an airway should not do any further harm provided care is taken to avoid any sideways movement or twisting. The jaw thrust is a better option for opening the airway in this situation. His head should be immobilized using plenty of padding.

A casualty with spinal injuries is normally left lying on his back. However, if the casualty is unconscious and there isn't the means to intubate him, he will have to be placed in a slightly modified Safe Airway Position. As much padding as possible is used to prop the casualty up in such a way that his spine is kept in as straight a line as possible.

▶ **SPINAL LOG ROLL**—This is a useful technique if a casualty needs to be turned over, to inspect or treat other injuries.

1 The first aider, who will coordinate the roll, holds the casualty's head firmly between his hands.

2 As many people as possible kneel down to one side of the casualty. They then lean across the casualty and grab hold of his clothing.

3 On the first aider's instruction every one pulls steadily on the casualty so that he rolls over towards them.

4 In this position the casualty's back can be checked/treated and insulation placed between him and the ground before he is rolled back onto it.

Figure 21-10 spinal log roll used to insulate a casualty from the ground.

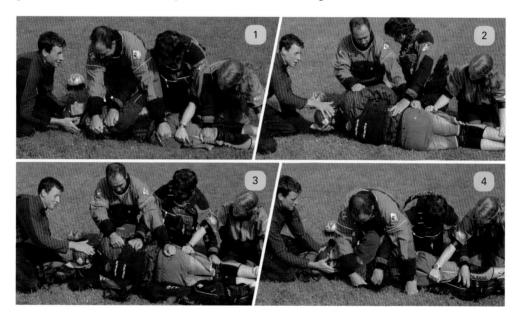

▶ **HANDS-ON CARRY**—This is a good technique for moving a badly injured person a short distance, either to get him out of the water or to a more sheltered location. It is also a good way to load people onto a stretcher.

1 The first aider, who will coordinate the lift, holds the casualty's head firmly between his hands.

2 As many people as possible squat each side of the casualty, reach under his body and grab a handful of clothing.

3 On the first aider's instruction "lift," everyone stands up straight.

4 The casualty is moved the short distance required, slowly and carefully.

5 At the required place the first aider gives the instruction "lower" and the team all squat and gently lower the casualty to the ground.

HEALTH WARNING

IF A PERSON IS BADLY INJURED, A HANDS-ON CARRY IS FAR MORE SUITABLE THAN ANY FORM OF NON-RIGID LITTER/STRETCHER.

Lower Leg Injuries

With upper limb injuries, the casualty will nearly always hold the injured limb in the position of most comfort. With lower limb injuries the casualty may not be able to do this unaided. A first aider may need to straighten an injured leg to reduce pain and prevent further injury or to make it physically possible to load the casualty onto a stretcher.

Do not straighten knee injuries or fractures where the bone is sticking out through the skin (compound fractures).

The first aider will need to get a firm hold and apply traction while straightening the limb into its anatomically normal position. One of the easiest ways to splint a leg is to strap it to the good leg. However, if the casualty is unconscious it will make it easier to load the casualty onto the stretcher in the SAP if the leg is splinted and kept separate from the other leg.

CHAPTER 22

Post Traumatic Stress

In recent years there has been a growing acceptance that members of emergency services who come face-to-face with horrific accidents can become overwhelmed by the psychological stresses involved. If suitable steps are not taken to help these people deal with these stresses a condition that is now known as Post Traumatic Stress Disorder can develop.

What is not so well recognized is the fact that anyone involved in an accident can find themselves in this position. This includes:

- **Victims**
- **Rescuers (whether members of the party or outsiders)**
- **Anyone who witnessed the accident or its aftermath**

POST TRAUMATIC STRESS DISORDER CAN ONLY OCCUR FOLLOWING A TRAUMATIC EVENT. MOST SURVIVORS, ALTHOUGH INITIALLY AFFECTED, DO NOT DEVELOP PTSD

Sources of Stress

The sources of the stresses involved can be divided into those caused by the accident itself and those that are hidden.

▶ **ACCIDENT STRESSES**—These can be caused by a number or combination of factors:

- **The sights, sound or smells associated with the accident**
- **The fact that the casualty may die**
- **The sheer physical effort required**
- **A feeling of helplessness induced by the enormity of the task or the inadequacy of the resources**
- **Enforced periods of inactivity such as when waiting for the first aider to do his bit or awaiting the arrival of the emergency services**

▶ **HIDDEN STRESSES**—These can range enormously, from the fact that the rescuer is already burdened with sufficient stresses from his everyday life, to his perceptions as to what can and can't be reasonably achieved by the rescuers.

Possible hidden stresses are:

- **Personal, financial or legal problems at home**
- **Pressures of work**
- **The rescuer being already weakened by illness or fatigue**
- **Unrealistic optimism on the possibility of a successful outcome**
- **A perception that the rescuer failed because he was not up to the task**
- **A perception that the rescue failed because other members of the team were not up to the task**

Normal Reactions

Everyone who has to deal with a bad accident will react to the stresses of the situation. These reactions are normal and should be recognised as such. Recognizing and accepting these reactions as normal is an important part of dealing with the aftermath of trauma.

▶ **IMMEDIATE REACTIONS**—These can be divided into emotional reactions, thinking (cognitive) difficulties and physical (physiological) signs and symptoms.

▶ **EMOTIONAL REACTIONS**—These may include all or any of:

- **Anxiety**
- **Apprehension**
- **Hopelessness and despair**
- **Doubting one's own abilities**

Many people also experience "dissociation." This is a defense mechanism where people block out their emotions and only allow the logical part of their brain to surface. It is a useful defensive tactic that many professional rescuers consciously develop.

DISSOCIATION CANNOT BE KEPT UP INDEFINITELY. AS SOON AS THE EMERGENCY IS DEALT WITH, EMOTIONS MUST BE ALLOWED TO RUN THEIR COURSE.

▶ **THINKING DIFFICULTIES**—Typical among these would be difficulty making decisions, difficulty concentrating and forgetting where one has just put something.

▶ **PHYSICAL SIGNS & SYMPTOMS**—The physical signs and symptoms usually fade away within a day or two but the underlying emotional cause cannot be ignored. The following are often reported:

- **A pounding sensation in the heart**
- **Nausea**
- **Headaches**
- **Muscles trembling**
- **Sweating profusely**
- **Cramps**
- **Chills**
- **Muffled hearing**
- **TATT (Tired All The Time)**

▶ **DELAYED REACTIONS**—Delayed reactions may occur a few hours or many years after a traumatic event. Once again this is perfectly normal and most people are able to work through these reactions. Reactions may be inward, that is suffered by the individual, or outward, that is directed at other people.

Inward reactions may include:

- **Feelings of guilt**
- **Apathy**
- **Depression**
- **Nightmares**
- **Insomnia**
- **Headache**
- **Loss of appetite**
- **Nausea**

Outward reactions may include:

- **Irritability**
- **A tendency to "flare up" easily**
- **Anger**

▶ **ABNORMAL REACTIONS**—Taking various forms, ranging from an immediate and complete mental breakdown, the signs of which are usually clear for all to see, to PTSD which can easily go undiagnosed. Superficially the victim may appear to be coping.

Post Traumatic Stress Disorder

If an individual is unprepared, unsupported and unable to undergo the normal reactions to traumatic stress, PTSD may develop.

Diagnosis

The table in Figure 22-1 (page 248) the criteria that are most widely used for the diagnosis of PTSD. These were developed by the American Psychiatric Association and are from their *Diagnostic and Statistical Manual* (DSM-IV).

The criteria that must be met are split into the following areas:

▶ **EXPOSURE TO AN ABNORMALLY STRESSFUL SITUATION**—It is important to realize that one doesn't have to be the victim of an accident to be a victim of PTSD.

▶ **RE-EXPERIENCING SYMPTOMS**—These are sometimes known as intrusive symptoms. The person experiencing them is unable to control when, where or in what form he is forced to relive the experience.

▶ **AVOIDANCE SYMPTOMS**—It is usually the victim's family and friends who are more aware of and likely to complain about these.

▶ **INCREASED AROUSAL**—The soldier's illustration of a startle response is the person who dives for cover when a car backfires. Another form of increased arousal is that the victim's family complains of how irritable the victim has become.

> **CRITERIA FOR DIAGNOSING POST TRAUMATIC STRESS DISORDER**

A Exposure to a traumatic event in which both the following were present:

i. The person experienced, witnessed or was confronted with an event(s) that involved actual or threatened death, serious injury or a threat to physical integrity.

ii. The person's response involved intense fear, helplessness or horror.

B The event is persistently experienced in one (or more) of the following ways:

i. Recurrent and intrusive distressing recollections of the event, including images, thoughts or perceptions. Note: In children there may be frightening dreams without recognizable content.

ii. Acting or feeling as if the event were recurring (includes a sense of reliving the experience, illusions, hallucinations and dissociative flashback episodes, including those that occur on awakening or when intoxicated). Note: In young children traumatic specific re-enactment may occur.

iii. Intense psychological distress at exposure to internal or external cues that symbolize or resemble an aspect of the traumatic event.

C Persistent avoidance of stimuli associated with the trauma and numbing of general responsiveness (not present before) as indicated by three or more of the following:

i. Efforts to avoid thoughts, feelings or conversations associated with the trauma.

ii. Efforts to avoid activities, places or people that arouse recollections of the trauma.

iii. Inability to recall an important aspect of the trauma.

iv. Markedly diminished interest in participation in significant activities.

v. Feeling of detachment or estrangement from others.

vi. Restricted range of affection (e.g. unable to have loving feelings).

vii. Sense of foreshortened future (e.g. does not expect to have a career, marriage, children or significant lifespan).

D Persistent symptoms of increased arousal (not present before the trauma), as indicated by two (or more) of the following:

i. difficulty in falling or staying asleep.

ii. Irritability or outbursts of anger.

iii. Difficulty in concentrating.

iv. Hypervigilance.

v. Exaggerated startle response.

E Duration of the disturbance is more than one month.

F The disturbance causes clinically significant distress or impairment in social, occupational or other important aspects of function.

Figure 22-1 DSM-IV diagnostic criteria for Post Traumatic Stress Disorder.

▶ **DURATION**—As mentioned earlier, most people show some stress-related symptoms at some time after a traumatic incident. For PTSD to be diagnosed these symptoms have to persist for over a month.

▶ **SOME DEGREE OF DISABILITY**—It is quite possible for someone to exhibit many of the symptoms and still continue to function as before. The thinking is that if there is no loss of function or disability then the person cannot be thought of as having a serious psychological disorder.

▶ **TREATMENT**—Once PTSD is diagnosed, treatment becomes the province of specialists. The role of friends, team members, leaders and family is at the preventative stage.

Prevention

Preventing what is a perfectly normal reaction to a traumatic situation from developing into Post Traumatic Stress Disorder can be approached in two phases:

1 **Preparation that can take place before a traumatic accident occurs**

2 **Team strategies that can be developed for supporting each other in the immediate aftermath of such an event**

▶ **PREPARATION**—This can take the form of appropriate training and mental preparation.

▶ **TRAINING**—Some of the most crippling symptoms that rescuers experience are those of helplessness and inadequacy when they have been unable to help the victim—often followed by a sense of guilt.

If we train and maintain our paddling, safety and rescue, and first aid skills we are better prepared in a number of ways:

1 **We are better able to offer assistance in the event of a traumatic accident.**

2 **We will, if the training is good, have a more realistic appreciation of what is and isn't possible.**

We are therefore less likely to blame ourselves if intervention is not successful or not possible.

▶ **MENTAL PREPARATION**—We need to prepare ourselves for the possibility that we may have to deal with a traumatic event in the future. We need to think about, discuss with friends and in groups at training sessions the possibility that we may have to face up to traumatic situations.

Topics that might be considered are:

1 **The fact that accidents do happen. That even if we conform to accepted safe practice we are involved in a risk sport.**

2 **The possibility that even if we are well trained and equipped, a rescue situation may develop that is beyond our resources to deal with.**

3 The fact that even if a first aider does everything that is possible, people might still die.

4 The fact that if a surgeon has no access to an operating room, or a paramedic to specialist equipment, they can do little more than a first aider can.

5 The possibility that we may see a friend, loved one or client we are responsible for who is badly injured or dead.

The very fact that these possibilities have been acknowledged and explored will lessen their impact should we be unfortunate enough to be faced with such situations.

Team Strategies

There are a number of steps that we can take as a group of paddlers, to lessen the impact of, and work through, traumatic stress.

▶ **SUPPORTIVE ENVIRONMENT**—It is important to develop a team approach to confronting problems. We need to foster an atmosphere where team members are able to discuss their emotions. In other words we need to drop this macho, "I don't like to talk about it" stuff and admit that we are only human.

Each member of the team should have the well-being of the rest of the team as their main priority.

During the Trauma

Whilst we are actually dealing with an accident there are some preventative steps that we can take if we have thought about the matter beforehand.

▶ **THE LEADER**—The leader can help protect everyone concerned in a number of ways. By standing back from the incident and keeping the whole picture in view, the leader will be able to organize the rescue more efficiently. This will lessen the effect of traumatic stress in three ways:

1 The incident will be dealt with more quickly which will benefit both the victims and the rescuers.

2 The leader can ensure that everyone has a job to do. This will help prevent feelings of helplessness and inadequacy.

3 The leader will be able to create time to keep everyone informed which will also help with feelings of helplessness.

▶ **TEAM MEMBERS**—Team members need to accept the fact that they may not be the best person to deal with a particular situation. For example it may be that the person who has been delegated to administer first aid is too emotionally involved with the accident victim. The rescuer concerned should ask the leader to delegate the first aid to someone else and be given another, equally vital job.

If a supportive atmosphere has been cultivated, the rest of the team will not see this as a weakness but as a show of strength of character. It takes strength to admit that you are not the best person for the job. The easy option would be to muddle on and hope for the best.

▶ **THE VICTIM**—The psychological well-being of the victim is dealt with in the chapter on first aid.

Debriefing

Everyone involved in a traumatic experience should realize that stress overload is almost inevitable if the accumulated emotions are not shared with others. This can be approached as individuals; it only takes someone who is a sympathetic listener to help an individual work through the emotions involved.

Full-time rescue teams are increasingly developing more structured approaches to psychological debriefing, which we would do well to adopt in the event of a traumatic accident. A typical approach would be as follows:

▶ **EXERCISE**—Within twenty-four hours the whole team takes part in some form of strenuous physical exercise. This helps flush out various fatigue and stress-related poisons that can build up in our bodies. It also relaxes the muscles and in itself provides a form of emotional outlet.

▶ **EMOTIONAL DEBRIEF**—Within one to three days, the whole team takes part in a group debrief. This is not a technical debrief. Everyone who was present at the traumatic event should take the opportunity to describe their feelings and emotional reactions to the event. Everyone present should be encouraged to share their emotions honestly and without embarrassment in a supportive and non-judgmental atmosphere.

The debrief should take place without alcohol being consumed, as mind altering drugs of any kind will lessen the effectiveness of the session. After these two sessions everyone involved should eat and rest well.

▶ **TECHNICAL DEBRIEF**—Only after the emotional and physical well-being of the team has been assured should any technical debrief take place. After a period of ten to fourteen days has elapsed, it is possible to analyze an incident and learn from the inevitable mistakes without the people involved feeling emotional and defensive.

Dealing with the Press

The press can become a major source of stress in itself. Most large organizations have a laid down procedure which they adopt in the event of a serious incident.

When dealing with the press, the following steps could be adopted by any group of people:

1 Appoint a press officer.

2 Prepare a press release.

▶ **THE PRESS OFFICER**—Ideally this will be someone who was not directly involved in the incident. That way the person concerned only has to deal with the stress of dealing with the Press. This will make it easier for him to think clearly and calmly.

Another advantage is that if the press officer is asked for the gory details that are not included in the prepared statement, he can in all honesty reply that he doesn't know and cannot give any further details at this time.

▶ **THE PRESS RELEASE**—If reporters are told nothing at all, they will simply make something up and attribute it to "local sources." Worse still, they may harass people who were involved in the incident or their relatives.

It is far better to give them something to be going on with. The advantage of issuing a press release is that the bare facts of the situation can be outlined in black and white. This effectively denies the less responsible members of the media the opportunity to write works of fiction.

Seeking Professional Help

If an incident has been particularly traumatic, it may well be worth considering the use of professional counselors to help with group and individual debriefs. Families, friends and team members can help individuals by simply being available and good listeners.

However, if an individual's reactions go beyond what is normal or show signs of developing into Post Traumatic Stress Disorder it is essential that he seeks professional help.

SECTION 4 ACCESS AND RECOVERY

CHAPTER 23

Specialist Equipment

As discussed earlier in the book, the vast majority of rescue and kayak recovery situations can be easily dealt with if each member of the team carries a throw bag, a knife, an 8-foot (2.5 m) sling and two karabiners. However, there are a number of situations in which more specialist equipment may be required:

1 The forces exerted on a broached raft or open canoe can be so great that pulleys are required to gain sufficient mechanical advantage.
2 Kayakers paddling in very small groups may need to employ mechanical advantage to make up for lack of numbers.
3 In steep-sided gorges, or other places where access may be only possible from above, the ropes we use for throw lines are totally inadequate.

Groups covered by situations one and two should consider carrying the following additional equipment:

- **Two pulleys**
- **A few extra screwgate karabiners (one per person in a small group and one between two people in a large group)**
- **Three prussik loops or specialist rope jamming/camming devices**
- **Two or more lengths of nylon tape**
- **A 150-foot (45 m) low-stretch caving or canyoning rope.**

It is best to have more than one set of specialist equipment within the team in case the boat carrying the gear is the one that gets into trouble. In situations where difficult vertical access problems are envisaged, the team should also consider adding:

- **A 150 feet (45 m) dynamic climbing rope**
- **A climbing or caving harness**
- **A figure-of-eight descender**

HEALTH WARNING

TOO MUCH EQUIPMENT CAN BECOME A HAZARD IN ITSELF, WEIGHING DOWN YOUR BOATS AND GETTING IN THE WAY. UNLIKE RESCUE TEAMS, PADDLERS RUNNING WHITEWATER NEED TO ADOPT A MINIMALIST APPROACH.

Low Stretch versus Dynamic Ropes

There are two types of rope designed for different purposes.

▶ **LOW STRETCH ROPES**—Low stretch ropes are designed for use in situations where the loads they will bear are increased slowly and are more or less constant. They are constructed in such a way that there is very little stretch. This makes them far more suitable for hauling, lowering and tensioning than dynamic ropes.

▶ **THROW LINES**—All throw line ropes are low stretch; however, due to the fact that they are required to float they are generally made out of polypropylene. This is a material that is not as strong as other ropes and has the disadvantages of a low melting point and a tendency to abrade easily. For anything that involves rescuers being suspended over a big drop they are unsuitable. Kevlar or spectra cored ropes are as strong as caving ropes, but still have the disadvantage of a polypropylene sheath with its low melting point.

HEALTH WARNING

IF THROW LINES ARE USED IN A DIRE EMERGENCY FOR SUCH PURPOSES IT IS WORTH WETTING THE ROPES AS A PRECAUTIONARY MEASURE.

▶ **CAVING / MOUNTAIN RESCUE ROPES**—These are designed expressly for rappelling, lowering and hoisting. They are stronger, more abrasion resistant and heat resistant than polypropylene floating ropes. They are therefore the rope of choice in many recovery or vertical access situations. These ropes vary in size from 0.35 to 0.47 inches (9-12 mm).

Figure 23-1 table of comparison of rope strengths and qualities.

descript.	polyprop. throw line	spectra core throw line*	canyon	caving	caving
diameter	0.40 in. (10 mm)	0.40 in. (10 mm)	0.37 in. (9.5 mm)	0.41 in. (10.5 mm)	0.43 in. (11 mm)
type	static	static	static	static	static
static strength	2,200 lb. (1,000 kg)	4,180 lb. (1,900 kg)	4,290 lb. (1,950 kg)	5,940 lb. (2,700 kg)	6,600 lb. (3,000 kg)
strength fig. 8 knot	—	—	—	4,290 lb. (1,950 kg)	4,510 lb. (2,050 kg)
pros	cheap floats handles well non-stretch	strong floats handles well non-stretch	strong, floats abrasion resistant non-stretch	v. strong abrasion resistant non-stretch	v. strong abrasion resistant non-stretch
cons	low melt point abrades easily	low melt point abrades easily	stiff	stiff sinks	stiff sinks

*polypropylene sheathed

Caving ropes sink in water, making them unsuitable for many water-based situations.

▶ **CANYONING ROPES**—A recent development is the arrival on the scene of ropes specifically designed for the activity of canyoning. This is the descent of mountain streams by abseiling and climbing down waterfalls, stream-beds and gorges. These ropes are usually 0.37 in. (9.5 mm) in diameter and have the advantages of caving ropes with the ability to float. This combination of qualities makes canyoning ropes ideal for recovery and vertical access in a water environment.

Unfortunately these ropes are too stiff for use as throw lines.

▶ **DYNAMIC ROPES**—These are nylon ropes that are designed for use by rock climbers and mountaineers. They are designed for situations in which a rope can be suddenly shock loaded as would happen if a climber fell some distance before the rope came tight. The rope is constructed in such a way that it stretches and absorbs energy. This means that much of the energy created by a falling climber is absorbed by the rope, rather than putting a massive and sudden load on the climber and the anchors that the rope is tied off to. A dynamic rope can stretch up to a third of its original length before it would break.

These qualities make dynamic ropes the first choice where a rope is being used as an additional safety back-up, in a situation where a slip or a rope system failure could result in a serious fall. The fact that energy has to be wasted taking up the stretch in the rope means that it is not particularly suitable for most recovery purposes.

These ropes also sink, which means that they are unsuitable for most whitewater rescue situations.

▶ **FULL WEIGHT ROPES**—A full weight rope is any rope designed to be used as a single rope and is what should be used in most rescue and recovery situations. They come in a variety of diameters from 0.39 to 0.43 inch (9.8 to 11 mm); 0.39 inch ropes are lighter, smaller and almost as strong as 0.43 ropes. Their disadvantages are that they are more expensive and wear out quicker than their heavier counterparts. Full weight ropes have the symbol **1/1** on them.

▶ **HALF ROPES**—Half ropes are between 0.32 and 0.35 inch (8 and 9 mm) in diameter and have the symbol of **1/2**. As the name implies they should only be used in pairs. Those with a rock climbing background will know how and where to use them—those without should stick to full weight ropes.

Nylon Tapes

In addition to the 8 foot sewn sling discussed in Chapter 13 it is useful to have a selection of lengths of tubular nylon tape (webbing). These can be bought off the reel at any climbing shop. These can be cut in different lengths but for most purposes a couple of 16-foot (5m) lengths are most useful. Professional rescue teams use color codes so that every member of the team knows how long a given color of tape is. These are mostly used for linking a number of anchors in order to create a strong point to attach a line to. The fact that these tapes are not pre-sewn makes them slower to use but more versatile. The tape can be threaded through or passed around the anchor and then knotted to form a sling.

Figure 23-2 (left) nylon tape and (right) chained for ease of storage.

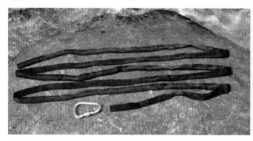 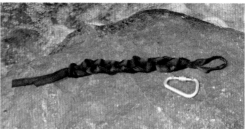

▶ **KNOTS FOR TAPE**—A simple overhand on the bight (see Appendix B) is fast and easy to tie. This knot is strong but will allow the tape to creep about 1.6 inches (4 cm) under load; it is therefore essential to leave a long tail when tying the knot. If time isn't an issue the knot of choice is the tape knot (water knot).

HEALTH WARNING

LIKE LOW STRETCH ROPES, **NYLON TAPE IS NOT** DESIGNED TO ABSORB ENERGY. IF RESCUERS TIE DIRECTLY INTO A TAPE FOR PROTECTION, THEY MUST DO SO IN SUCH A WAY THAT THE TAPE IS ALREADY UNDER TENSION & THE ANCHOR OR RESCUER CANNOT BE SHOCK LOADED. IN CERTAIN CIRCUMSTANCES A FALL OF ONLY 4 FEET (1.2 M), **CAN SNAP A FULL-WEIGHT, LOW-STRETCH ROPE OR TAPE.**

Prussik Loops

These are 3 to 4 foot (1 to 1.5 m), lengths of 0.2 in. (5mm) line tied with a Double Fishermans knot to form a sling. (Figure 23-3). These prussik loops are wrapped around a rope in such a way that a combination of friction and a camming action grip a tensioned rope. This means that ropes or slings can be attached to a rope without the use of knots.

Larger and smaller diameters of line can be used but the following must be borne in mind:

1 Smaller diameter line grips better but is less strong and therefore could fail by breaking.

2 Larger diameter line is stronger but doesn't grip well and therefore could fail by slipping.

▶ **PRUSSIK KNOTS**—There are a large number of different prussik knots of which I will describe three. They have different characteristics which between them cover every situation we are likely to use them in (see Appendix B for how to tie them).

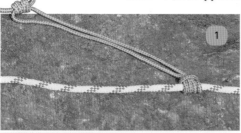

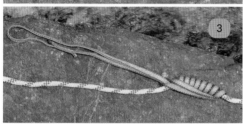

▶ **CLASSIC PRUSSIK**—This is the most reliable form of prussik in that it cannot be released once it has gripped the rope unless it is slackened off. This makes it most suitable for use wherever it is essential that the knot doesn't release once it is under load.

▶ **FRENCH PRUSSIK**—This knot grips the rope well when it is under tension and releases quickly and easily when it is not. It can be released even when it is under tension if pressure is applied on the end of the knot farthest from the anchor and pulling towards the anchor. (This is very useful in certain applications.)

The French Prussik should not be used where it might be accidentally released, for example where a rope runs over an edge.

▶ **KLEMHEIST KNOT**—This knot is useful in that it cannot be released accidentally but frees off easier than a Classic Prussik. It is also useful in that a tape sling can be used instead of prussik loops.

With any prussik, in certain conditions such as where ropes are wet or icy, it is worth putting in an extra wrap or two more than usual, to compensate for the lack of friction.

Figure 23-3 1 *Classic Prussik.*

Figure 23-3 2 *French Prussik.*

Figure 23-3 3 *Klemheist Knot.*

Figure 23-4 (bottom) dangerous misuse of a French Prussik. The critical part of the knot pushes against the rock and is released.

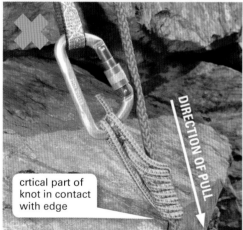

crtical part of knot in contact with edge

DIRECTION OF PULL

PRUSSIK KNOTS SHOULD NEVER BE LEFT UNATTENDED UNLESS THE ROPE THEY ARE SECURING **IS TIED OFF WITH A KNOT OR HITCH AS A SAFETY BACK-UP.**

▶ **MECHANICAL DEVICES**—There are a host of mechanical jamming and camming devices available to perform the same tasks as prussik loops. The problem is that they are all designed for fairly specific situations, uses and rope diameters. If you do use these, be sure to check that the use you are putting them to falls within the manufacturers' design specifications.

Prussik loops are lighter, cheaper and more versatile. For most recreational paddlers carrying a minimum of specialist equipment, they are a far better bet.

Pulleys

Although it is possible to set up a pulley system using karabiners instead of pulleys, much of the mechanical advantage gained is lost because of the increased friction. Pulleys developed for industrial uses are too heavy and those designed for yachting are not designed to be used in rescue situations. The pulleys that are best suited for whitewater rescue or recovery are designed for caving or mountain rescue and made of aluminum.

*Figure 23-5
1- and 2-inch (25 mm and 50 mm) swing cheek pulleys.*

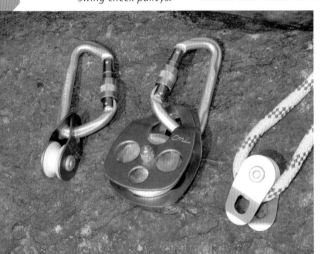

▶ **SIZE**—For most purposes 1-inch (25 mm) lightweight caving pulleys are fine. However, in situations where the pulley is going to bear high loads or where failure would be disastrous, it is better to use 2-inch (50 mm) rescue pulleys. The latter are stronger, and because of the increased radius of the pulley, less prone to twisting which can in certain circumstances damage the rope.

▶ **SWING OR FIXED CHEEK**—Most pulleys designed for rescue and recovery purposes are swing cheeked. This allows pulleys to be quickly clipped on to a line at any point, without the need to thread the whole length of the line through the pulley as would be the case with a fixed cheek pulley.

Karabiners

Most karabiners have a rating of between 4,800 and 5,500 lb. (2,200 and 2,500 kg). However, if they are loaded sideways instead of lengthways, their strength is reduced to about 1,100 lb. (500 kg).

This is also the case if the gate is open when they come under load. Therefore for any activity involving people suspended over drops it is best to use screwgate karabiners.

CHAPTER 24

Rope Dynamics

*Figure 24-1
rope damage on an
edge.*

It is essential to have an understanding of what forces are involved when we load ropes and other equipment, if we are to work efficiently and avoid disaster. The various items of climbing, caving or rescue equipment we might use are manufactured to extremely high standards, and in Europe are covered by PPE (Personal Protective Equipment) laws. When we link items together they form a chain; these links are designed to be of similar strength. Weak links can occur through poor understanding of the dynamics involved and subsequent misuse of equipment.

Due to the nature of the topic, it is important that the reader consults the diagrams closely throughout this chapter.

Ropes

The difference between static and dynamic ropes has already been explained in Chapter 23. Rope failures are rare.

▶ **EDGES**—Investigations into rope failures in both climbing and caving situations show that the most common cause is when ropes that are under tension rub on a sharp or angular edge. Ideally the rope system is set up so that the rope doesn't run over an edge—if this is not possible then the rope can be protected by:

- Padding the rope
- Padding the edge
- Improvising a roller

- Using a pulley to change the direction in which the rope travels

▶ **PAD THE ROPE**—A rope that is not being hoisted or lowered can still move enough to damage the rope. However, if the rope is limited in its movement it may be easier to pad the rope than the edge. Professional rescue teams carry rope protectors made of strips of heavy duty material.

A simple and effective alternative is to protect the rope by wrapping a few layers of repair tape around the area that needs protecting.

▶ **EDGE PADDING**—A spare article of clothing, (preferably a cheap one as it is going to get trashed), or a dry bag, can be draped over the offending edge and tied in place using any old pieces of rope. Rescue teams carry edge protectors which can be made cheaply by using old carpet squares or short sections of old fire hose.

▶ **IMPROVISED ROLLERS**—Although padding an edge prevents rope damage it also increases the friction and therefore the effort required when tensioning or hoisting a rope. Rescue teams sometimes use edge rollers to allow a rope to be run over an edge without causing damage or increasing the amount of friction.

You can improvise by tying a smooth driftwood log in position.

Figure 24-2 (left) edge padding.

Figure 24-3 (right) driftwood roller.

Knots & Hitches

A hitch can only be tied around an object, such as a karabiner. If you remove the karabiner the hitch unravels. A knot is free standing; this means that a knot can be tied with just a piece of rope.

To retain 100 percent of its original strength a rope must not be made to curve through an arc of a diameter of less than four times its own diameter. Most knots will therefore create a link in the chain that is weaker than the rope itself.

The rope is also weakened where the rope is passed around a karabiner which is only about $^3/_8$ inch (9-10 mm) in diameter. If a $^1/_2$-inch (12 mm) low-stretch rope, with a breaking strain of 8,800 lb. (4,000 kg), is tied around a karabiner with a breaking strain of 4,840 lb. (2,200 kg), it doesn't really matter if the rope loses 20 percent of its original strength as it will still be as strong as the karabiner. If, however, we are using a $^3/_8$ inch (9.5 mm) canyoning rope its breaking strain is 4,290 lb. (1,950 kg). Reduced by 20 percent it becomes 3,432 lb. (1,560 kg). While this is still more than strong enough for most situations, there are some situations where creating such a weakness in the chain would be undesirable. An example would be when rigging a high-line Tyrolean (see Chapter 26).

*Figure 24-4
the No Knot.*

▶ **NO KNOT**—When making the end of a rope fast to a large tree, the rope can be simply wrapped around the tree several times until the friction is so great that the rope is as securely tied as if a knot were used. Because the diameter of the tree is far more than four times the diameter of the rope there is no loss of strength. The other advantage is that it can, if necessary, be released even when the rope is under tension by simply unwrapping the rope and reducing the amount of friction.

▶ **OTHER KNOTS**—I have deliberately kept the number of knots used in this book to a minimum. (See Appendix B.) This is to keep things simple, quick and easier to get right in a stressful situation. Although the knots I suggest will always be suitable, there will be situations where an ideal, even better knot could be used in its place. Those who have a good working knowledge of knots should feel free to use their judgment and use any appropriate knot that they are familiar with.

Karabiners

Karabiners should be used as the link between ropes and tapes and not clipped to each other. If a twisting action is induced when a system is loaded, karabiners can be levered one against the other. The effect is similar to loading a karabiner sideways and the chain is massively weakened.

Anchors

An anchor is a strong point to which a rope is fastened. These can be strong points on a boat or raft, or trees or rocks on the bank.

▶ **ANCHOR SELECTION**—When selecting an anchor the following points should be borne in mind:

• Strength of the anchor

• Direction of pull

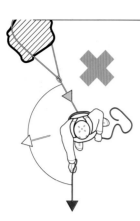

Figure 24-5
▶ *direction of pull on rope*
▷ *direction of pull on anchor*
▷ *direction of pull on belayer should form a straight line.*

▶ **STRENGTH**—Never take it for granted that an anchor is strong enough. There are three ways to inspect an anchor:

1 We can look at it. If it is a tree, is it big, is it healthy, has the root system been exposed by erosion? If it's a rock, is it large and heavy enough, does it slope in such a way that a rope would roll over it rather than stay put, has it got any sharp edges?

2 We can listen to it. If we thump it does it sound hollow?

3 We can physically test it. Push it for all you are worth! This can produce real surprises; sometimes rocks that looked "bombproof" can turn out to be precariously balanced. Boulders that appeared to be jammed solid can be moved with ease.

▶ **DIRECTION OF PULL**—It is vital that we don't lose sight of the whole picture. The strongest anchor in the world is of no use if it doesn't allow us to exert force in the required direction. When using an anchor to safeguard a belayer, the system should be set up so that the anchor, belayer and swimmer form a straight line. If this is not done, when a load is applied, the belayer will be dragged along the bank until he is in line and may get hurt or let go of the rope he is holding on to.

▶ **SINGLE POINT ANCHORS**—Are simple and quick to set up. The disadvantage is that all your eggs are in one basket. An anchor that is going to be used on its own must be 100 percent reliable, such as a large healthy tree or a massive rock.

▶ **MULTIPLE ANCHORS**—If there is the slightest doubt about the reliability of an anchor, two or more anchors should be linked together. The aim is to spread the load between the anchors.

▶ **ANGLES**—Anchors should ideally be close enough together that the angle formed between the anchors and centralized anchor point is less than 60˚. Once the angle reaches 120˚, the load is the same as if only one anchor was used. Once the angle reaches 160˚, the leverage caused by what is known as a "vector pull" is such that the force on each of the anchor points is nearly three times the force pulling on the centralized anchor point.

Figure 24-6 the effects of angles on forces.

IDEAL ANGLE OF PULL ON ANCHORS = LESS THAN 60˚

220 lb. (100 kg) 220 lb. (100 kg)	253 lb. (115 kg) 60˚ 253 lb. (115 kg)	310 lb. (141 kg) 90˚ 310 lb. (141 kg)	440 lb. (200 kg) 120˚ 440 lb. (200 kg)	440 lb. (200 kg) 160˚ 440 lb. (200 kg) 1,267 lb. (576 kg) 1,267 lb. (576 kg)
440 lb. (200 kg)	440 lb. (200 kg)	440 lb. (200 kg)	440 lb. (200 kg)	440 lb. (200 kg)

Linking Anchors

Figure 24-7 (above) a twist is put in the loop of rope or tape sling to ensure that if one of the anchors fails the karabiner will remain in the system. When the direction of pull changes the tape slides around and self-equalizes.

There are two approaches to linking anchors; each is suited to different situations.

▶ **SELF-EQUALIZING ANCHORS**—The aim here is that the load on the anchors is evenly spread even if the angle of pull varies.

Figure 24-8 (right) the painter of an open boat used to link several strong points. By using a self-equalizing technique the risk of breaking any of the anchor points is reduced.

Figure 24-9 the end of the haul rope used to make a self-equalizing system (with inset).

Self-equalizing anchors have advantages and disadvantages:

Pros:

+ This system is great when used in a situation such as hauling a wrapped boat. Here, should anything in the anchor system fail, the slack introduced would ensure that the forces on the other anchors would decrease as the boat settles back onto the rock.

Cons:

– This system should not normally be used in any situation where gravity is involved, such as raising, lowering, high-line Tyrolean, rapelling or belay ropes. This is because, should an anchor fail and slack be introduced into the system, the remaining anchor(s) will be shock loaded. The resulting forces would be far in excess of the original load.

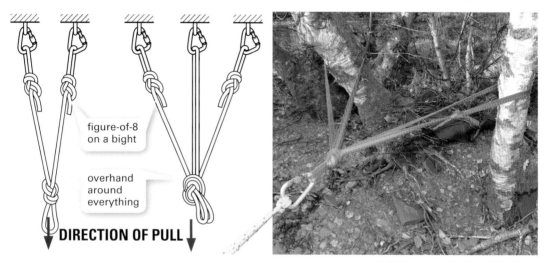

figure-of-8 on a bight

overhand around everything

DIRECTION OF PULL

Figure 24-10 (left) spare rope used to link independent anchors. (right) Two anchors independently linked using a tape sling.

▶ **LINKED INDEPENDENT ANCHORS**—The aim here is that the load is evenly spread and each anchor is entirely independent. Therefore should any anchor fail the others would not be shock loaded.

Cons – **If the direction of pull changes, the load will come on to one anchor. Therefore if there is no way to avoid the direction of pull changing, it may be better to use a self-equalising belay even in situations involving gravity.**

Figure 24-11 Italian Hitch in use.

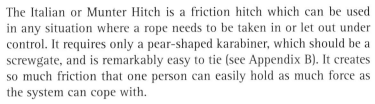

Italian Hitch

The Italian or Munter Hitch is a friction hitch which can be used in any situation where a rope needs to be taken in or let out under control. It requires only a pear-shaped karabiner, which should be a screwgate, and is remarkably easy to tie (see Appendix B). It creates so much friction that one person can easily hold as much force as the system can cope with.

Figure 24-12 Italian Hitch locked-off with two half hitches.

▶ **LOCKING OFF**—By simply holding on tight to the dead end of the rope, the Italian Hitch locks and will not allow any movement until the operator allows rope to feed through. It can be locked off by using a bight of the dead rope to tie two half hitches around the live rope. This frees the operator to perform other tasks .

As it can be easily released without losing control, a locked off Italian Hitch is an excellent way to fasten a rope that may need to be released later or in an emergency.

Mechanical Advantage

Mechanical advantage allows us to increase the amount of force that we can exert for a given amount of muscle power. However, as will become clear, there is a price to pay for these gains.

▶ **NO ADVANTAGE 1:1**—If a 220-lb. weight is to be pulled a distance of 33 feet (10 m), a force of 220 lb. will have to be applied and 33 feet of rope will pass through the rescuer's hands.

▶ **2:1 PULLEY SYSTEM**—If a 220-lb. weight is to be pulled a distance of 33 feet, a force of 110 feet (50 kg) will have to be applied but 66 feet (20 m) of rope will pass through the rescuer's hands.

Note that in a 2:1 pulley system the end of the rope is tied to the anchor and the pulley is tied to the object to be moved. If the system is rigged the other way around the pulley simply changes the direction of pull.

Figure 24-13 1:1 (no advantage).

Figure 24-14 (above)
1 *2:1.*
2 *The more parallel the ropes are kept the more efficient the pull will be.*

Figure 24-15 (above right) 3:1 pulley system.

▶ **3:1 PULLEY SYSTEM**—If a 220 lb. weight is to be pulled a distance of 33 feet, a force of 73 lb. (33.3 kg) will have to be applied but 98 feet (30 m) of rope will pass through the rescuer's hands.

▶ **4:1 PULLEY SYSTEM**—There are two ways to create a 4:1 pulley system. One involves using three pulleys and an extremely long rope, the other needs only two pulleys and works by multiplying one 2:1 system by another. The less kit we have to carry the better, so this is the one illustrated in Figure 24-19. It is known as a "pig rig" because it uses a separate rope piggybacked onto the haul rope, in this case using a French Prussik.

Practical Pulley Systems

▶ **DIRECT**—It is only possible to attach a pulley system directly to a boat if the distance involved is very short. With a 66-foot (20 m) line, a 2:1 system would have to be attached to an anchor less than 33 feet away.

▶ **"Z" DRAG**—A "Z" drag allows all but the last few feet of a rope to be used. Two prussik loops are used.

1 Prussik A is used to attach the second pulley to the rope that is being pulled.

2 Once the rope has been pulled as far as it will go, the rope is let out a few inches until the French Prussik (B) takes the strain on the live rope. (Prussik B is pushed against the pulley and releases automatically when the rope is pulled in.)

3 Prussik A is then shunted back along the live rope and the procedure started again.

If you are short of prussiks you can use a knot instead of the second prussik. However this is time consuming and frustrating as you have to keep untying and retying a knot that has been pulled very tight indeed.

Figure 24-16 "Z" drag.

Figure 24-17 (above)

① *when the line is taken in the prussik loosens and allows the rope to run.*

② *when the line is released the prussik becomes tight and holds fast.*

Figure 24-18 (left) using a single prussik and (right) a knot in place of a prussik.

▶ **PIG RIG**—A "piggyback" system allows a full rope length—or even two or more ropes tied together—to be used. It can even be used to tension one rope and then be transferred to a second rope.

locked off friction hitch

1 A rope is tied to the boat and either "no knot-ted" around a tree or attached to a karabiner with an Italian Hitch.

2 A separate pulley system is then attached to the rope using a prussik loop, (A). This example shows a 4:1 system in use, but if the force needed is less, a 3:1 or 2:1 would be more appropriate.

3 As the pulley system hauls the rope, the slack created is taken in by feeding the rope around the tree or by operating the Italian Hitch.

4 When the pulley system can go no further the strain can be taken by the "no knot" or by locking off the Italian Hitch.

5 Prussik A is then shunted back along the live rope and the procedure started again.

Figure 24-19 "pig rig" pulley system, 4:1.

A

▶ **PASSING A KNOT**—Passing a knot that has been tied to join two ropes through the system doesn't present a problem. When the knot comes up against prussik A (see Figure 24-19) the strain is taken by the Italian Hitch, allowing the prussik to be released and retied on the other side of the knot.

When the knot reaches the karabiner of the Italian Hitch, the strain is taken by the piggyback rig and the Italian Hitch is released and retied on the other side of the knot. Note that if the ropes have been joined using an overhand knot (see Appendix B), the knot can be worked through the karabiner without having to untie and retie the Italian Hitch.

Key Points:

1   If the rope that is being pulled on is tied off at the object being moved, the mechanical advantage is uneven, e.g. 1:1, 3:1.
2   If the rope that is being pulled on is tied off at the anchor, the mechanical advantage is even, e.g. 2:1, 4:1.
3   If a pulley system divides the force required by a factor of 3, it also multiplies the amount of pulling needed and the length of rope needed by a factor of 3. If you choose to use a 3:1 pulley system where you could have managed without, allowing for the extra time it takes to rig, it will probably take five times as long to get the job done.

Friction

To simplify the figures used to explain how pulley systems work, we have conveniently ignored friction. In fact, even with pulleys, we lose a little of the advantage gained. If we use karabiners instead of pulleys, a 3:1 system will in fact only have the same effect as a 2:1 system that uses a pulley.

▶ **DIMINISHING RETURNS**—Although adding extra pulleys increases the theoretical mechanical advantage, the percentage of the gain that is lost to friction also increases. If you construct a pulley system using karabiners instead of pulleys, more force is lost than gained if a system involving more than two pulleys is used.

CHAPTER 25

Recoveries

Many recovery situations are made far more difficult than they need be. It is important to remember that we are no longer in a rescue situation. We can afford to take as much time as is necessary over planning our actions. What is more, we should do so for reasons of safety as well as efficiency.

In a rescue situation we need to find the fastest solution that is within acceptable limits of risk. In a recovery situation, speed is not an issue. The solution we use must be the one that offers the least risk to those attempting the recovery.

Planning a Recovery

Once the leader has gathered the team and ensured that everyone is safe, the team will have to carry out the following tasks:

1 Assess the situation.

2 Work out which way the stuck object will have to be pushed or pulled.

3 Work out how the object will be brought to shore once it is free of the obstacle.

4 Work out how to attach lines and/or place rescuers.

5 Decide if and how any downstream hazards need to be covered.

6 Decide whether an upstream lookout is needed to warn other paddlers about lines and other hazards.

▶ **INCIDENT MANAGEMENT**—All the points covered in Chapter 18 apply. The plan must be communicated to the team. Each member of the team must be clear as to who their boss is and what their job is. Most importantly of all, it is essential that the leader does not get physically involved, and stays detached, so as to keep the whole picture in view.

If the team is very small this may not be possible. In this case leaders should allocate themselves the least involving job, with the clearest view of the whole situation.

Attaching a Line

This is the part of the operation that potentially involves the most risk to rescuers. If it is possible for a rescuer to quickly paddle, wade or swim to a point where he can easily attach a line at no risk to himself, then he should do so. However, if this involves any real risk to the rescuer another way must be found. If a safe way cannot

Figure 25-1 recovering a broached kayak.

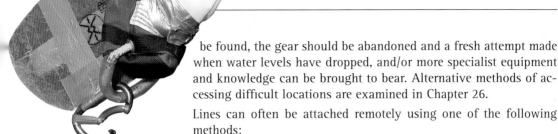

Figure 25-2 improvised paddle hook.

be found, the gear should be abandoned and a fresh attempt made when water levels have dropped, and/or more specialist equipment and knowledge can be brought to bear. Alternative methods of accessing difficult locations are examined in Chapter 26.

Lines can often be attached remotely using one of the following methods:

▶ **PADDLE HOOKS**—Paddle hooks can either be improvised as shown in Chapter 14, and don't have to be attached to a paddle. By using a canoe pole or a piece of driftwood we can extend our reach even farther.

▶ **DRIFT LINES**—A line is floated down the current in such a way that the middle of the line is caught against the object. The free end of the line is then recovered and, by pulling on both ends of the line simultaneously, the object can be moved.

▶ **WEIGHTED LINE**—As above except that the end of the line is weighted so that the line goes under the object concerned.

▶ **SINGLE LINE CINCH**—After either a drift line or a weighted line has been deployed, instead of pulling on both lines simultaneously, the bag end of the rope is clipped to the other end of the line. This is then pulled tight till the object involved is effectively lassoed.

▶ **TWO LINE CINCH**—This is the same system that is described in Chapter 16 for use in foot entrapments. It is particularly useful for recovering paddles that are snagged in midstream.

Using the Force

In this case, the forces we are concerned with are either the power of the current or gravity. If we find a way to work with, rather than against these forces we are far more likely to be successful. More often than not, if a boat can't be moved, it is because the rescuers are pulling or pushing in the wrong direction. All else being equal, it will be necessary to relieve some of the pressure between the boat and the rock, as well as pull the boat towards the bank. A good rule of thumb is to pull at an angle of 45° to the flow of the current.

▶ **OFF-CENTER BROACH**—More often than not, a boat will broach in such a way that the current exerts more pressure on one side of the boat than on the other. In Figure 25-3 (page 272) it will be easier to pull the boat off to river left so that it pivots. Less obvious is the exact direction in which the rescuers need to pull to get it to move. Some experimentation may be necessary, but taking the time to try and work it out will save a good deal of time and effort.

Figure 25-3
causing an off center
broached canoe to
pivot into the current.

▶ **CENTER BROACH**—If the current has broached a boat or raft in such a way that the pressure is exerted equally on both sides, there are a number of possible solutions:

▶ **LIFT**—It may be possible to simply reach and lift one end clear of the current or it may be effective to lift from another angle with ropes.

Figure 25-4
two lifting methods
for recovering a
broached canoe.

Photos: Whitewater
Consultancy

▶ **WEAK CURRENT**—If the current is weak, it may be possible to pull it off in either direction. In which case it makes sense to choose the side that is easiest to get to.

▶ **RAFTS**—With rafts it is possible to deliberately relieve the pressure on one side of the raft by deflating the appropriate air tubes. The advantage here is that we can choose on which side the current will exert the most pressure. This means that we can sometimes choose which bank to work on.

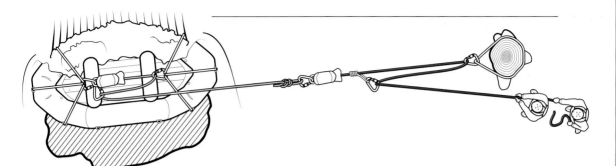

*Figure 25-5
internal "Z" drag set
up between two self-
equalizing anchors at
either end of the raft,
which is then con-
nected directly to the Z
drag on the bank.*

*Figure 25-6
a self-equalizing
anchor has been
rigged and a haul line
attached which has
reduced the sagging
of the raft around the
rock—however it may
be necessary to pull
from a different angle
to release the broach.
Bhote Khosi, Nepal.*

▶ **PEEL & PULL—**The best angle of pull on a broached raft will usually be parallel with the broach angle, sliding the raft off the obstruction. This is made a lot easier if the raft is tensioned internally with a "Z" drag so it no longer sags around the rock. An internal Z drag can be simply and effectively combined with a bankside Z drag to combine the "peel" and "pull" into one system.

Photo: www.swiftwaterrescue.at

▶ **TWO POINT BROACH—**These situations can usually be dealt with in much the same way as a one point broach. On some occasions it so happens that the easiest solution is to lift one end of the boat over one of the two objects on which it is stuck. This operation may be so simple that one rescuer can stand on the obstacle and heave the boat off.

▶ **VERTICAL PINS**—A vertical pin usually occurs because the bow of a kayak is trapped behind a small projection in a ledge. Usually all that is required is for the boat to be pulled back a short distance and then released. Once again it may be better to attach a second rope with which to recover the boat.

On the other hand it may require running a line through a pulley attached to a tree branch to change the direction of pull. A second line is also attached so that, once the end of the boat is lifted clear, the first line is let go so that the second line can be used to bring the boat into the side.

Vector Pulls

When a rope has been tensioned in an unsuccessful attempt to pull a boat off a rock and then locked off, a vector pull (simply pulling on the tensioned rope at 90° to the direction of pull) can be used to good effect. It gives two major advantages:

1 The force already being exerted on the line is multiplied by a factor of 3–4.

2 A small but significant change in the direction of pull is achieved.

Roll Over

In wrap situations, rafts and open boats offer a huge surface to the power of the water. This is particularly the case if the inside of the hull is facing upstream, trapping the power of the water.

Figure 25-7 attaching the line for a roll-over release from a broach.

If a line is attached as shown in the photos the boat can be rolled over (a roller is in itself a form of mechanical advantage), so that the bottom of the boat faces the current. When this line is pulled on, it acts as a 2:1 pulley (see Chapter 24), further increasing the mechanical advantage. Which way the boat is rolled depends on the shape of the rock that it is up against.

Figure 25-8 rolling the boat and pulling it to the side. Photos: Whitewater Consultancy

Combined Tactics

When a boat is really stuck it may be necessary to combine a number of techniques. Every situation is different, so take your time assessing the possibilities and formulating a plan. It will save you time in the long run.

Figure 25-9 line A is pulling the boat across the rock, line B is helping the boat to pivot around the rock and line C is rolling the boat.

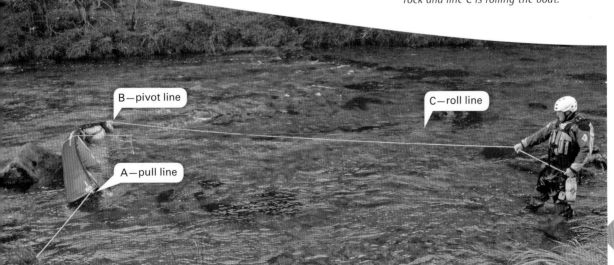

B—pivot line

C—roll line

A—pull line

CHAPTER 26
Other Access Techniques

In this chapter we will look at some techniques that might be used to gain access to a location. This may be because other, more usual (for paddlers), methods won't work or that these methods are quicker or safer.

Figure 26-1 the consequences of losing a single item of equipment halfway through a three day trip into a siphon-filled grade 5 canyon with 9,843-foot (3,000 m) walls meant that it was worth setting up a tensioned ropeway. It helped that three out of four of the paddlers are climbers and it therefore didn't take that long to set up. Colca Canyon, Peru.

Water-based Access

▶ **WADING**—If the current is not too powerful and is no more than knee deep, wading is an option. It is worth remembering that the heavier a person is, the less likely it is that the current will sweep him off his feet. There are a number of methods that can be used to improve the chances of success and to move groups of people in this way.

▶ **POLE**—A pole can be used to gain stability. The wader faces upstream and leans forward on to the pole so that a kind of tripod is formed. Only one "leg" of the tripod is moved at a time.

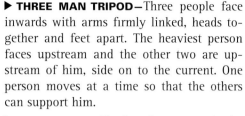

▶ **THREE MAN TRIPOD**—Three people face inwards with arms firmly linked, heads together and feet apart. The heaviest person faces upstream and the other two are upstream of him, side on to the current. One person moves at a time so that the others can support him.

▶ **LINE ASTERN**—The heaviest person in the group uses a pole and stands at the upstream end of the line. The others get in line behind him, hold the shoulder straps of the person in front of them and lean forward so as to hold the front person firmly on the river bed.

▶ **THE WEDGE**—Useful for larger groups. Once again the heaviest person stands at the upstream end and leans on the pole. This time the remainder of the group form a wedge formation. Once again everyone leans onto the person in front of them to help give them a firm footing. Heaviest people at the front, lightest at the rear.

Note that by adapting it a little, the wedge can be used to ferry a stretcher across shallows. The victim must be wearing a PFD and a helmet and must not be strapped into the stretcher.

Figure 26-2 (top) supported wading.

Figure 26-3 (middle) three man tripod.

Figure 26-4 (bottom) line astern.

Figure 26-5 (right) the wedge.

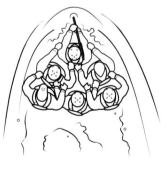

THERE IS A GOOD RULE OF THUMB WHEN DECIDING TO USE THE ABOVE GROUP TECHNIQUES, WHICH LEAVES A MARGIN FOR ERROR. ASSUME THAT **IF THE HEAVIEST PERSON IN THE GROUP CAN'T WADE ACROSS ON HIS OWN, IT IS TOO RISKY.**

Rope-assisted Access

. . . .

Figure 26-6 handrail.

I have deliberately omitted a number of roped river crossing techniques from this section. This is because I believe them to be unnecessarily risky. As paddlers we can always find another way. The two methods suggested here are useful and relatively safe.

▶ **PENDULUM TRAVERSE**—A line is rigged as for a handrail (see Chapter 14), and the wader uses it for support to wade out into the current. If he loses his footing he will be swung back into the side.

Points to note:

1 The longer the handrail the smaller the angle formed and the more support is provided.

2 The wader must not be tied into the system other than with a releasable chest harness.

▶ **TENSIONED DIAGONAL**—A line is tensioned so that it is out of the water but low enough to be easily reached by a swimmer. The angle that the rope forms in relation to the main flow must be 45° or less. Note that the diagonal can only be used to move across in one direction, downstream. To cross back again a second rope has to be rigged.

People cross by one of four methods:

1 The swimmer lies in the water on his front and, holding on with both hands, shuffles down the line allowing his body to "stream" in the current.

2 A tape sling is clipped to the line with a karabiner and the swimmer lies on his back and allows the current to ferry glide him to the far side. If the swimmer holds on with the sling over the shoulder nearest the start point, his body will assume a better ferry angle.

3 The cow's tail of a chest harness is clipped on to the rope and the rescuer surfs on his back as he ferry glides across.

4 A raft or a catamaran made by lashing two canoes together is clipped to the rope and used to ferry people across. If canoes are used they should be attached with bridles.

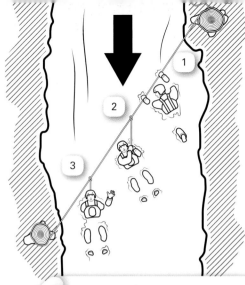

Note

If there is enough person power available, only the upstream end of the rope need be tied off. The team can then tension the rope by hauling "tug of war" fashion. When there is a lack of convenient anchors, this makes it easier to position a rope accurately enough to get a rescuer to a precise location.

Figure 26-7 tensioned diagonal.

HEALTH WARNING

IT IS NOT A GOOD IDEA TO SET UP A TENSIONED DIAGONAL ON A BEND, UNLESS YOU HAVE A GOOD EYE FOR HOW THE ANGLE OF THE MAIN FLOW CHANGES AS IT GOES AROUND THE BEND. THE ANGLE TO THE FLOW OF THE CURRENT WILL VARY AND THE PERSON CROSSING MAY FIND HIMSELF STUCK IN MIDSTREAM.

Swimming Aids

If swimming is one of the options you are prepared to consider then it makes sense to increase efficiency.

▶ **WEBS**—These are simply neoprene gloves with webbed fingers. Playboaters sometimes use them as hand paddles.

▶ **FINS**—Small fins as used by surfers can be used. Anyone planning to carry them should become well practiced in their use on a safe rapid before using them in a real rescue.

▶ **RIVER BOARDS**—These are small boards, similar to but more buoyant than the belly boards used in surf. Rafters who are not accompanied by safety kayakers should consider these for access purposes. Inflatable versions are sometimes used. People using these need fins and once again should become proficient in their use before using them in a rescue or recovery situation.

High-line Tyrolean with Tethered Raft

This is more complicated and time consuming to set up than two or four point tethered raft systems. However it does provide a great deal more control and unlike the others can be used on more technically difficult and complex rapids.

Figure 26-8 training exercise, Lower Oetz, Austria. Note the 2:1 pulley system being used which is not really necessary and requires a very long rope. Also note the stern lines to prevent the raft being pulled into the stopper. Photos: Paul O'Sullivan

Points to note:

1 **The crew must keep their weight well back so that the bow rides high and the water flows under the raft.**
2 **If this technique is used in a stopper rescue, two lines will have to be used to stop the raft being sucked in by the undertow.**
3 **The crew can use a guide's paddle to help fine-tune the positioning of the raft.**
4. **Organization and communication are the key to success.**

Vertical Access

I strongly recommend that if you do not have a climbing or caving background, you organize a training session supervised by someone who does, before attempting these techniques. Practice sessions should take place only a short distance above the ground so that if mistakes are made nobody gets hurt.

Figure 26-9 as they don't weigh all that much, getting kayaks in and out of steep places is simple.

HEALTH WARNING

WITH ALL OF THESE TECHNIQUES IT IS GOOD PRACTICE TO PROVIDE A SAFETY BACK-UP BY BELAYING THE PERSON(S) BEING LOWERED OR HOISTED WITH A SEPARATE LINE AND AN ITALIAN HITCH.

HANDRAIL LINE—When access involves descending or ascending a steep slippery bank, all that may be required is a fixed rope to hold on to and steady oneself, so that a slip does not become a fall.

Figure 26-10 (left) hand rail used to descend a steeply sloping bank.

clove hitch

figure-of-8 on a bight

Figure 26-11 (above) improvised sling chest harness.

Figure 26-12 (left) improvised sit harness. Pass the sling around like a belt, then make a third loop through the legs from the lower part of the sling behind.

Figure 26-13 (right) combined improvised full body harness.

▶ **IMPROVISED HARNESS**—The drawing shows how to make an improvised sit harness and the photos show an improvised chest harness and how to link the two to make a full body harness. The latter is particularly for raising or lowering an injured person. This is because it provides more support and helps the victim remain upright.

Lowering & Hoisting

If a rescuer needs to get to a place where vertical access is required there are a number of advantages in being lowered and hoisted by other team members:

1 The techniques involved are ones that even non-climbers will be familiar with from recovery situations.

2 The rescuer on the end of the rope has his hands free and can concentrate on the task.

▶ **2:1 LOWER/HOIST**—The rescuer is lowered using a 2:1 pulley system connected directly to his harness and hoisted using the same set up.

Pros:

+ This system is simple, quick and has the advantage of changing from a lower to a hoist with no change of the system or tying and untying of knots.

Cons:

– The disadvantage is that it can only be used if the distance is half the length of the rope or less.

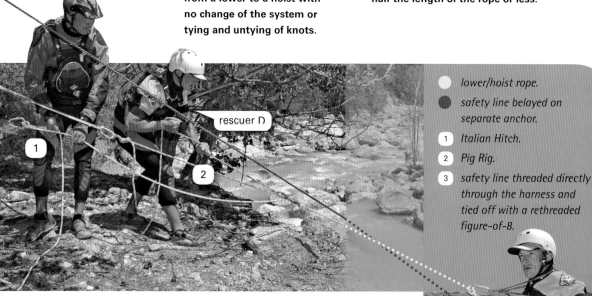

rescuer C rescuer B

rescuer D

● lower/hoist rope.

● safety line belayed on separate anchor.

① Italian Hitch.

② Pig Rig.

③ safety line threaded directly through the harness and tied off with a rethreaded figure-of-8.

Figure 26-14 pig rig used in lower/hoist system.

▶ **LOWER/PIG RIG**—In this system Rescuer A is tied to the end of a rope and lowered using an Italian Hitch by Rescuer B. When Rescuer A is in place the Italian Hitch is locked off and a piggyback rig is attached to the line with a prussik. This is then used to hoist him back up.

Pros: + Can work over more than one rope length.

Cons: – Needs at least two people to operate it (three with a safety line)

rescuer A

Description of lower and raise with a pig rig, with safety line:

1 Rescuer A is lowered by Rescuer C using an Italian Hitch on a low stretch rope (the yellow canyoning rope). At the same time Rescuer D safeguards his descent using an Italian Hitch on a dynamic safety line (the purple climbing rope).

2 When Rescuer A is ready, Rescuer B attaches a 2:1 pulley system using another low stretch rope (the yellow and red throw line) and hoists him back up. Rescuer C takes in the slack and locks off the Italian Hitch when the prussik needs adjusting and once again the safety line is operated by Rescuer D.

overhand on a bight

▶ **"Y" HANG**—If an injured person is being hoisted, a Y hang allows a rescuer to travel up with him and support him.

Figure 26-15 the end of the loop of rope created by the "Y" hang is connected via a karabiner to the casualty's harness.

Single Rope Technique

live rope

dead rope

Single rope techniques are the only methods that allow a rescuer to operate solo in a vertical access situation.

▶ **DESCENDING**—Rappelling involves the rescuer lowering himself down a fixed rope and controlling his rate of descent by means of the friction provided by an Italian Hitch, figure-of-eight descender.

Figure 26-16 rappelling on an Italian friction hitch (inset).

1 The upper hand is held loosely around the "live" rope for balance.

2 The lower hand holds the "dead" rope and controls the rate of descent by tightening or loosening its grip. Whatever happens, the abseiler must not let go with the lower hand.

Continued . . .

3 The rappeller's feet are kept flat against the rock and more than shoulder width apart so that he doesn't overbalance.

4 The descent should be made as smoothly as possible, avoiding any jumping or sudden movements that might shock-load the system.

Figure 26-17 ascending.

▶ **ASCENDING**—Ascending involves the rescuer using two prussik loops or mechanical ascenders to ascend a fixed rope. A Klemheist (see Appendix B) or Classic prussik knot is used for the knot that is attached to the harness because they do not release under load. A French prussik can be used for the stirrup, as in this case the ease of movement is an advantage.

1 He bends his knee so that the weight comes slowly on to the harness, ensuring that the harness prussik is holding before committing his weight to it.

2 While sitting in the harness he lifts his stirrup leg and slides the stirrup prussik up the rope as far as it will go.

3 The ascender stands up in the stirrup, loosens the harness prussik and slides it as far up the rope as it will go.

4 Stages 1–3 are repeated as often as is required.

IF YOU ANTICIPATE USING THESE TECHNIQUES AND DO NOT HAVE A CLIMBING OR CAVING BACKGROUND, I STRONGLY ADVISE THAT YOU GET SOME EXPERT INSTRUCTION. ALL YOUR EGGS ARE IN ONE BASKET AND A SINGLE MISTAKE **CAN BE FATAL.**

APPENDIX A
Glossary of Terms

Air Bag: a bag that is inflated with air through a valve so that it fills the unused spaces in a kayak or canoe and provides buoyancy in the event of swamping.

Backwash: the water that is flowing back into a stopper.

Bight: a loop of rope.

Bow: front end of a boat.

Broach: when a boat is held sideways against an obstruction by the force of the current.

C1: a closed deck one person canoe. (The paddler uses a single-bladed paddle and is kneeling.)

Cow's Tail: a short length of nylon tape (webbing) that extends from the chest harness attachment point on the back of a paddler's PFD to the front, making it easier for the paddler to attach himself to a line.

Duct Tape: strong, wide sticking tape. Used by paddlers for all sorts of emergency repairs. Also, carpet tape, duct tape.

Eddy: zone of recirculating water that forms behind an obstacle, out of the main current. Usually, but not always, relatively quiet and safe.

Eddy In: to paddle out of the main current and into an eddy.

Eddy line/fence: the border between the calm or upstream flowing water in an eddy and the fast downstream flowing water in the main flow of the river.

Eddy Out: to paddle out of an eddy and into the main current.

End grab/loop: a strong point on the end of a boat that can be used as a handle, or an attachment point for a recovery line.

Ferry glide angle: to paddle at an angle of 45° to the current so as not to lose ground while crossing a river.

Float Boat: any canoe or kayak that is not a squirt boat.

Gunwale: the rim of an open canoe. Where the sides stop and the top or deck would start, if it had one.

Hair Boater: extreme whitewater paddler.

Hydraulic: a dangerous form of stopper from which there is little outflow.

Hole: a surface stopper.

Hyperthermia: literally, too much heat. Heat exhaustion and heat stroke.

Hypothermia: literally, too little heat. Cold injury sometimes referred to as "exposure."

Line: any cord or rope, from the thinnest twine to the thickest cable.

Loom: the shaft of a paddle.

Low Head Dam: a weir.

OC1: a specialist whitewater open canoe, fitted out with a saddle and full length buoyancy bags and paddled by one person.

Outwash: the water flowing out of a stopper.

Painter: a length of line that is attached to the bow or stern of a boat. Traditionally used to tie the boat to the bank.

Play Hole: a 'friendly' hole, safe enough to play in.

Play Wave: a well shaped-standing wave, which can be surfed.

Portage: to carry a boat around a rapid or obstacle.

Rope: thick line. For the purposes of this book, any line with a diameter of $5/16$ inch (8 mm) or more.

Setting In: to paddle into an eddy by reverse ferry gliding rather than forward paddling.

Squirt Boat: an extremely low volume kayak or C1, with so little buoyancy that the craft barely floats and spends as much time underwater as on the surface.

Thwart: on an open canoe it is a length of wood or metal that spans the gap between the gunwales and strengthens the boat by keeping the sides apart. Though not designed as such it can be used as a seat. On a raft a thwart is an inflated tube that runs across the width of the raft for the same purpose.

Siphon: where the water has worn a pothole right through the bedrock and flows through this hole. Also, sump.

Stern: back end of a boat.

Stopper: a recirculating wave that can hold a boat or swimmer.

Strainer: any obstruction that has holes through which the current can flow but a swimmer can't. Strainers act like nets and are extremely dangerous.

Surface Stopper: a hole.

Transom: a flat square-cut stern, as opposed to a 'canoe' or pointed stern.

Weir: a low head dam.

Wrap: term used to describe what happens in a bad broach when a boat is 'wrapped' around the obstacle by the force of the water, often resulting in considerable damage.

APPENDIX B

Knots and Hitches

All knots or hitches that are tied on the end of a rope must have at least 12 inches (30 cm) of tail left over. This is because, as knots are pulled tight, there is some slippage. A short tail could work its way through and the knot come undone.

▶ **FIGURE EIGHT ON A BIGHT** - This knot is used to create a loop or 'bight' on the end of a rope. It is the strongest knot that can be used for this job and is easier to untie after use than an Overhand on a Bight.

Figure B-1 Figure Eight on a Bight.

▶ **OVERHAND ON A BIGHT** - This knot is used to tie a loop away from the ends of a rope, where there may be a pull on both ends of the rope (a Figure Eight tends to be pulled apart and weakened by this).

Other, more specialized knots that could be used are the In-line Figure Eight or the Alpine Butterfly.

Figure B-2 Overhand Knot on a Bight.

▶ **RETHREADED FIGURE EIGHT** - This is simply a different way of tying a Figure Eight on a Bight so that it can be threaded through something, rather than be clipped in via a karabiner.

Figure B-3 Rethreaded Figure Eight.

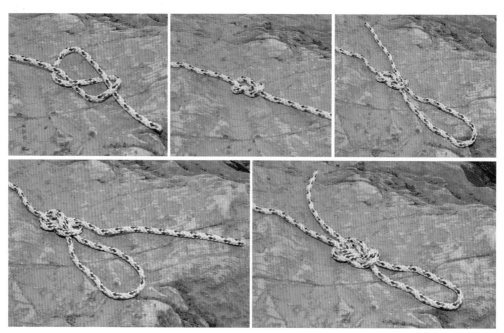

Figure B-4 Double Fisherman's Knot.

▶ **DOUBLE FISHERMAN'S KNOT** - A strong way to join two ropes, used to tie prussik loops. Can be used to join ropes of unequal diameters.

▶ **OVERHAND ON A DOUBLE ROPE** - This is a fast and simple way to tie two ropes together. It also produces a knot that is easier to pass around or through karabiners and other obstructions than others. The only proviso is that at least 2 feet (60 cm) of tail must be left to prevent slippage. An alternative is a Double Fisherman's Knot.

Figure B-5 Overhand on a Double Rope.

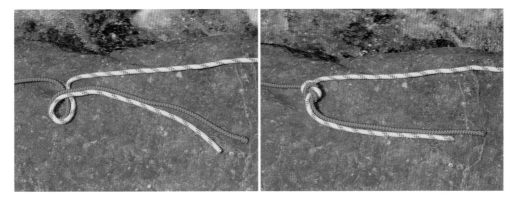

▶ **CLOVE HITCH** - A Clove Hitch can be adjusted without the need to take it out of the karabiner. It also encourages 'clean line' as hitches collapse as soon as they are removed from a karabiner.

Figure B-6 Clove Hitch.

WHITEWATER SAFETY AND RESCUE

*Figure B-7 Italian or
Munter Hitch.*

▶ **ITALIAN OR MUNTER HITCH** - The Italian Hitch is used for belaying, lowering, and rappelling.

*Figure B-8
Classic Prussik.*

▶ **CLASSIC PRUSSIK OR PRUSSIK KNOT** - Two wraps around the rope and then pull the knot through the loop. It cannot be released under tension.

*Figure B-9
French Prussik.*

▶ **FRENCH PRUSSIK** - Simplicity itself! The prussik loop is wrapped around the rope four to six times depending on conditions and the ends of the loop are clipped together with a karabiner. It can be released even when there is tension on the rope which is its strong and its weak point.

Figure B-10 Klemheist Prussik.

▶ **KLEMHEIST** - A prussik that can be tied with tape.

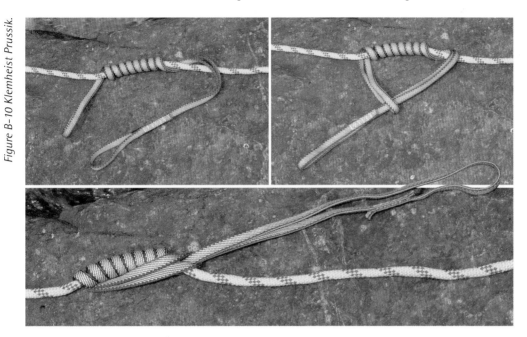

▶ **TAPE KNOT OR WATERMAN'S KNOT** - Leave at least 2 inches (5 cm) of tail and pull the knot as tight as you can after tying it. Check periodically to ensure that the knot doesn't work loose.

Figure B-11 Tape Knot or Waterman's Knot.

APPENDIX C

Index